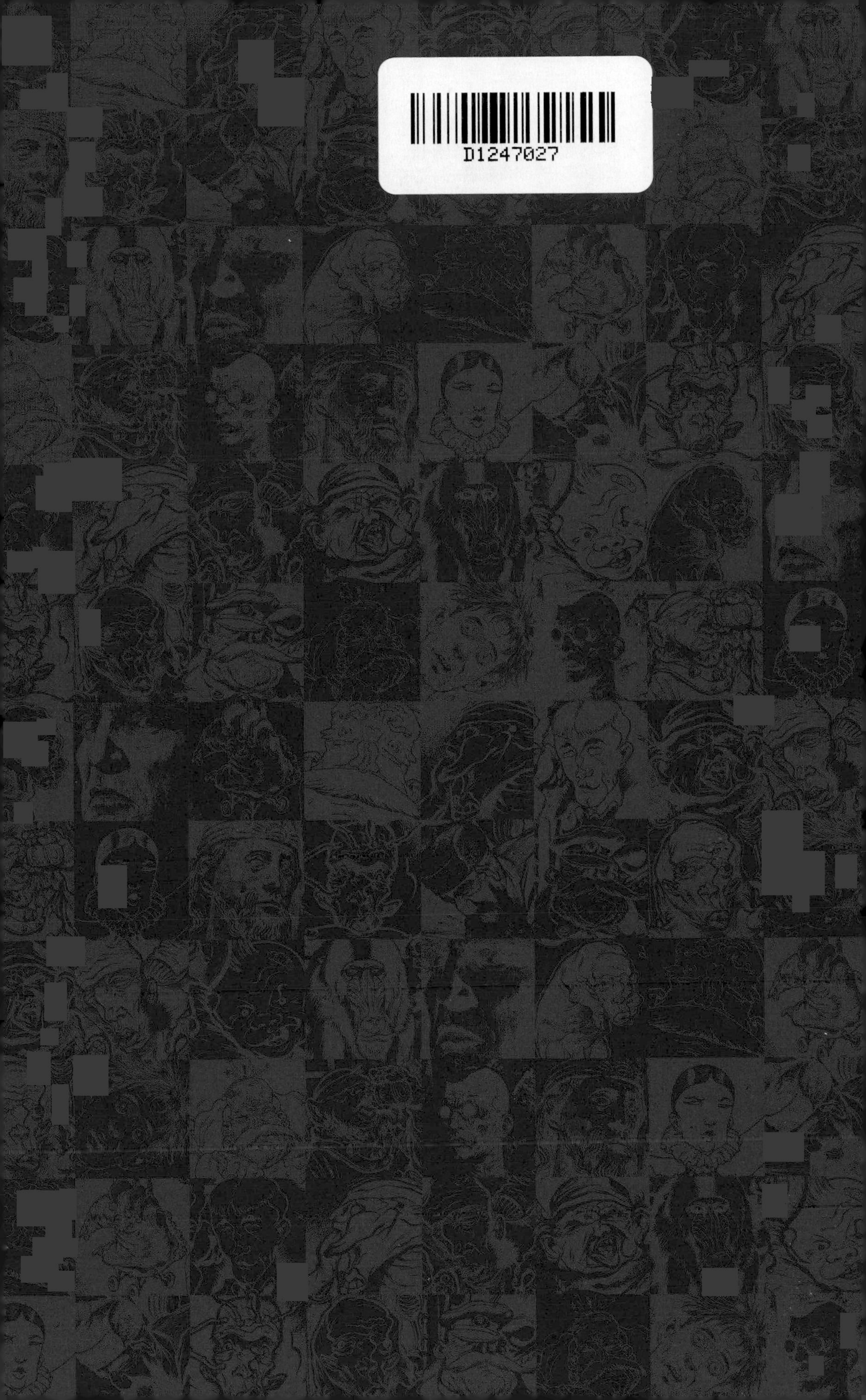

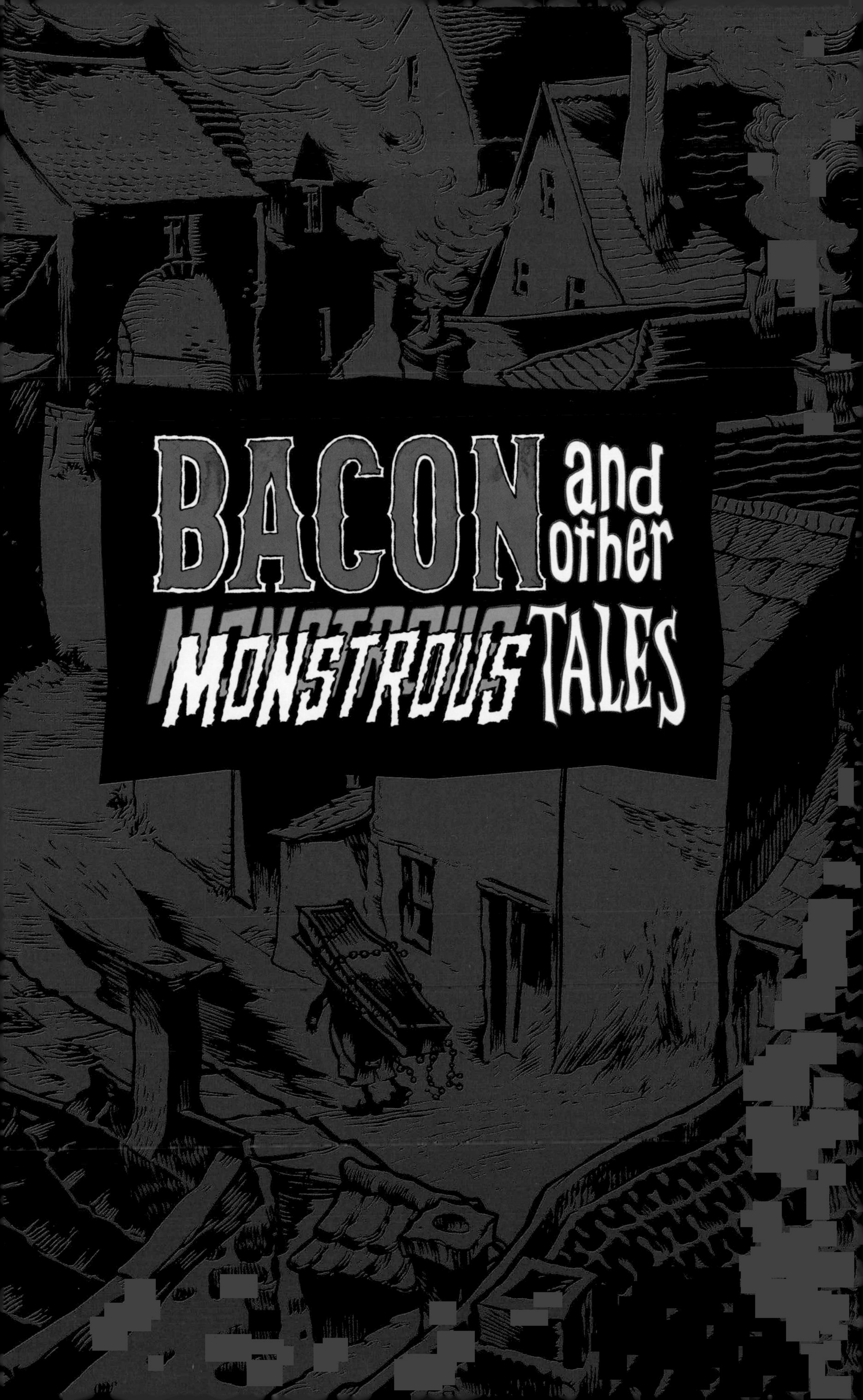
BACON and other MONSTROUS TALES

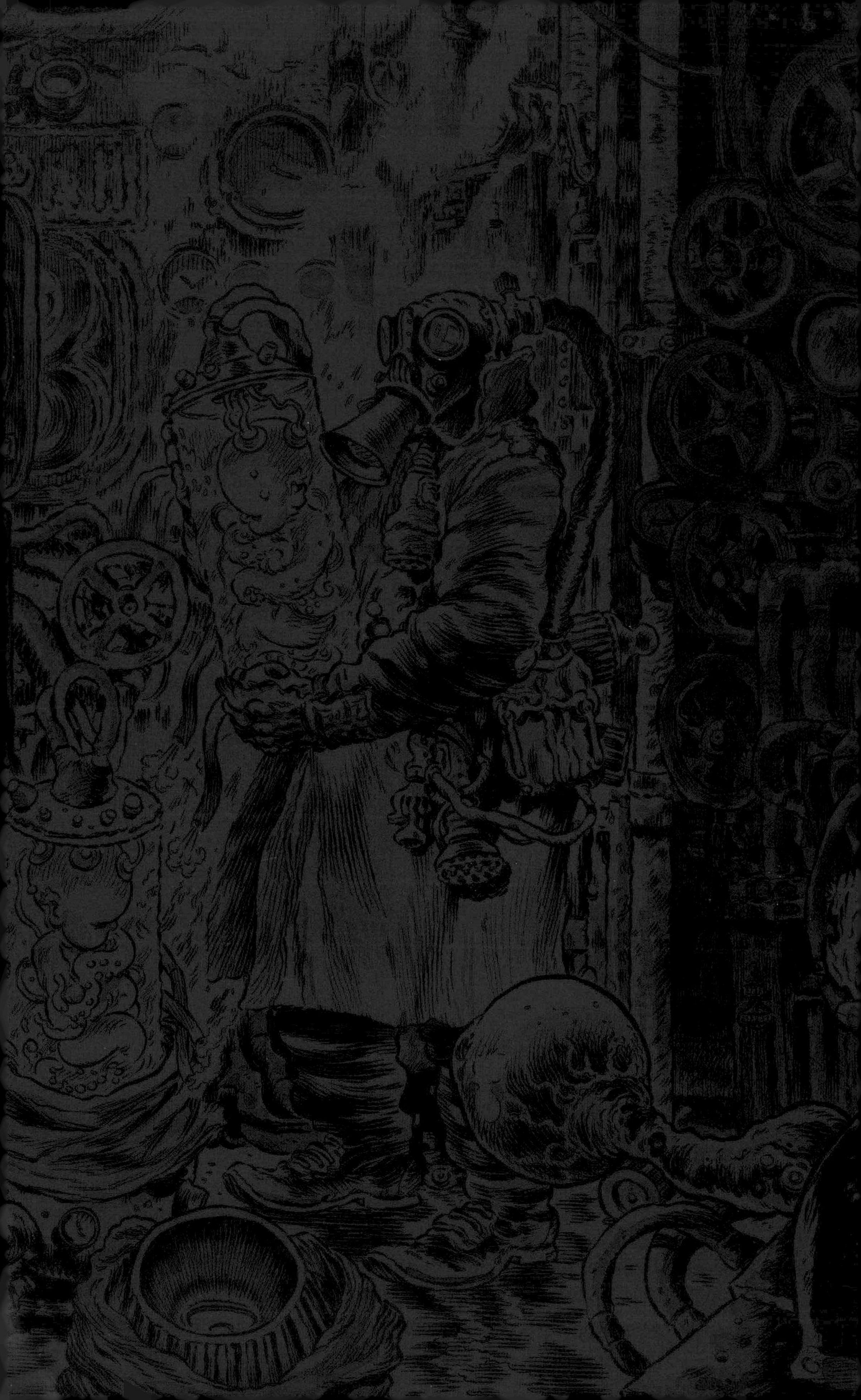

BACON and other MONSTROUS TALES

By TROY NIXEY

Letters for "Bacon" and
"Boogie Picker" stories by
SEAN KONOT
Cover art by
TROY NIXEY
and **MICHELLE MADSEN**

DARK HORSE BOOKS

PRESIDENT AND PUBLISHER
MIKE RICHARDSON

EDITOR
BRETT ISRAEL

ASSISTANT EDITOR
SANJAY DHARAWAT

DIGITAL ART TECHNICIAN
ALLYSON HALLER

COLLECTION DESIGNER
PATRICK SATTERFIELD

EXECUTIVE VICE PRESIDENT
NEIL HANKERSON

CHIEF FINANCIAL OFFICER
TOM WEDDLE

VICE PRESIDENT OF PUBLISHING
RANDY STRADLEY

CHIEF BUSINESS DEVELOPMENT OFFICER
NICK McWHORTER

CHIEF INFORMATION OFFICER
DALE LaFOUNTAIN

VICE PRESIDENT OF MARKETING
MATT PARKINSON

VICE PRESIDENT OF
PRODUCTION AND SCHEDULING
VANESSA TODD-HOLMES

VICE PRESIDENT OF
BOOK TRADE AND DIGITAL SALES
MARK BERNARDI

GENERAL COUNSEL
KEN LIZZI

EDITOR IN CHIEF
DAVE MARSHALL

EDITORIAL DIRECTOR
DAVEY ESTRADA

SENIOR BOOKS EDITOR
CHRIS WARNER

DIRECTOR OF SPECIALTY PROJECTS
CARY GRAZZINI

ART DIRECTOR
LIA RIBACCHI

DIRECTOR OF DIGITAL ART AND PREPRESS
MATT DRYER

SENIOR DIRECTOR OF LICENSED PUBLICATIONS
MICHAEL GOMBOS

DIRECTOR OF CUSTOM PROGRAMS
KARI YADRO

DIRECTOR OF INTERNATIONAL LICENSING
KARI TORSON

DIRECTOR OF TRADE SALES
SEAN BRICE

BACON AND OTHER MONSTROUS TALES

Bacon and Other Monstrous Tales™ © 2021 Troy
Nixey. Dark Horse Books® and the Dark Horse logo
are registered trademarks of Dark Horse Comics LLC.
All rights reserved. No portion of this publication
may be reproduced or transmitted, in any form or by
any means, without the express written permission of
Dark Horse Comics LLC. Names, characters, places,
and incidents featured in this publication either are
the product of the author's imagination or are used
fictitiously. Any resemblance to actual persons (living
or dead), events, institutions, or locales, without satiric
intent, is coincidental.

Published by Dark Horse Books
A division of Dark Horse Comics LLC
10956 SE Main Street
Milwaukie, OR 97222

First edition: August 2021
Ebook ISBN 978-1-50672-067-8
Hardcover ISBN 978-1-50672-066-1

10 9 8 7 6 5 4 3 2 1
Printed in China

Comic Shop Locator Service: comicshoplocator.com

Names: Nixey, Troy, author, artist.
Title: Bacon : and other monstrous tales / by Troy Nixey.
Description: First edition. | Milwaukie, OR : Dark Horse Books, 2020. |
    Summary: "Superstar artist Troy Nixey will take you on a journey through
    the creepy and otherworldly in this collection of never before collected
    tales! From alien invasions to monsters lurking in the unseen, this
    beautifully illustrated book is a must have for any horror and science
    fiction fan! Collecting stories from Nixey's early days at Oni Press and
    Dark Horse to the relaunch of Fangoria, as well as never-seen-before
    material and a bonus sketchbook section!"-- Provided by publisher.
Identifiers: LCCN 2020011219 | ISBN 9781506720661 (hardcover) | ISBN
    9781506720678 (ebook)
Subjects: LCSH: Graphic novels.
Classification: LCC PN6727.N59 B33 2020 | DDC 741.5/973--dc23
LC record available at https://lccn.loc.gov/2020011219

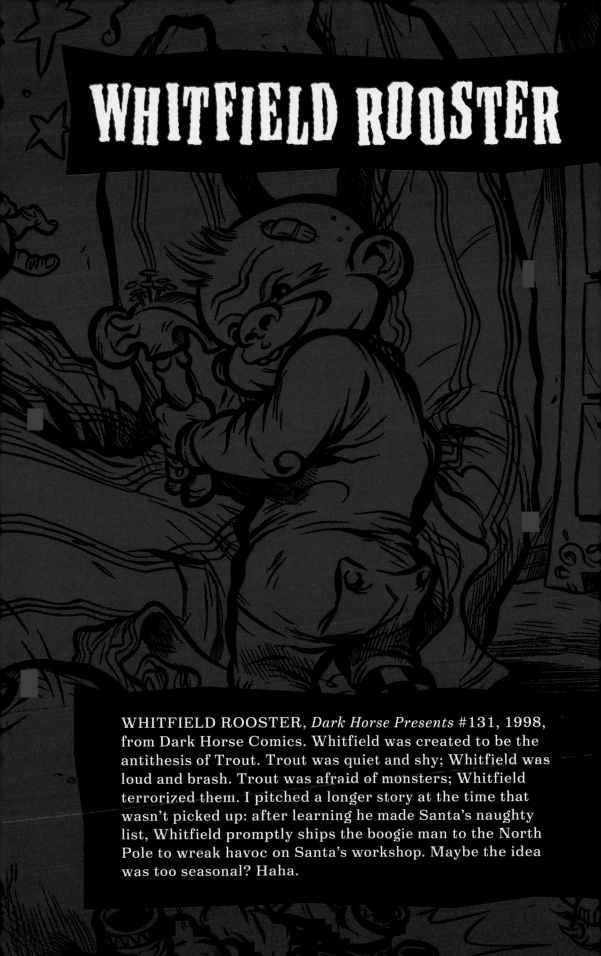

WHITFIELD ROOSTER

WHITFIELD ROOSTER, *Dark Horse Presents* #131, 1998, from Dark Horse Comics. Whitfield was created to be the antithesis of Trout. Trout was quiet and shy; Whitfield was loud and brash. Trout was afraid of monsters; Whitfield terrorized them. I pitched a longer story at the time that wasn't picked up: after learning he made Santa's naughty list, Whitfield promptly ships the boogie man to the North Pole to wreak havoc on Santa's workshop. Maybe the idea was too seasonal? Haha.

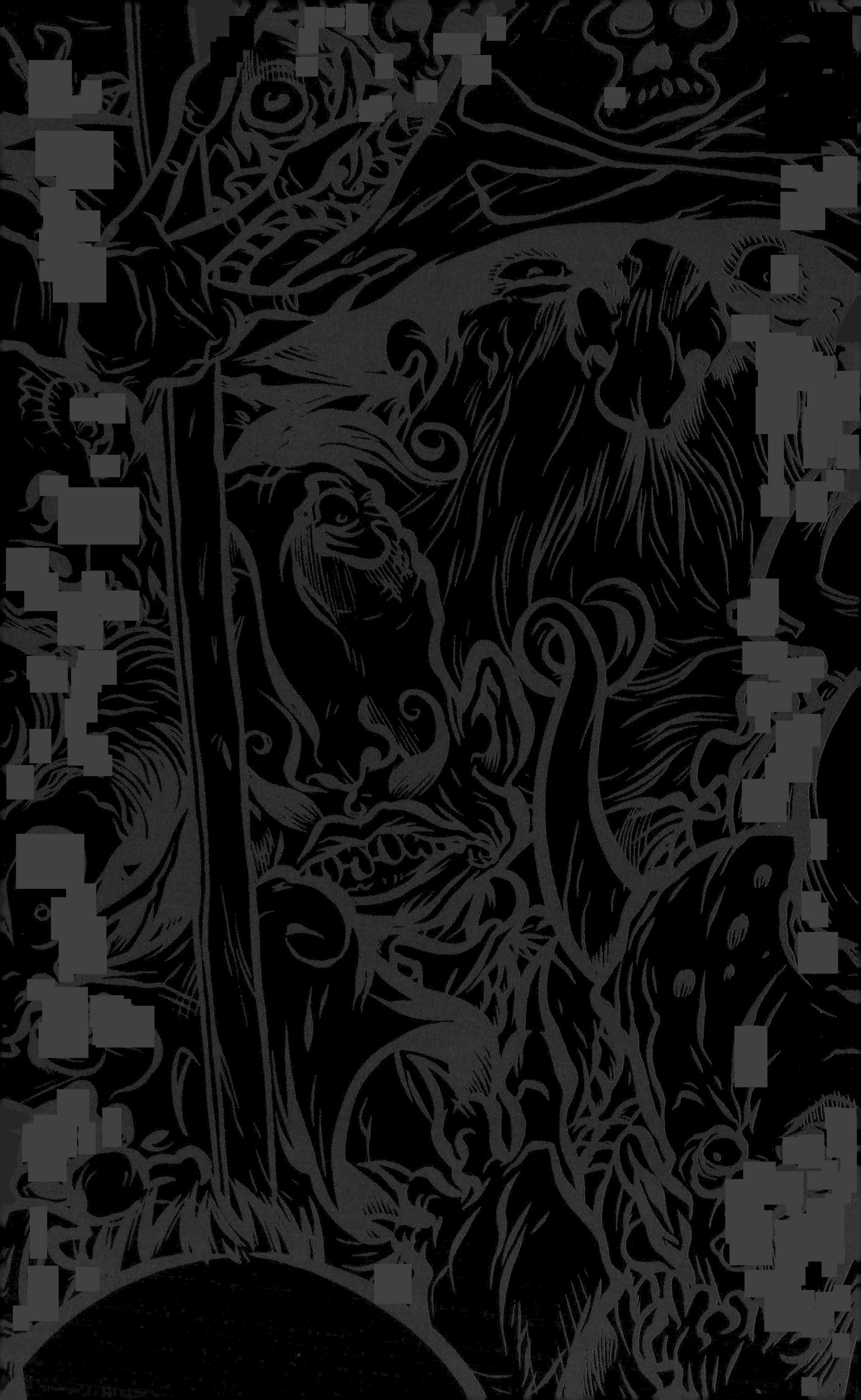

Whitfield · Rooster in:

Boogie Picker

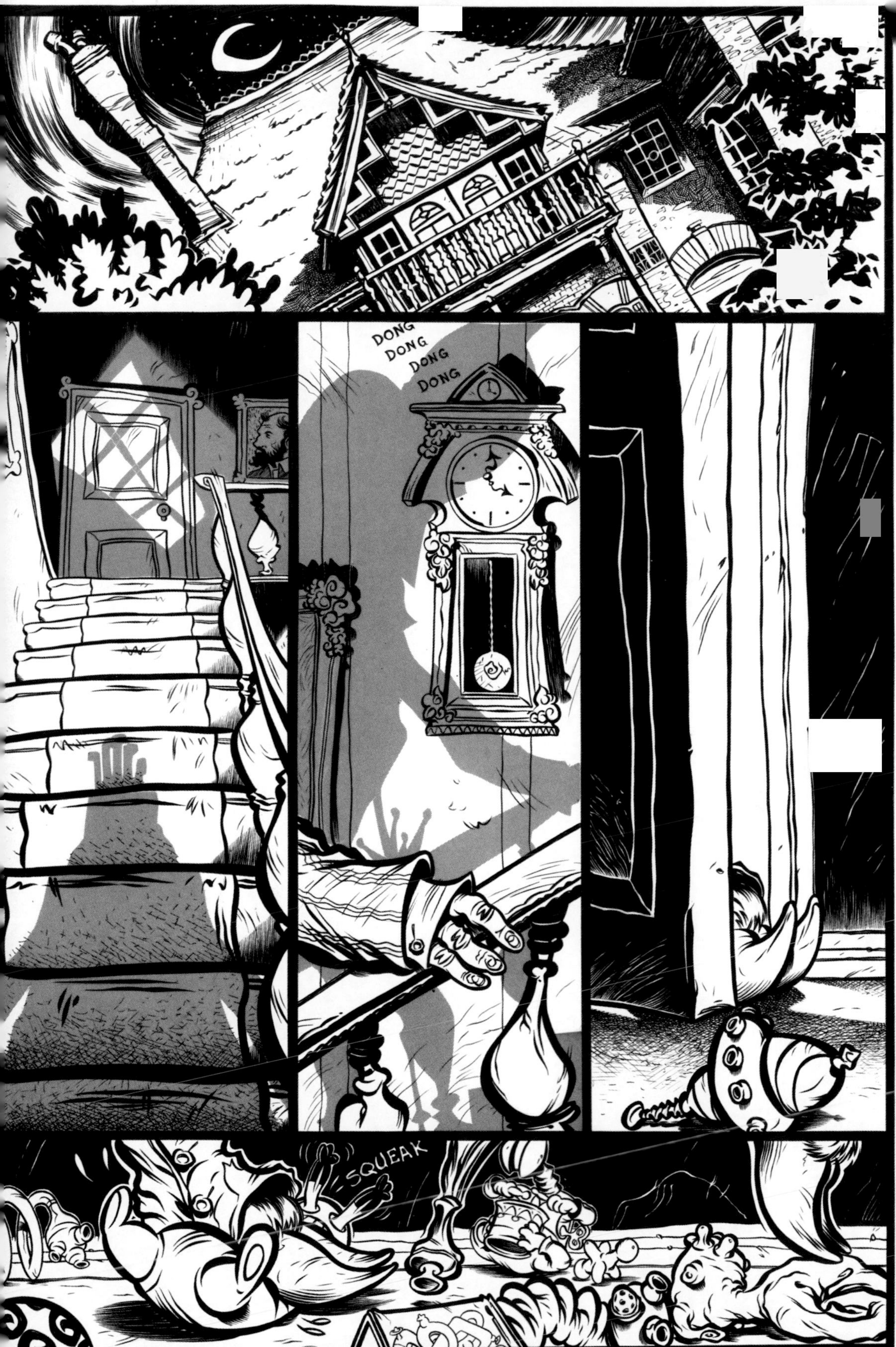

DONG
DONG
DONG
DONG
SQUEAK

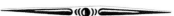

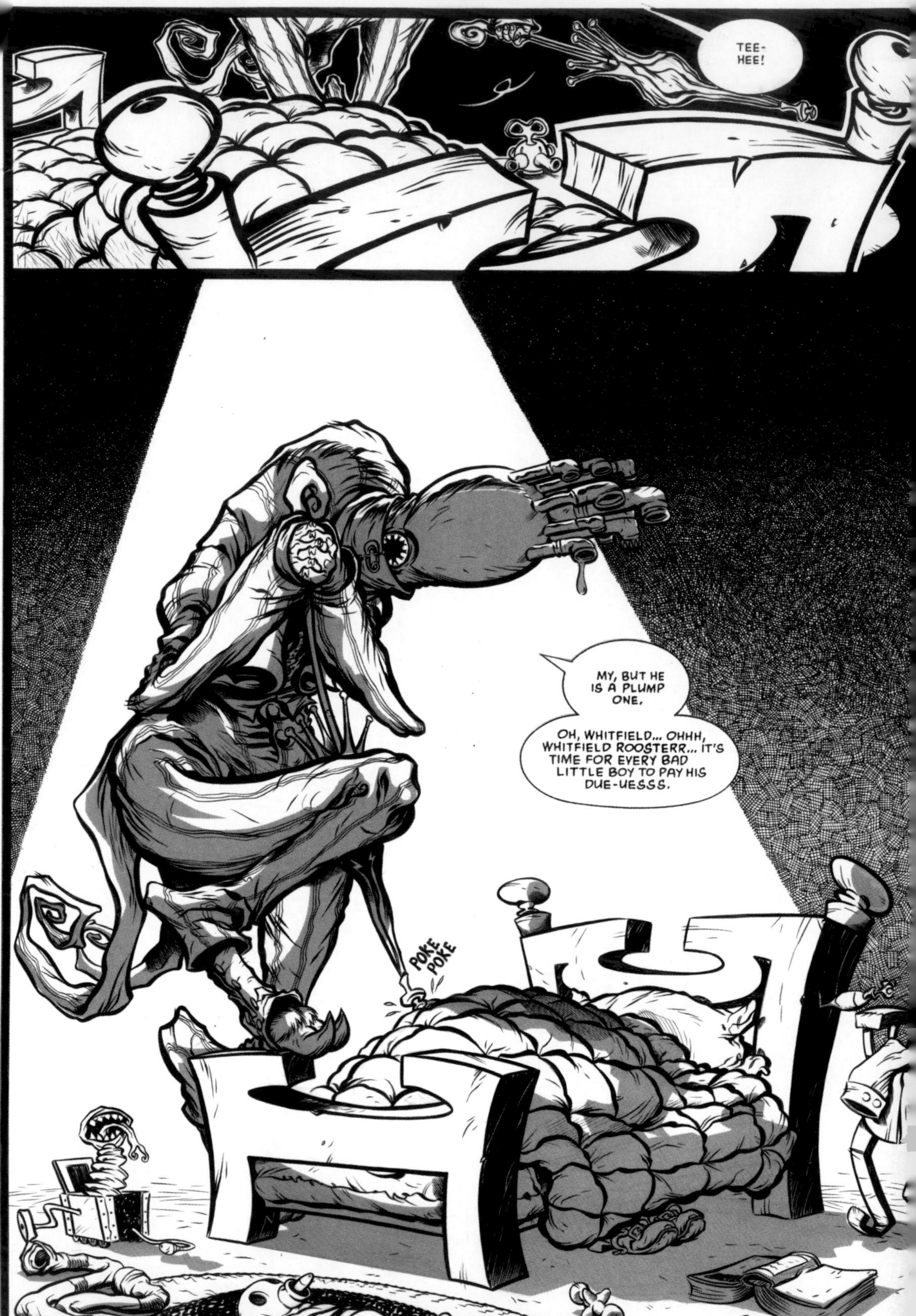
TEE-HEE!
MY, BUT HE IS A PLUMP ONE.
OH, WHITFIELD... OHHH, WHITFIELD ROOSTERR... IT'S TIME FOR EVERY BAD LITTLE BOY TO PAY HIS DUE-UESSS.
POKE POKE

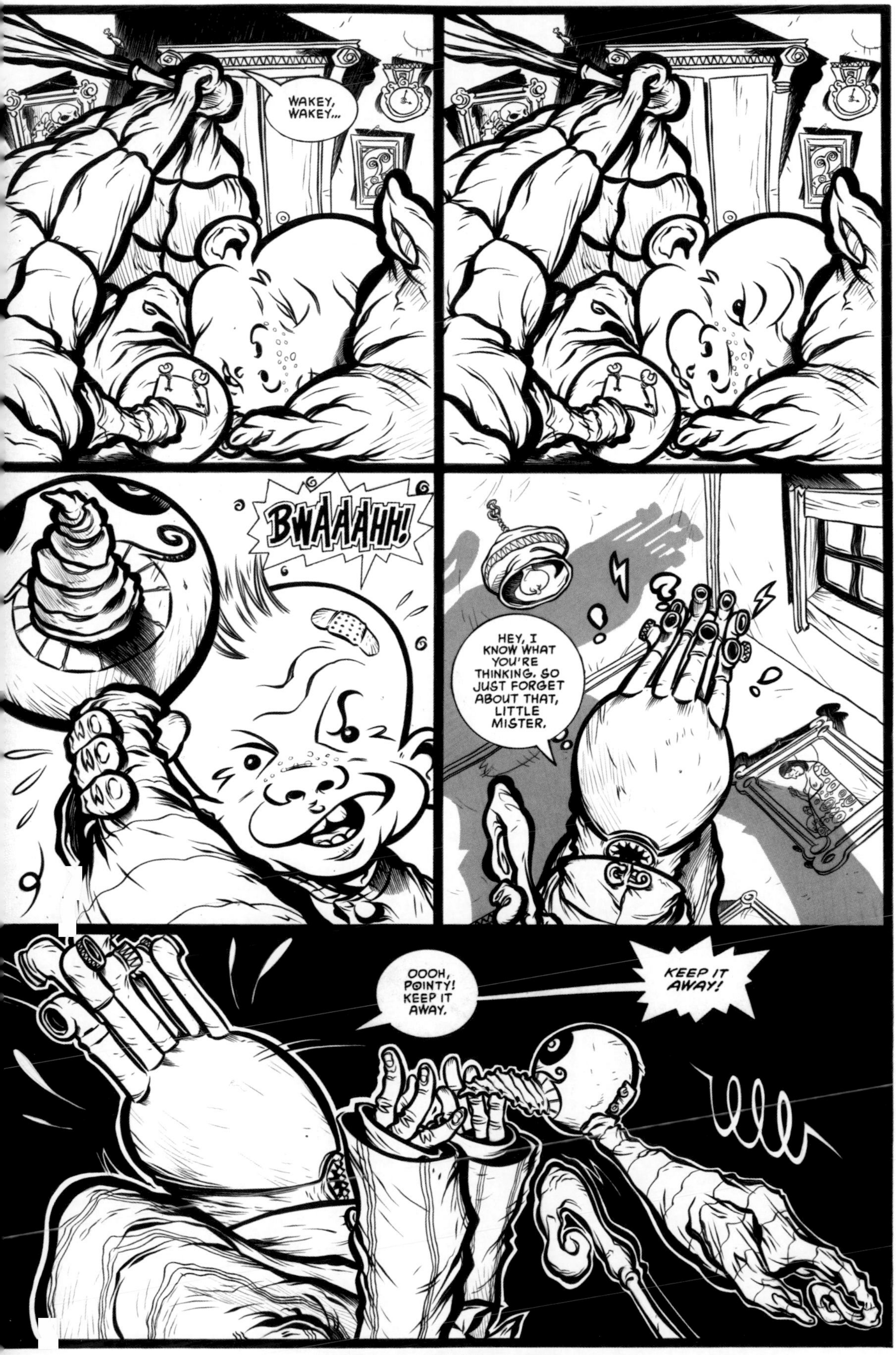
WAKEY, WAKEY...
BWAAAHH!
HEY, I KNOW WHAT YOU'RE THINKING. SO JUST FORGET ABOUT THAT, LITTLE MISTER.
OOOH, POINTY! KEEP IT AWAY.
KEEP IT AWAY!

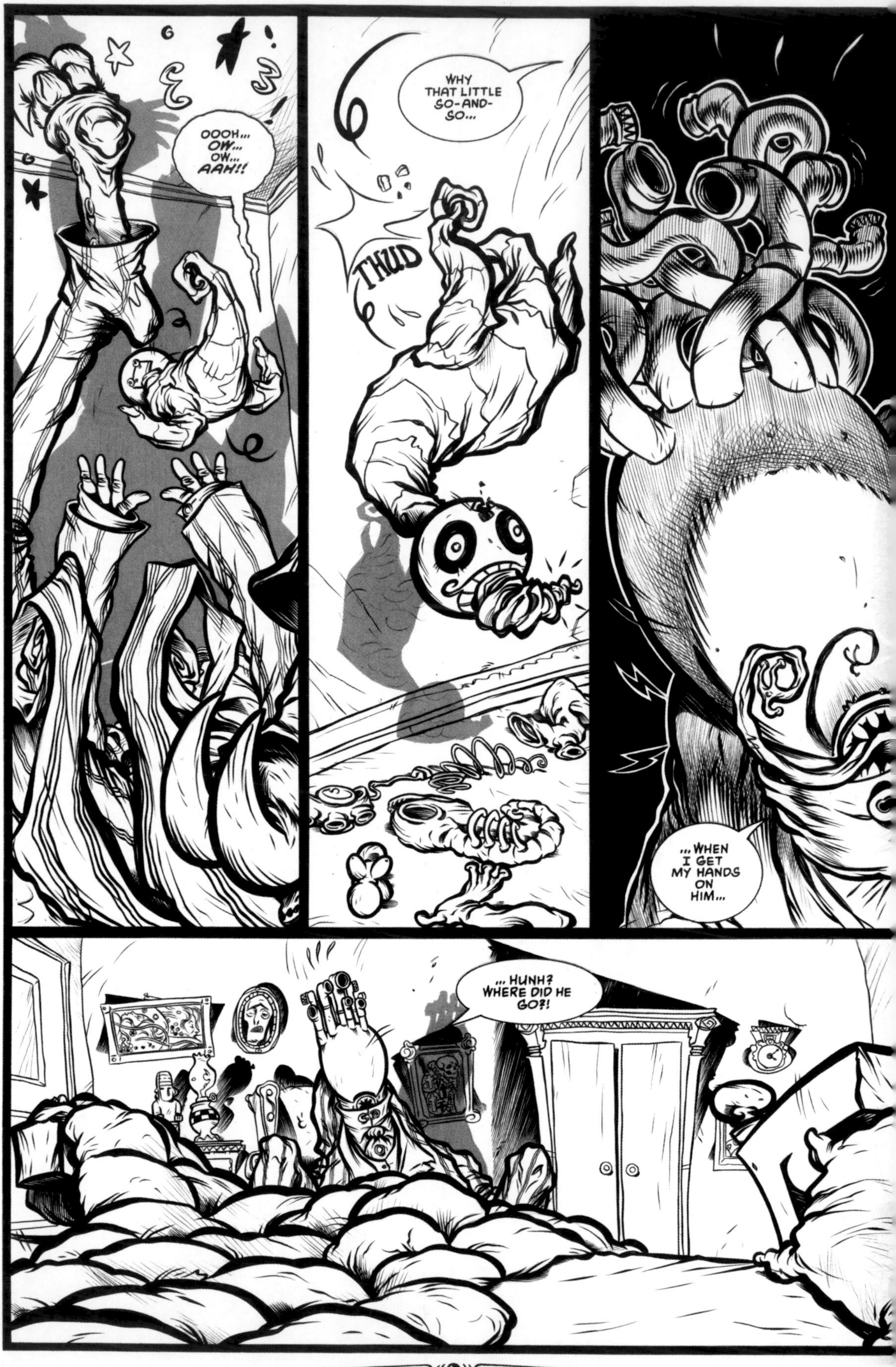
OOOH... OW... OW... AAH!!
WHY THAT LITTLE SO-AND-SO...
THUD
...WHEN I GET MY HANDS ON HIM...
...HUNH? WHERE DID HE GO?!

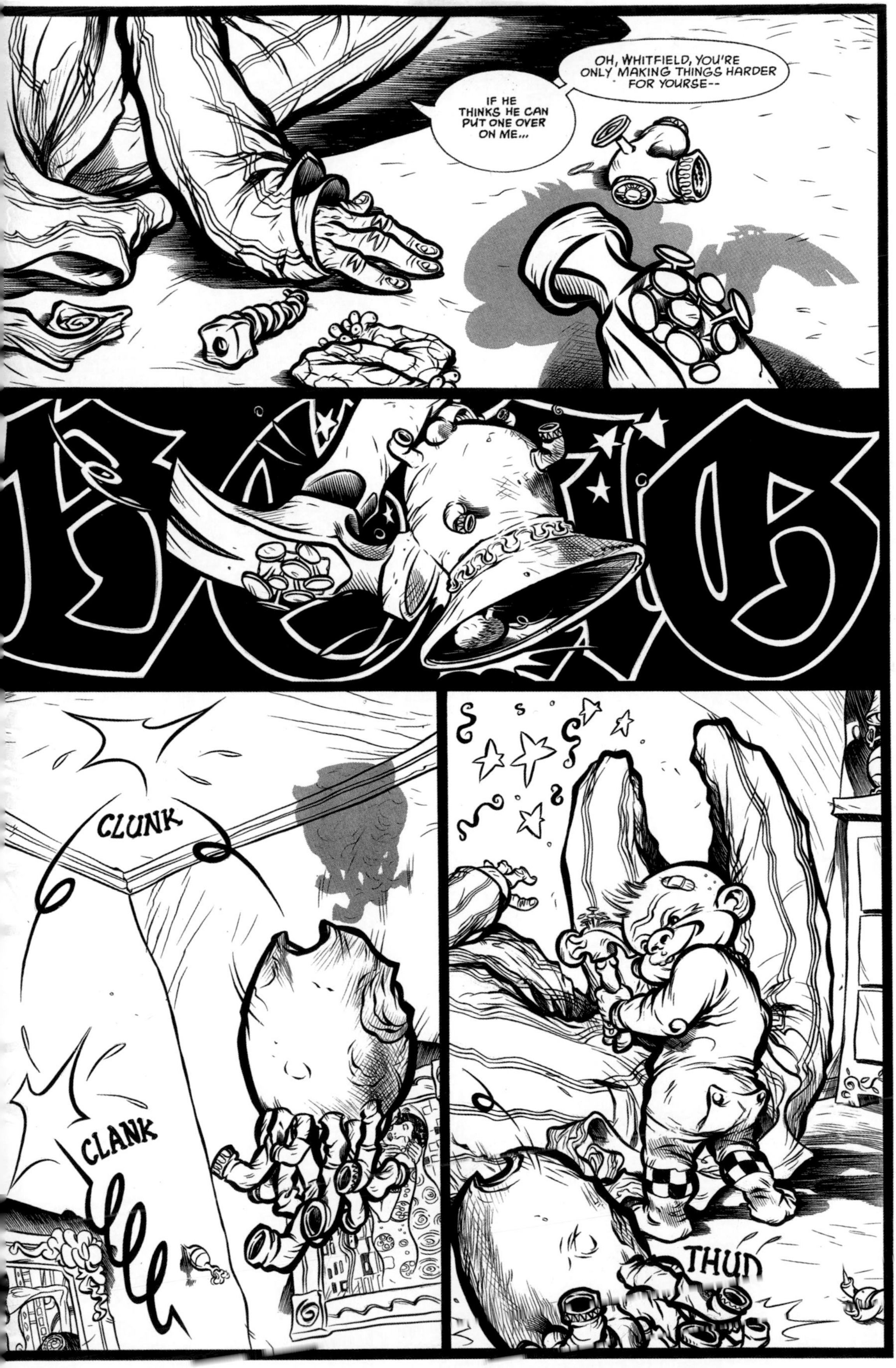
IF HE THINKS HE CAN PUT ONE OVER ON ME...
OH, WHITFIELD, YOU'RE ONLY MAKING THINGS HARDER FOR YOURSE--
CLUNK
CLANK
THUN

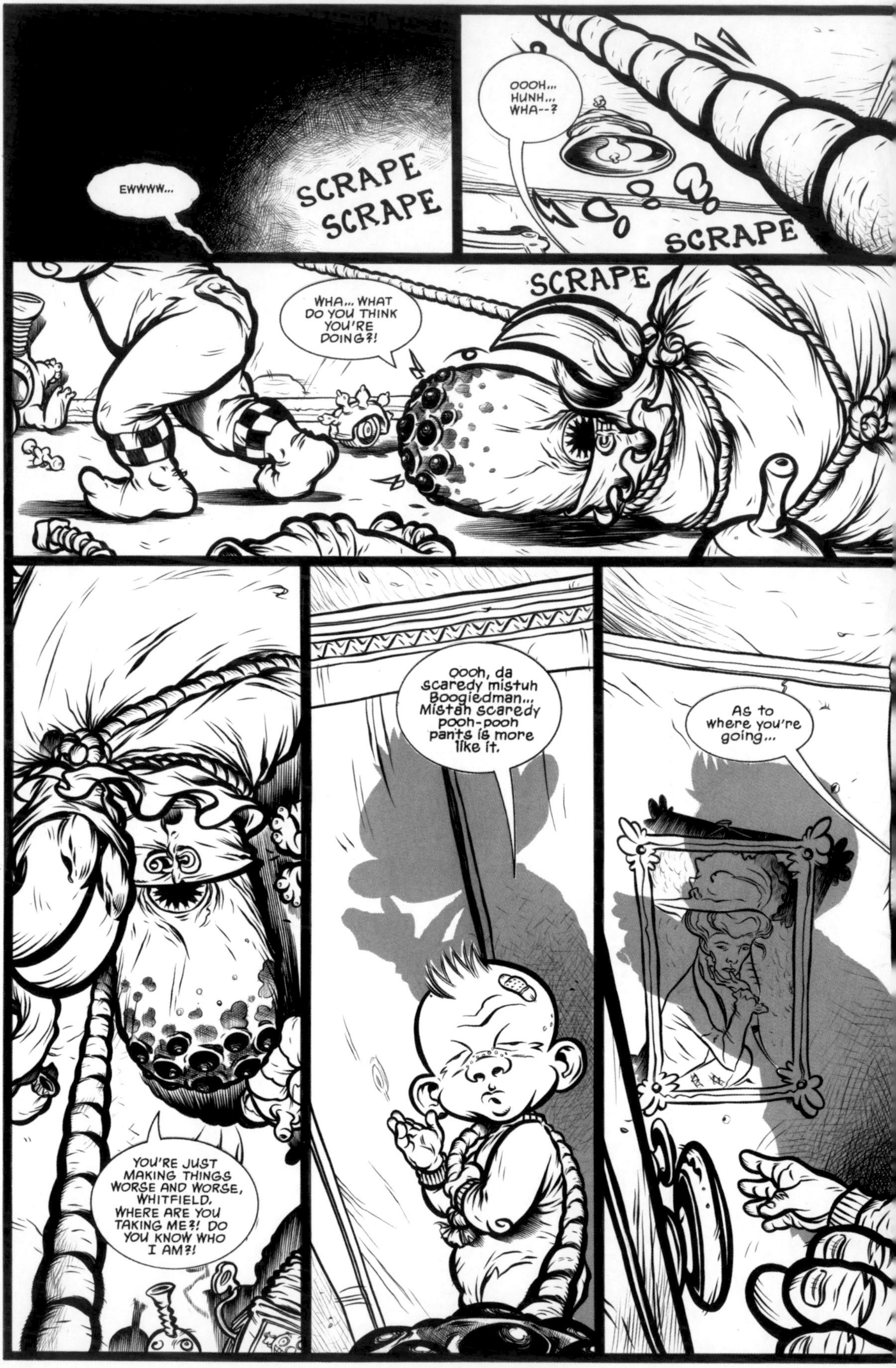
EWWWW...
SCRAPE
SCRAPE
OOOH... HUNH... WHA--?
SCRAPE
SCRAPE
WHA... WHAT DO YOU THINK YOU'RE DOING?!
YOU'RE JUST MAKING THINGS WORSE AND WORSE, WHITFIELD. WHERE ARE YOU TAKING ME?! DO YOU KNOW WHO I AM?!
Oooh, da scaredy mistuh Boogiedman... Mistah scaredy pooh-pooh pants is more like it.
As to where you're going...

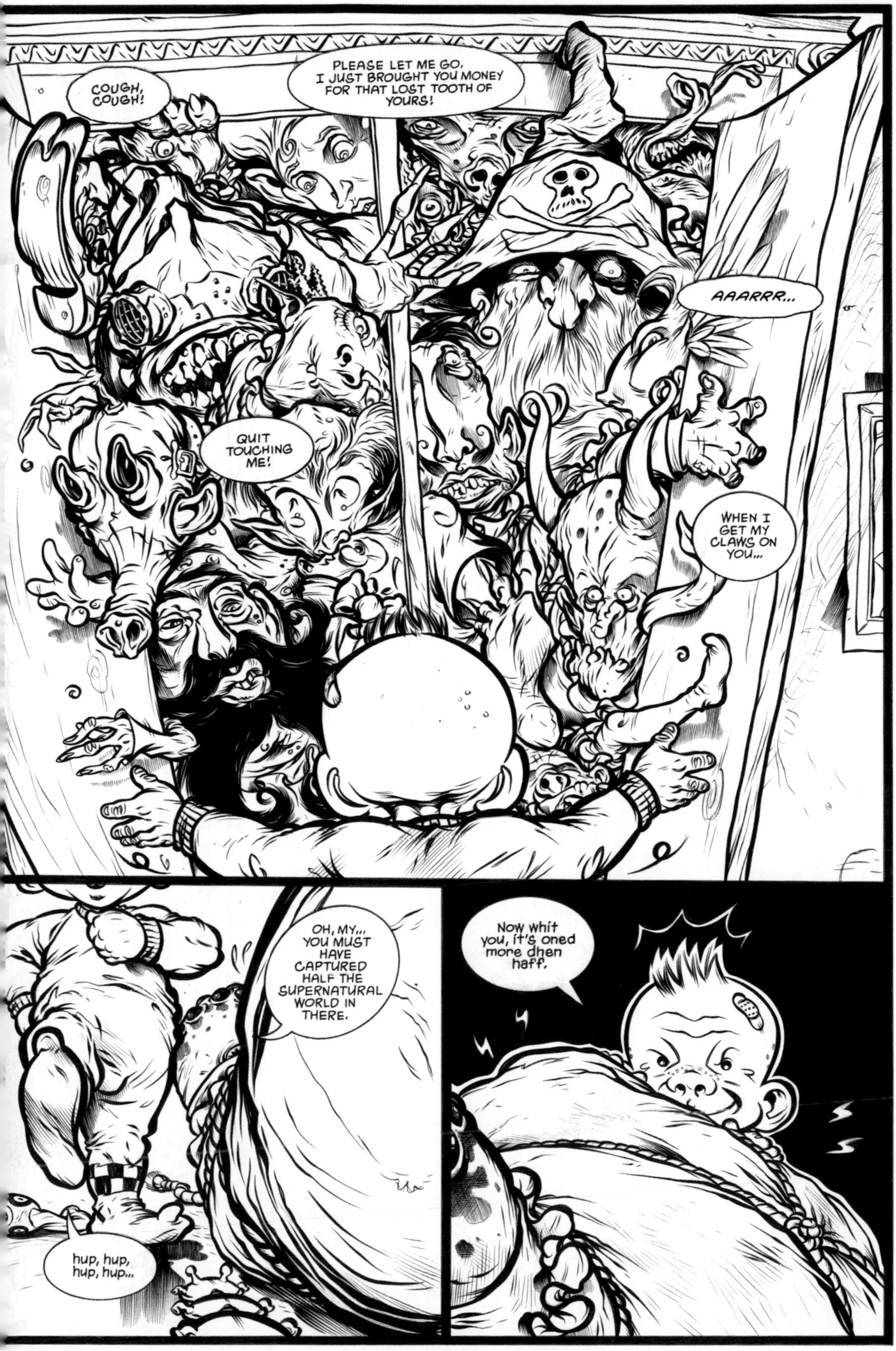
COUGH, COUGH!
PLEASE LET ME GO, I JUST BROUGHT YOU MONEY FOR THAT LOST TOOTH OF YOURS!
AAARRR...
QUIT TOUCHING ME!
WHEN I GET MY CLAWS ON YOU...
OH, MY... YOU MUST HAVE CAPTURED HALF THE SUPERNATURAL WORLD IN THERE.
hup, hup, hup, hup...
Now whit you, it's oned more dhen haff.

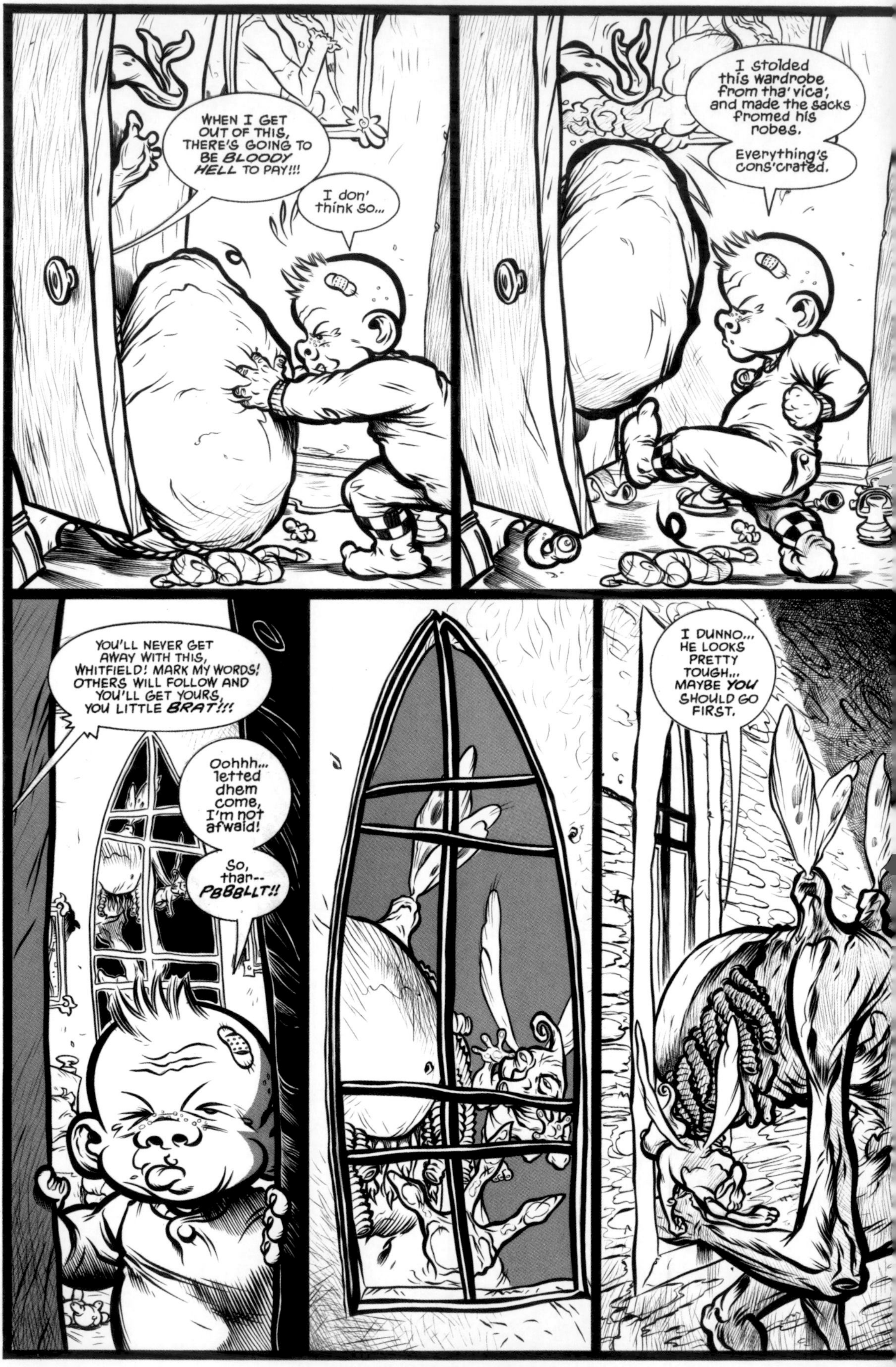
WHEN I GET OUT OF THIS, THERE'S GOING TO BE BLOODY HELL TO PAY!!!
I don' think so...
I stolded this wardrobe from tha' vica', and made the sacks fromed his robes.
Everything's cons'crated.
YOU'LL NEVER GET AWAY WITH THIS, WHITFIELD! MARK MY WORDS! OTHERS WILL FOLLOW AND YOU'LL GET YOURS, YOU LITTLE BRAT!!!
Oohhh... letted dhem come, I'm not afwaid!
So, thar-- PBBBLLT!!
I DUNNO... HE LOOKS PRETTY TOUGH... MAYBE YOU SHOULD GO FIRST.

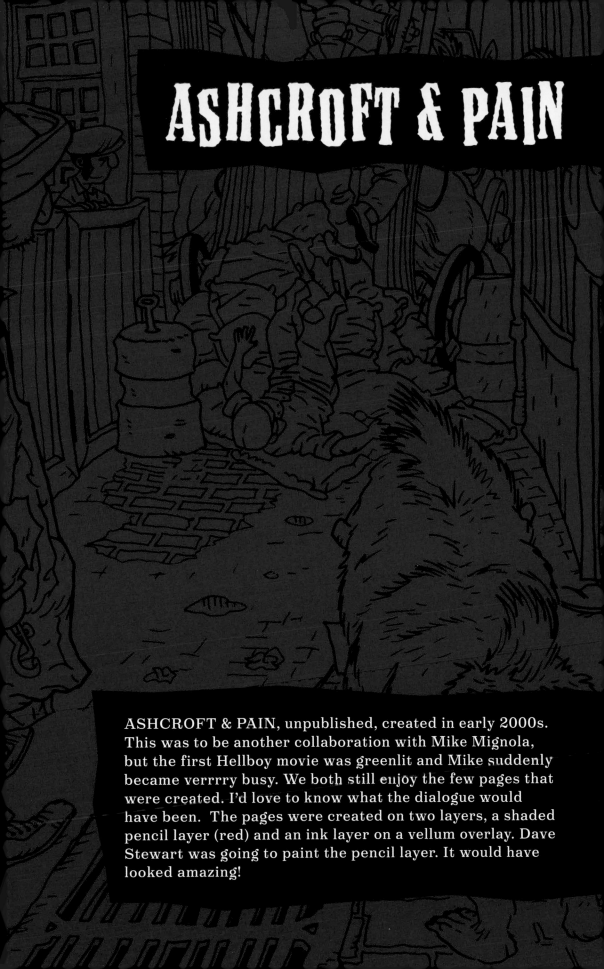

ASHCROFT & PAIN

ASHCROFT & PAIN, unpublished, created in early 2000s. This was to be another collaboration with Mike Mignola, but the first Hellboy movie was greenlit and Mike suddenly became verrrry busy. We both still enjoy the few pages that were created. I'd love to know what the dialogue would have been. The pages were created on two layers, a shaded pencil layer (red) and an ink layer on a vellum overlay. Dave Stewart was going to paint the pencil layer. It would have looked amazing!

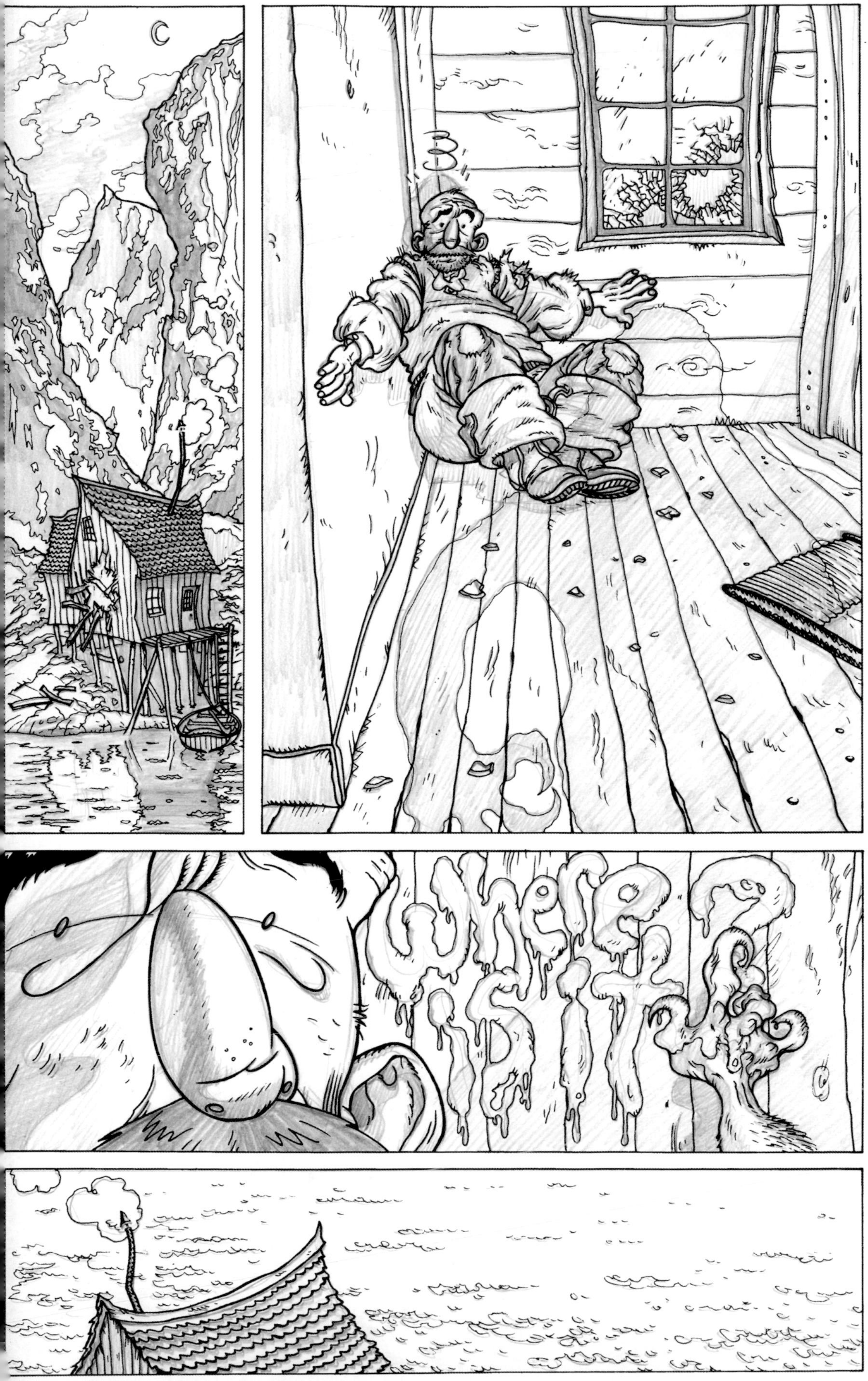
where? is it?

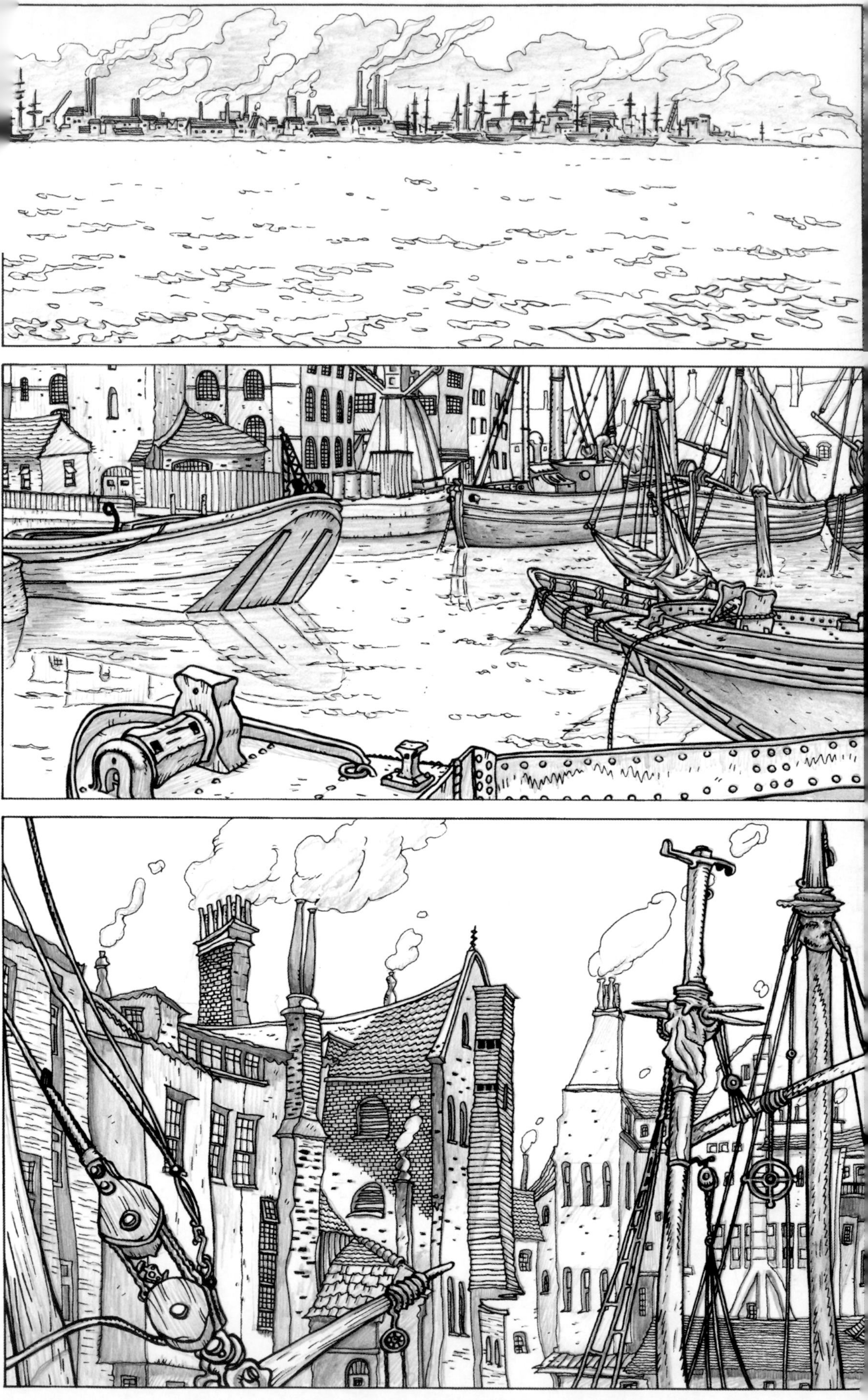

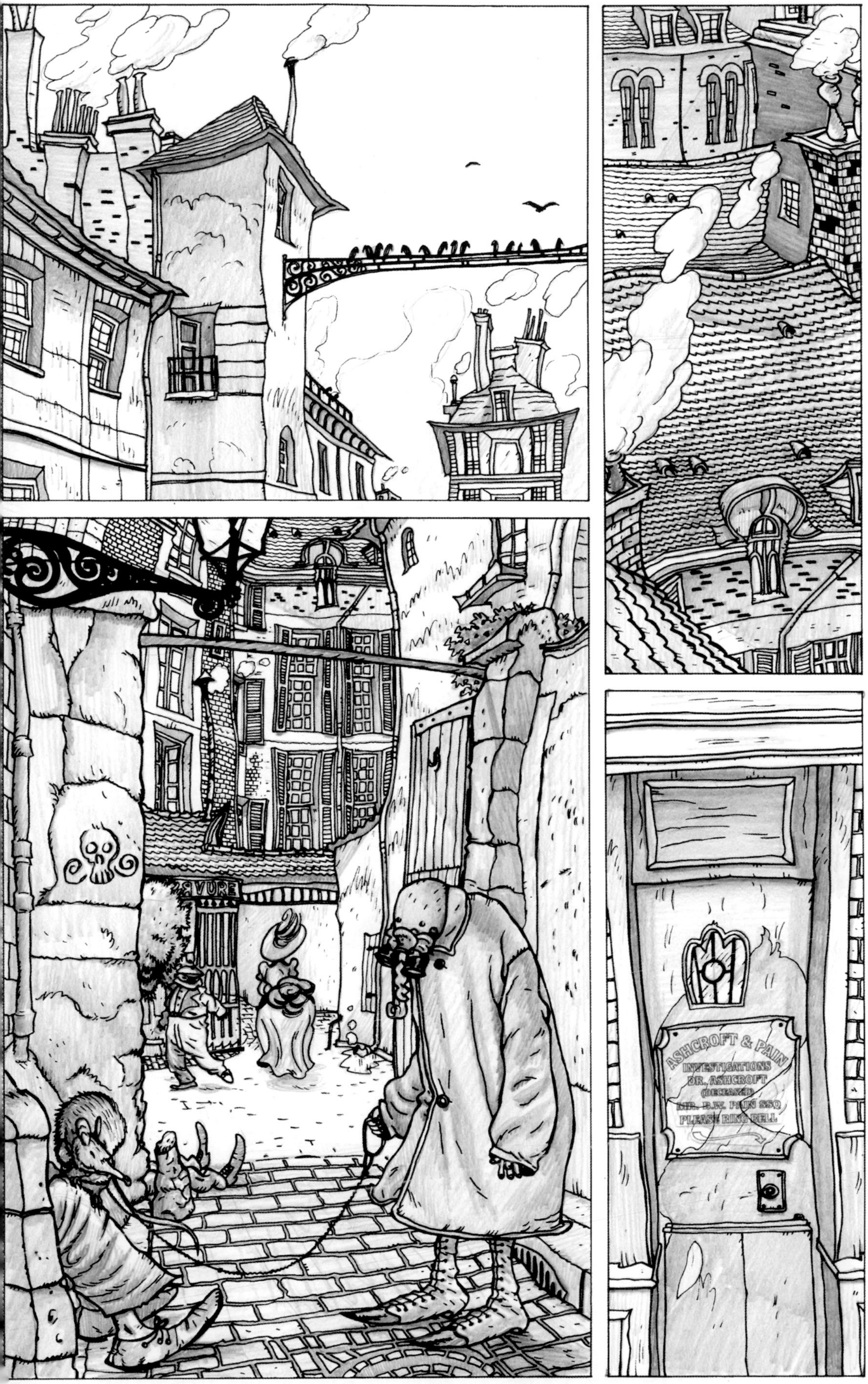
ASHCROFT & PAIN
INVESTIGATIONS
DR. ASHCROFT
(DECEASED)
MR. B.W. PAIN ESQ
PLEASE RING BELL

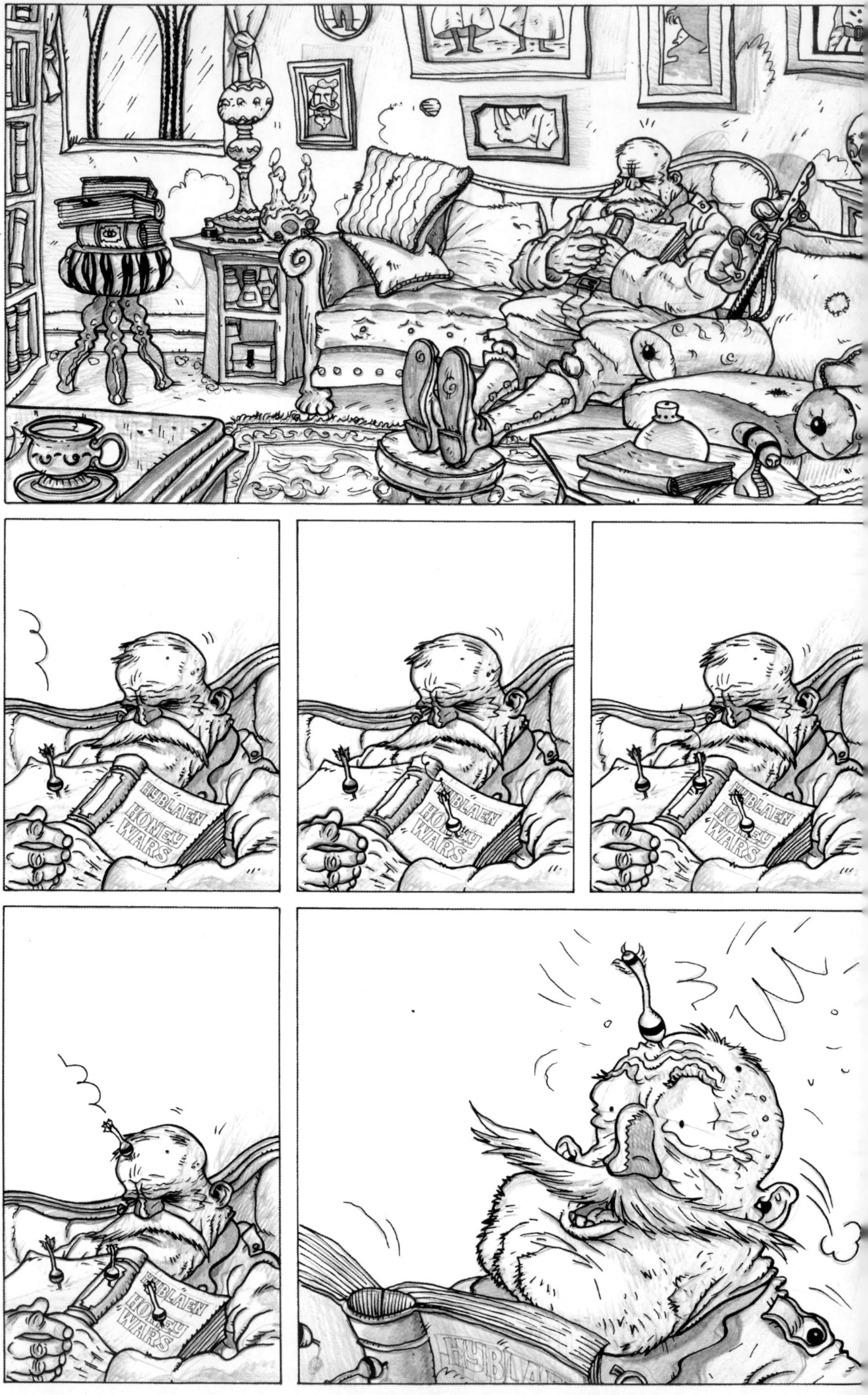
HYBLAEN
HONEY
WARS

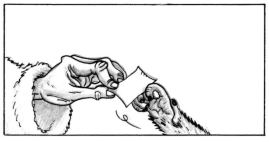

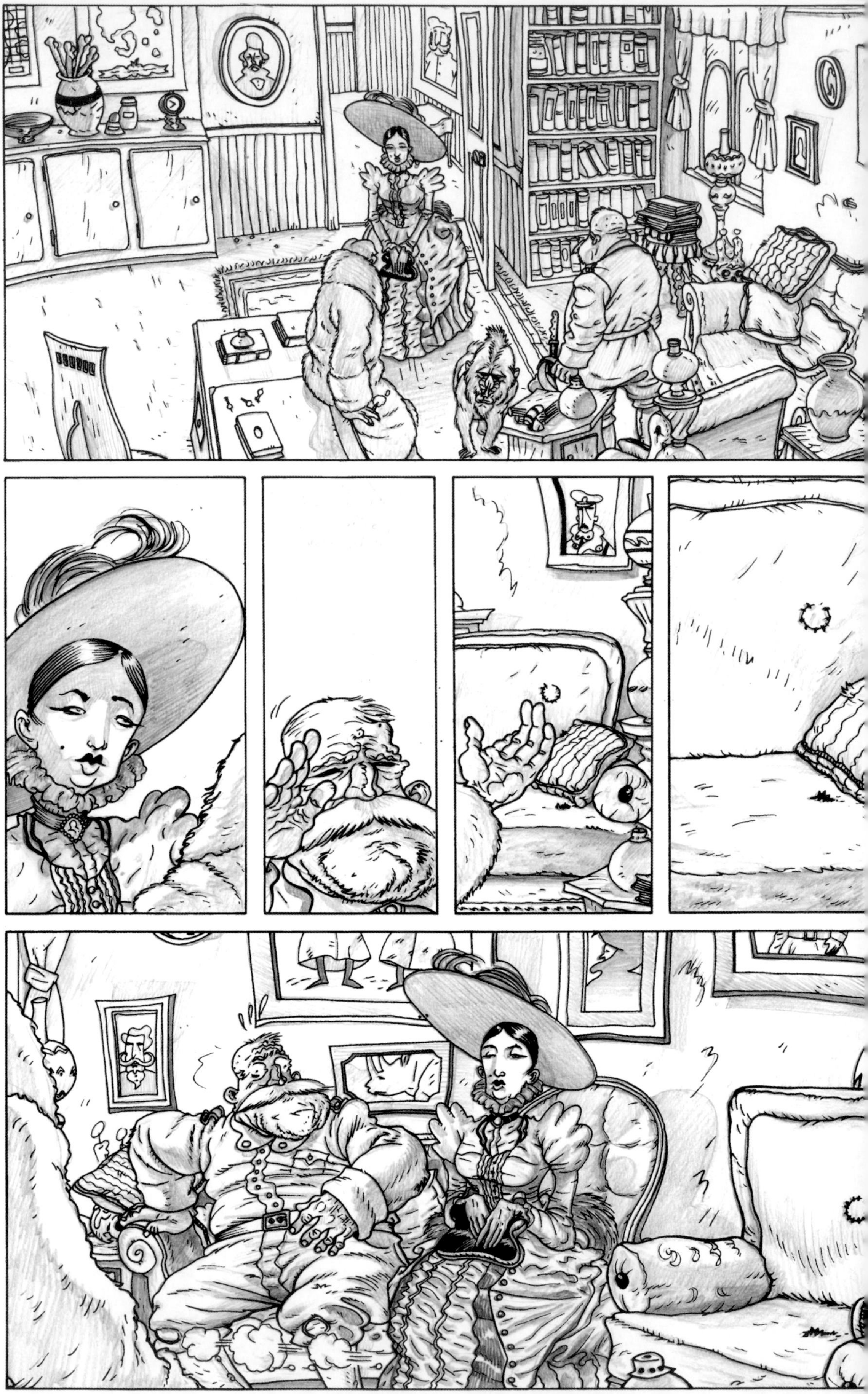

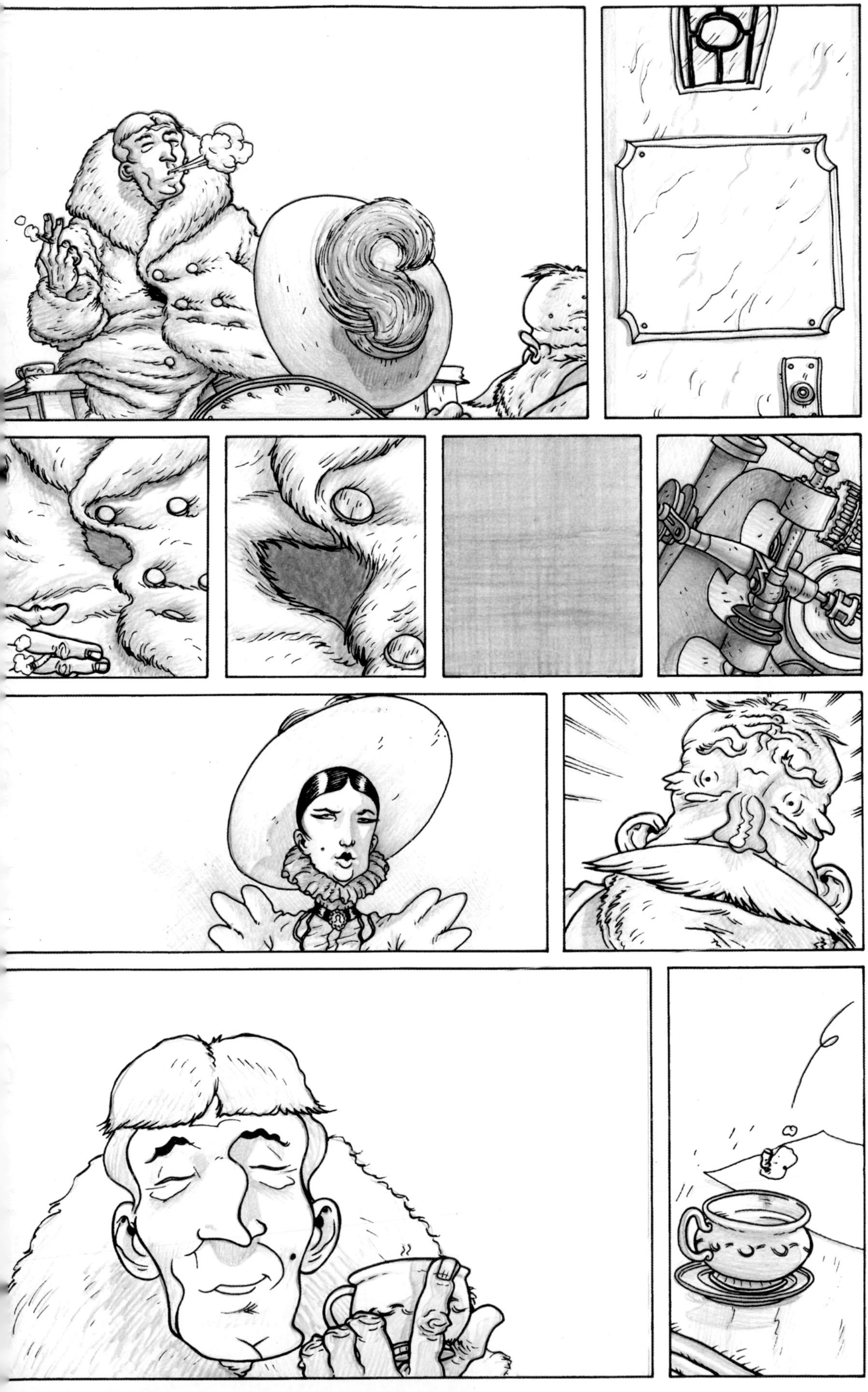

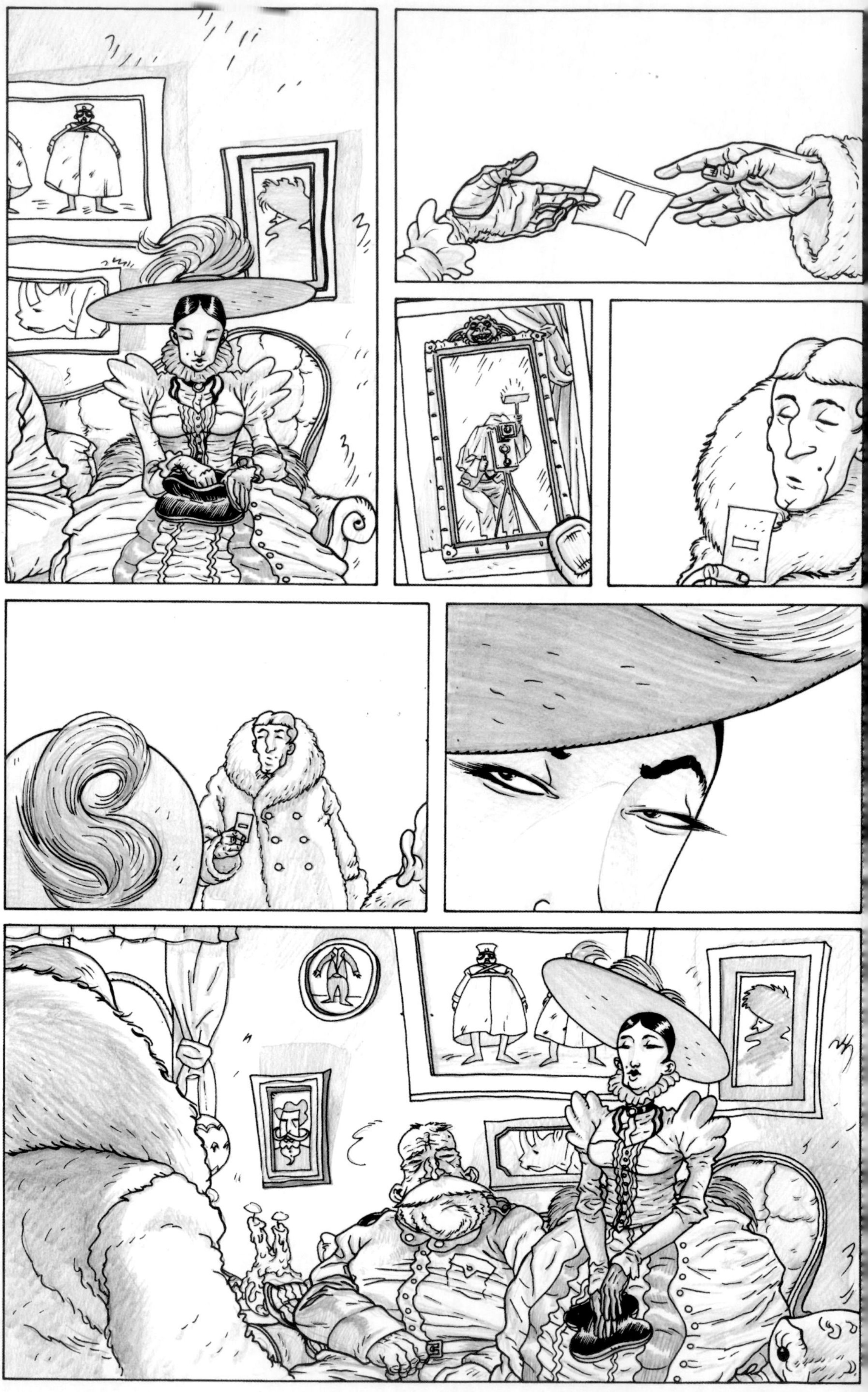

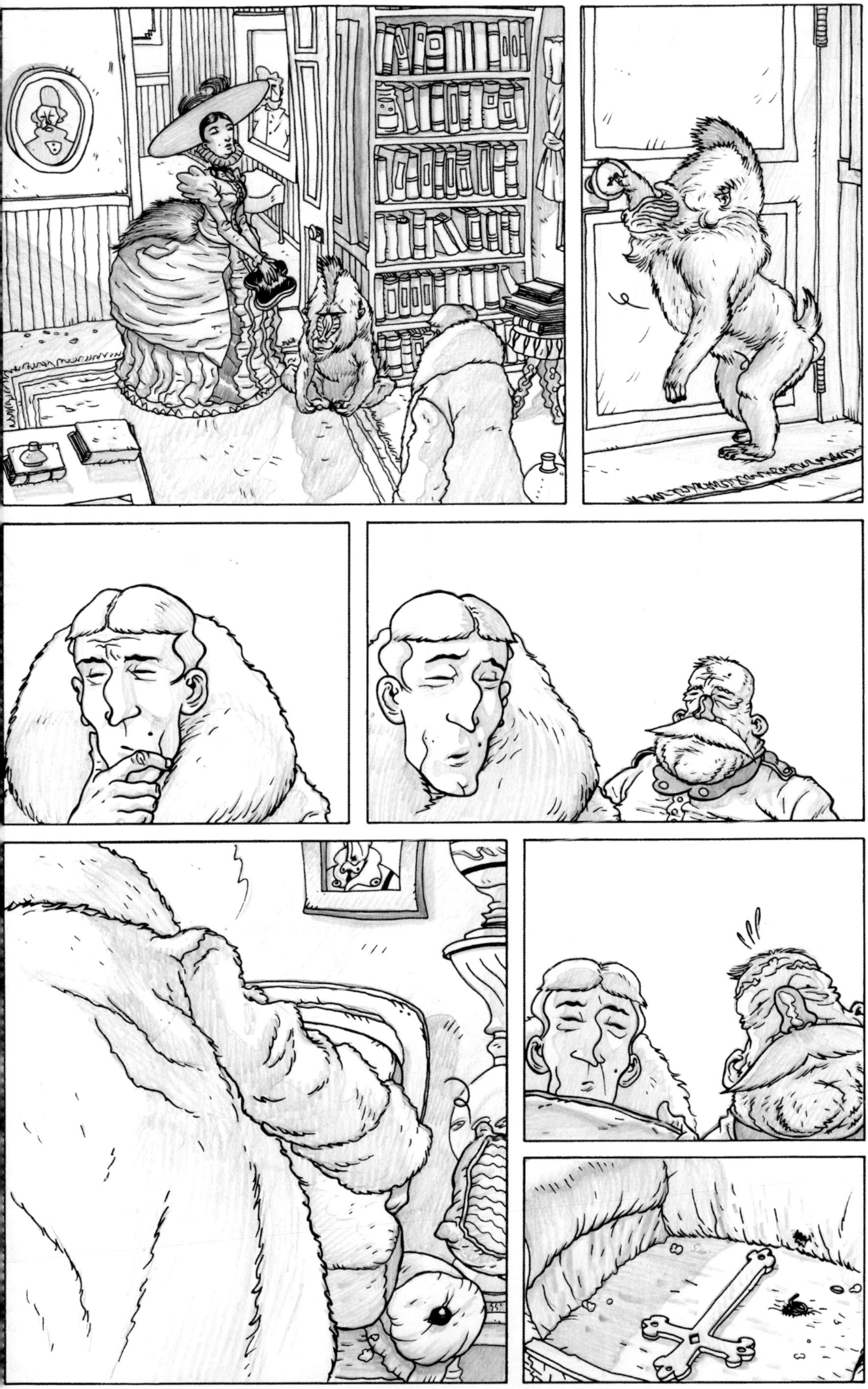

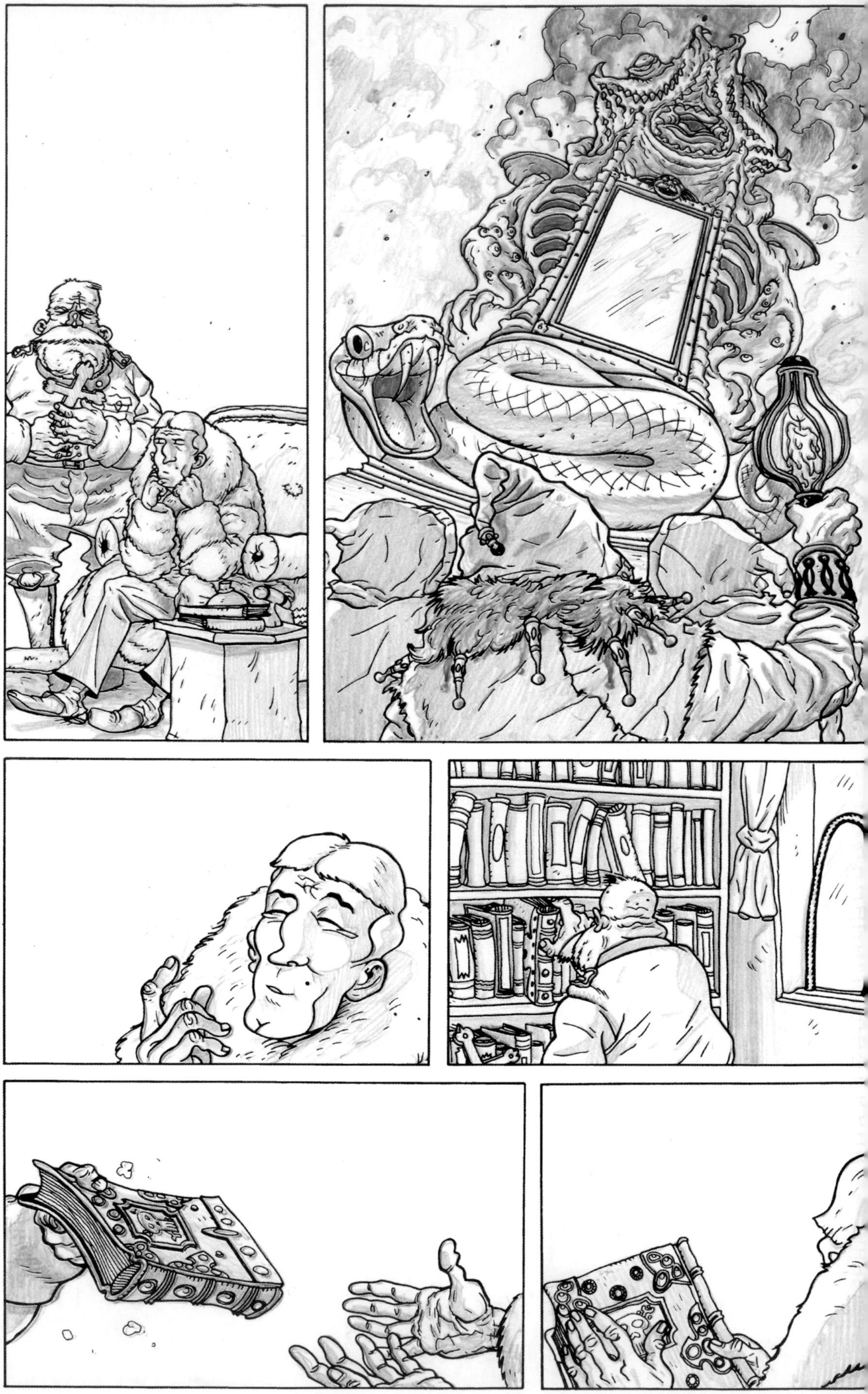

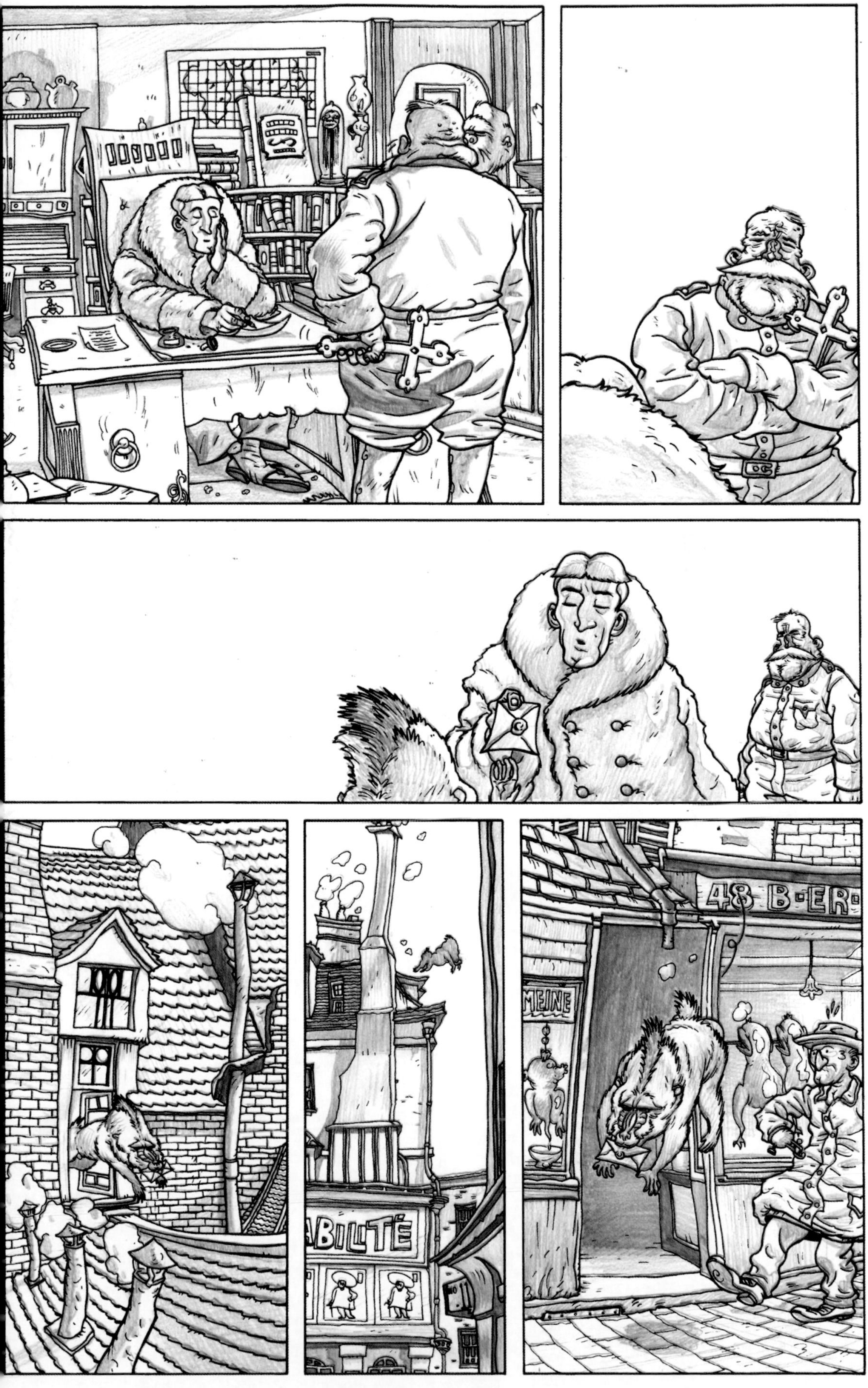
ABILITÉ
MEINE
48 B·ER

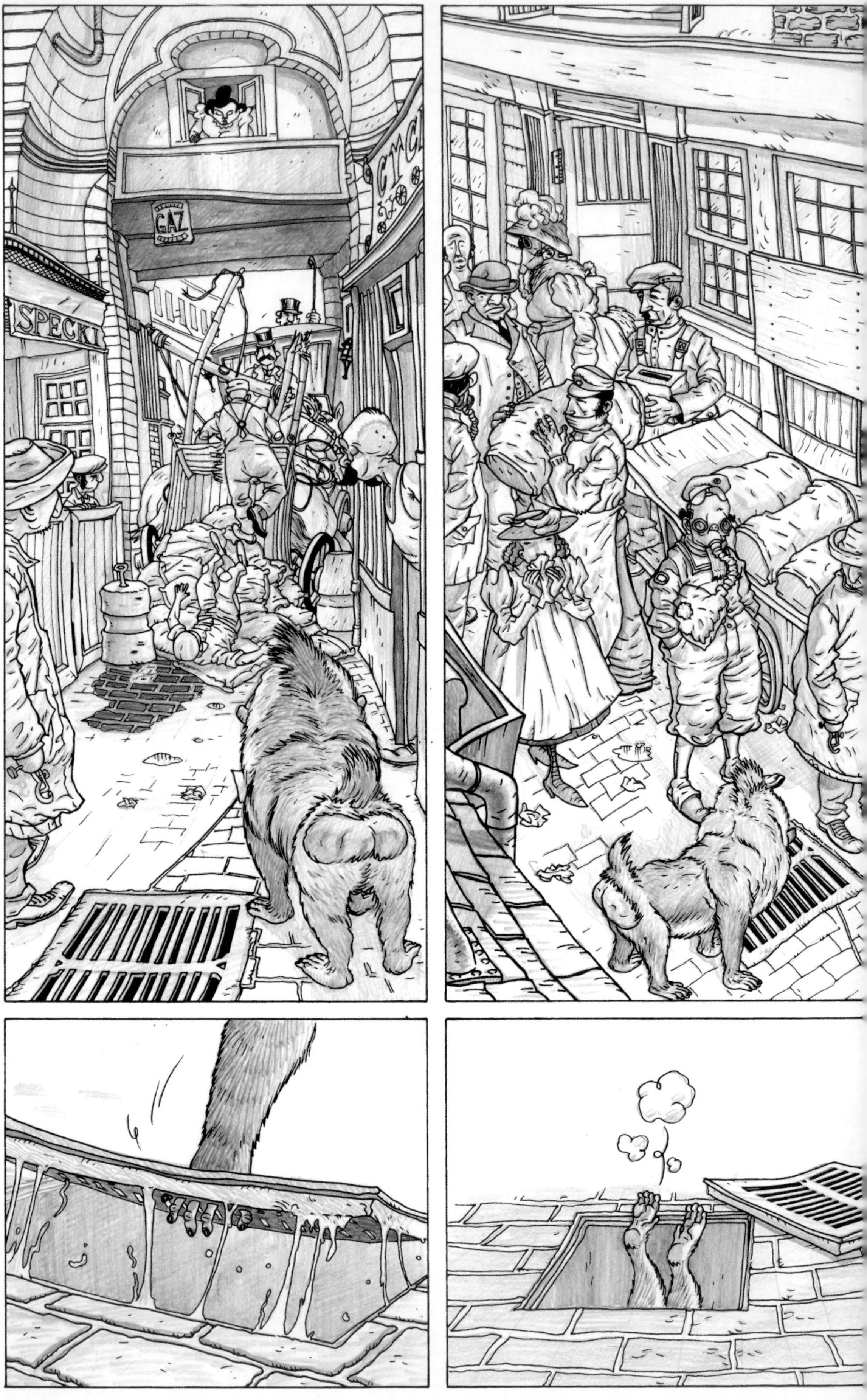

GAZ
SPECKI

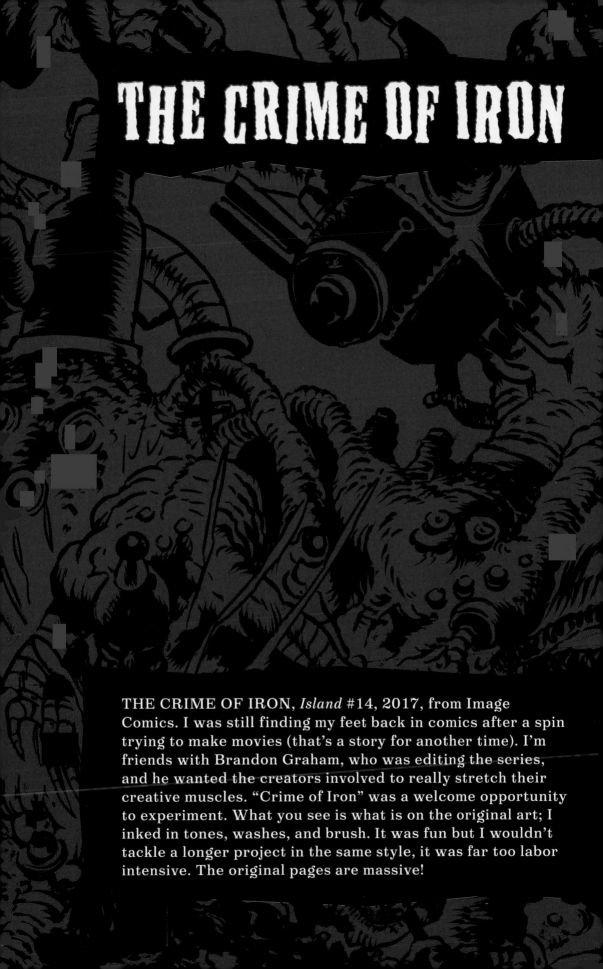

THE CRIME OF IRON

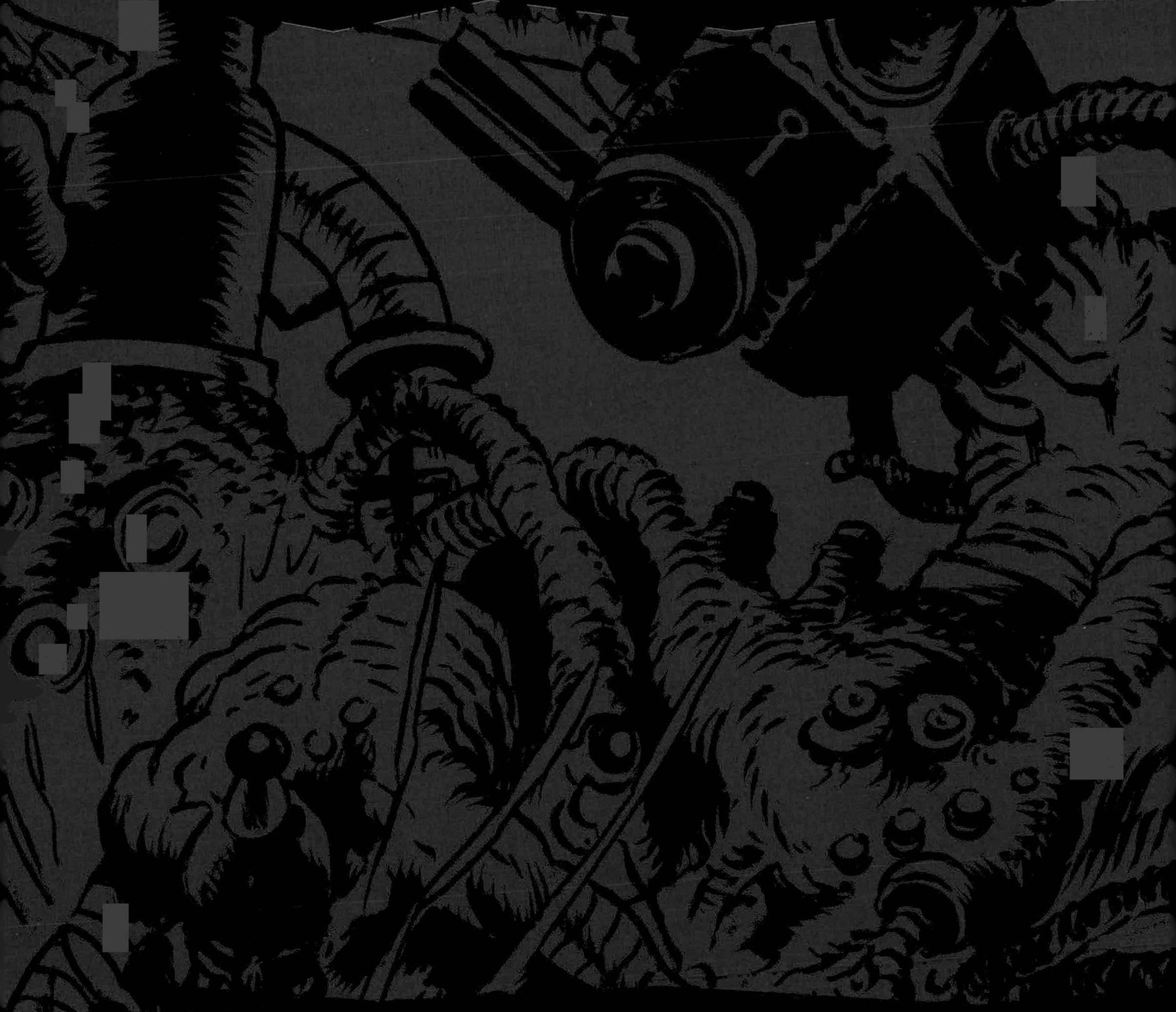

THE CRIME OF IRON, *Island* #14, 2017, from Image Comics. I was still finding my feet back in comics after a spin trying to make movies (that's a story for another time). I'm friends with Brandon Graham, who was editing the series, and he wanted the creators involved to really stretch their creative muscles. "Crime of Iron" was a welcome opportunity to experiment. What you see is what is on the original art; I inked in tones, washes, and brush. It was fun but I wouldn't tackle a longer project in the same style, it was far too labor intensive. The original pages are massive!

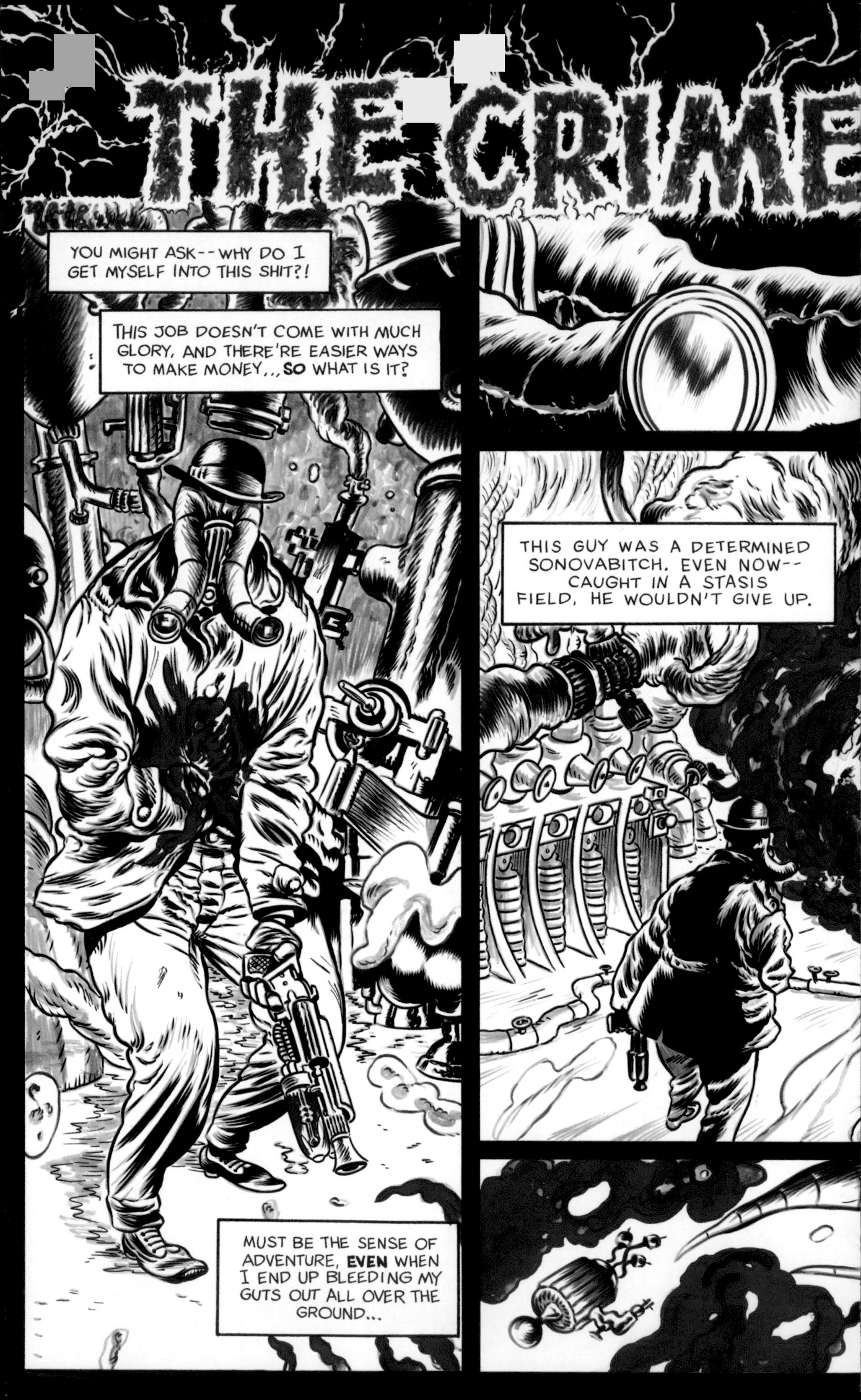
THE CRIME
YOU MIGHT ASK--WHY DO I GET MYSELF INTO THIS SHIT?!
THIS JOB DOESN'T COME WITH MUCH GLORY, AND THERE'RE EASIER WAYS TO MAKE MONEY,,, SO WHAT IS IT?
MUST BE THE SENSE OF ADVENTURE, EVEN WHEN I END UP BLEEDING MY GUTS OUT ALL OVER THE GROUND...
THIS GUY WAS A DETERMINED SONOVABITCH. EVEN NOW--CAUGHT IN A STASIS FIELD, HE WOULDN'T GIVE UP.

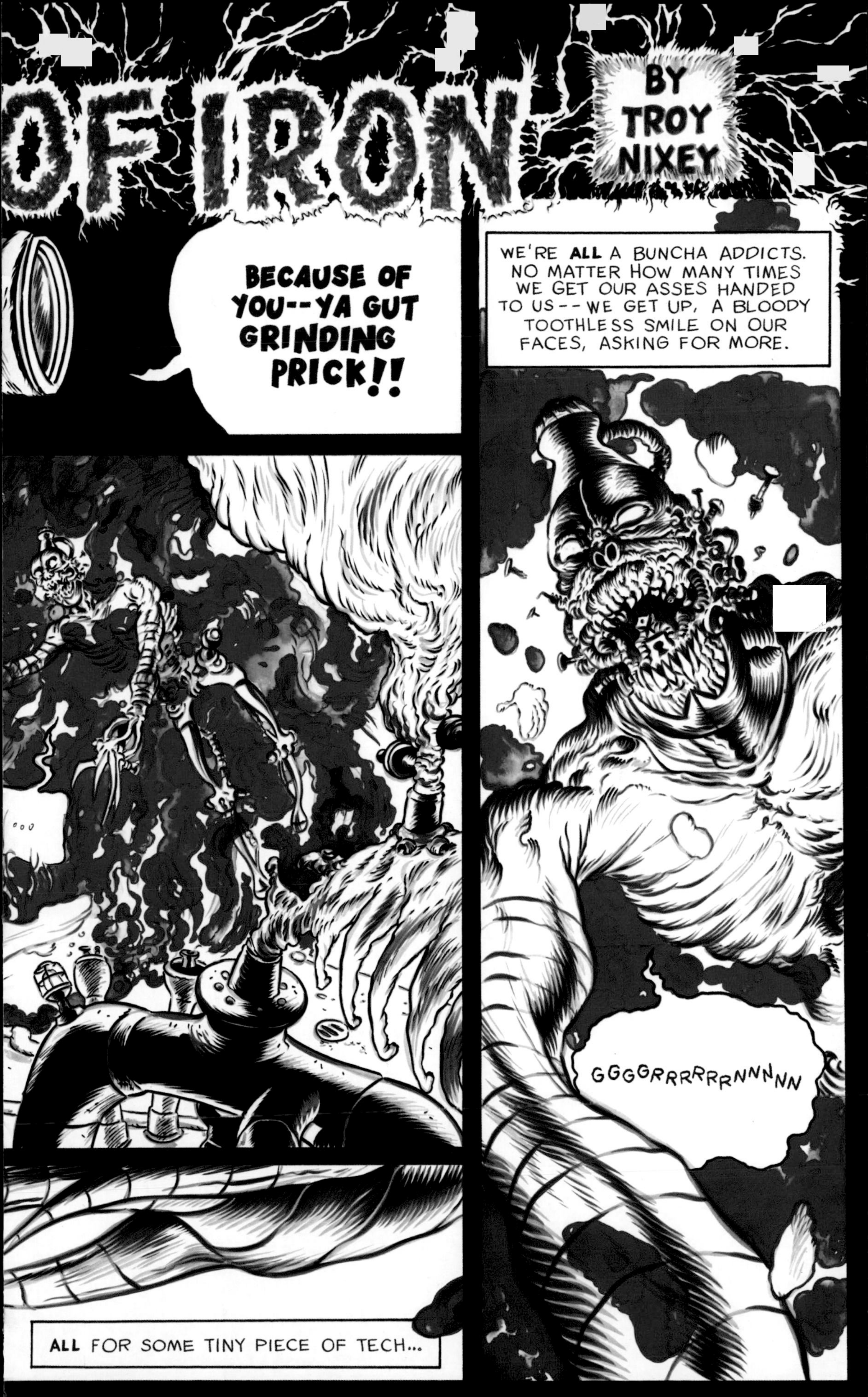
OF IRON
BY TROY NIXEY
BECAUSE OF YOU--YA GUT GRINDING PRICK!!
ALL FOR SOME TINY PIECE OF TECH...
WE'RE ALL A BUNCHA ADDICTS. NO MATTER HOW MANY TIMES WE GET OUR ASSES HANDED TO US--WE GET UP, A BLOODY TOOTHLESS SMILE ON OUR FACES, ASKING FOR MORE.
GGGGRRRRRRRNNNNNN

THIS JOB WAS JUST LIKE ALL THE REST- - RECOVER SOMETHING STOLEN OR LOST, IN THIS CASE STOLEN.

FFFOOOOSSSHHH

BEEP BEEP BEEP BEEP

IS TEN MILLION BLEAMS ENOUGH?

AN OLD MAN HAD A BLIP OF TECHNOLOGY PILFERED AND NEEDED IT BACK, HE WAS NUTS-- AND DESPERATE.

BLEAMS!? LOOK AT MY HAT--DO I LOOK LIKE SOMEONE WHO DEALS IN HOLO-CURRENCY?!

GLEEP! WHAT IS YOUR PREFERRED METHOD OF PAYMENT??

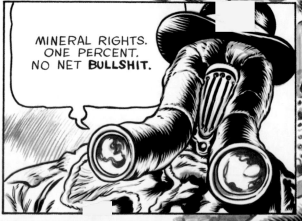

MINERAL RIGHTS. ONE PERCENT. NO NET BULLSHIT.

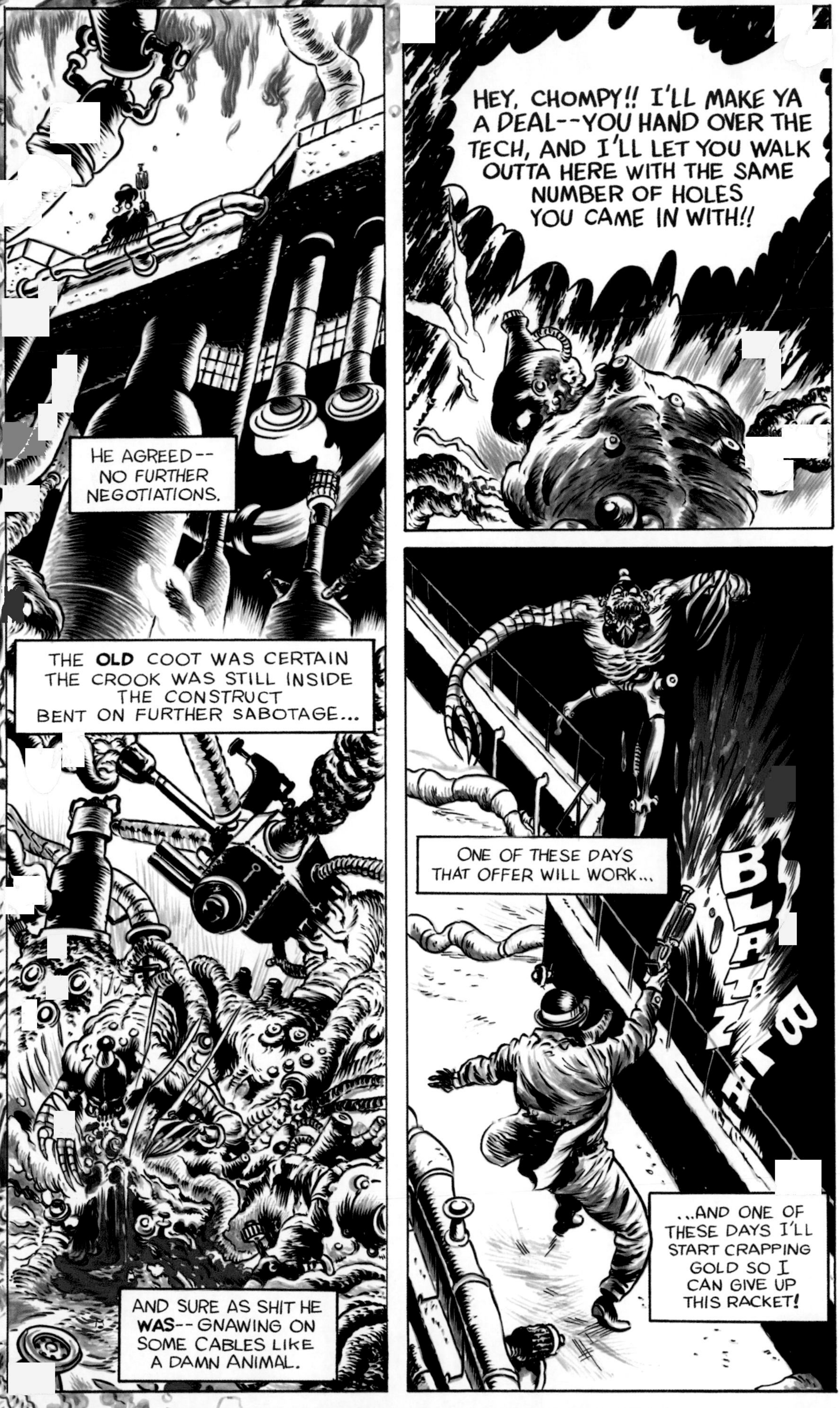
HE AGREED-- NO FURTHER NEGOTIATIONS.
THE OLD COOT WAS CERTAIN THE CROOK WAS STILL INSIDE THE CONSTRUCT BENT ON FURTHER SABOTAGE...
AND SURE AS SHIT HE WAS--GNAWING ON SOME CABLES LIKE A DAMN ANIMAL.
HEY, CHOMPY!! I'LL MAKE YA A DEAL--YOU HAND OVER THE TECH, AND I'LL LET YOU WALK OUTTA HERE WITH THE SAME NUMBER OF HOLES YOU CAME IN WITH!!
ONE OF THESE DAYS THAT OFFER WILL WORK...
...AND ONE OF THESE DAYS I'LL START CRAPPING GOLD SO I CAN GIVE UP THIS RACKET!

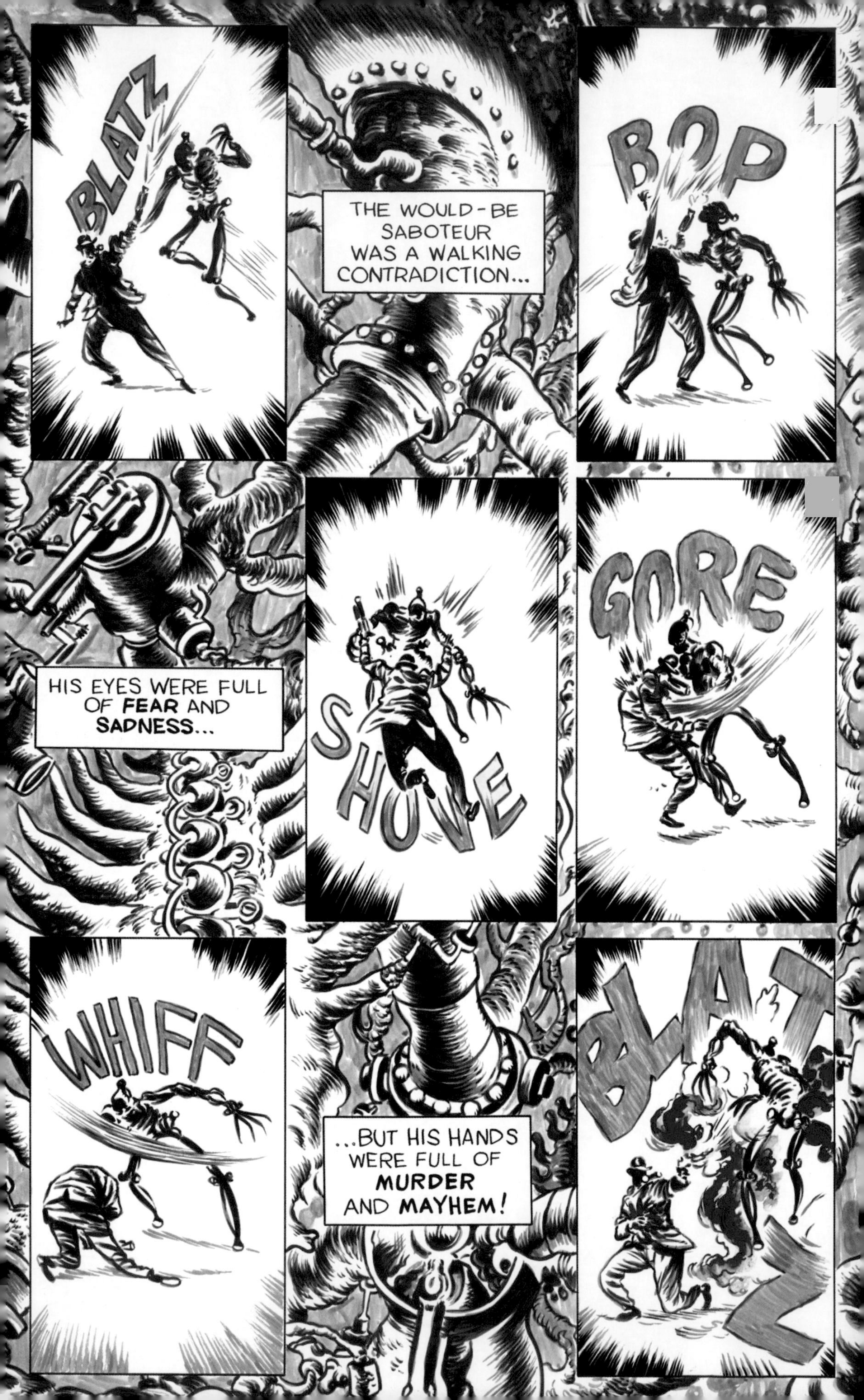
BLATZ
THE WOULD-BE SABOTEUR WAS A WALKING CONTRADICTION...
BOP
HIS EYES WERE FULL OF **FEAR** AND **SADNESS**...
SHOVE
GORE
WHIFF
...BUT HIS HANDS WERE FULL OF **MURDER** AND **MAYHEM**!
BLAT

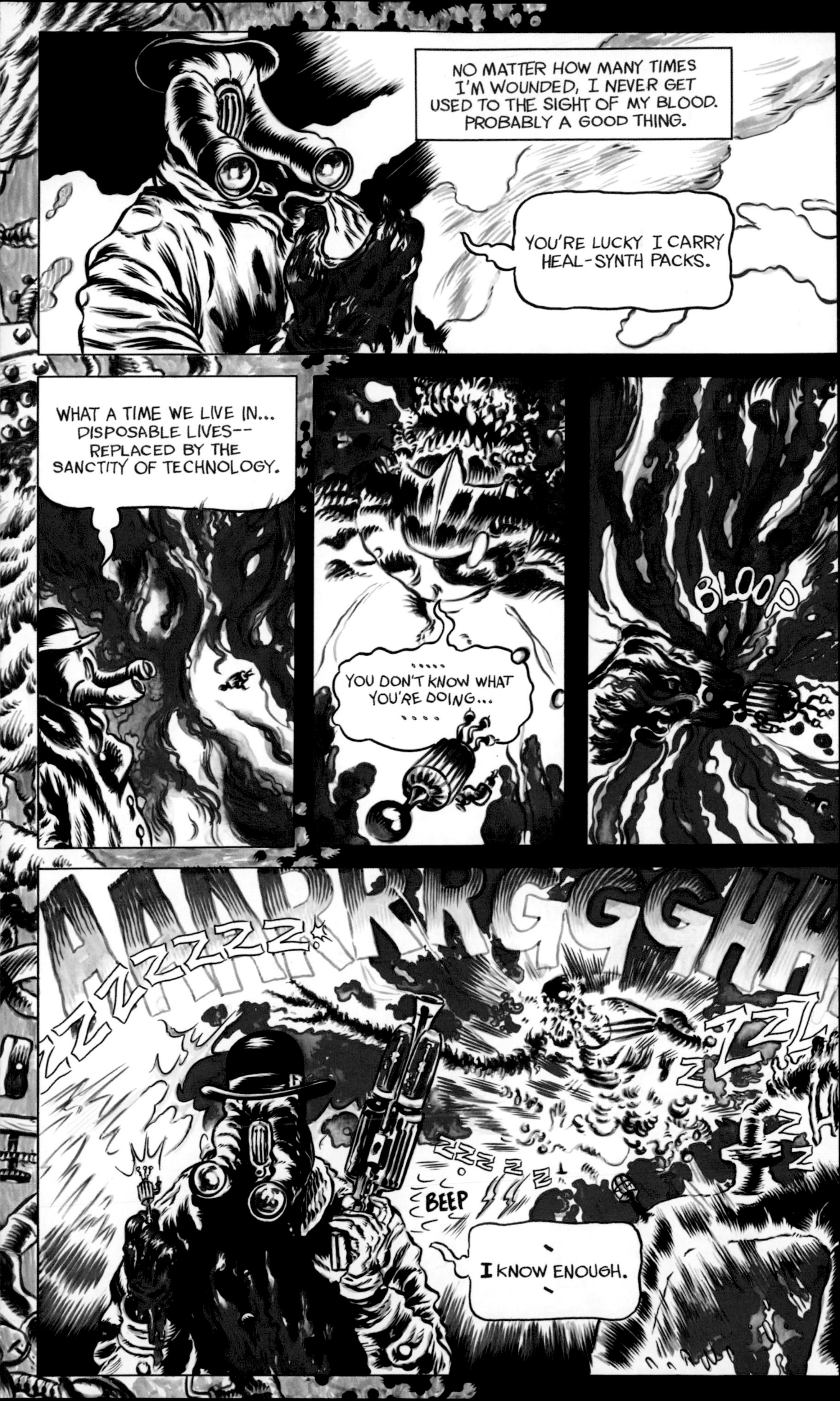
NO MATTER HOW MANY TIMES I'M WOUNDED, I NEVER GET USED TO THE SIGHT OF MY BLOOD. PROBABLY A GOOD THING.
YOU'RE LUCKY I CARRY HEAL-SYNTH PACKS.
WHAT A TIME WE LIVE IN... DISPOSABLE LIVES-- REPLACED BY THE SANCTITY OF TECHNOLOGY.
..... YOU DON'T KNOW WHAT YOU'RE DOING... ....
BLOOP
AAARRGGGH
ZZZZZZZZ
BEEP
I KNOW ENOUGH.

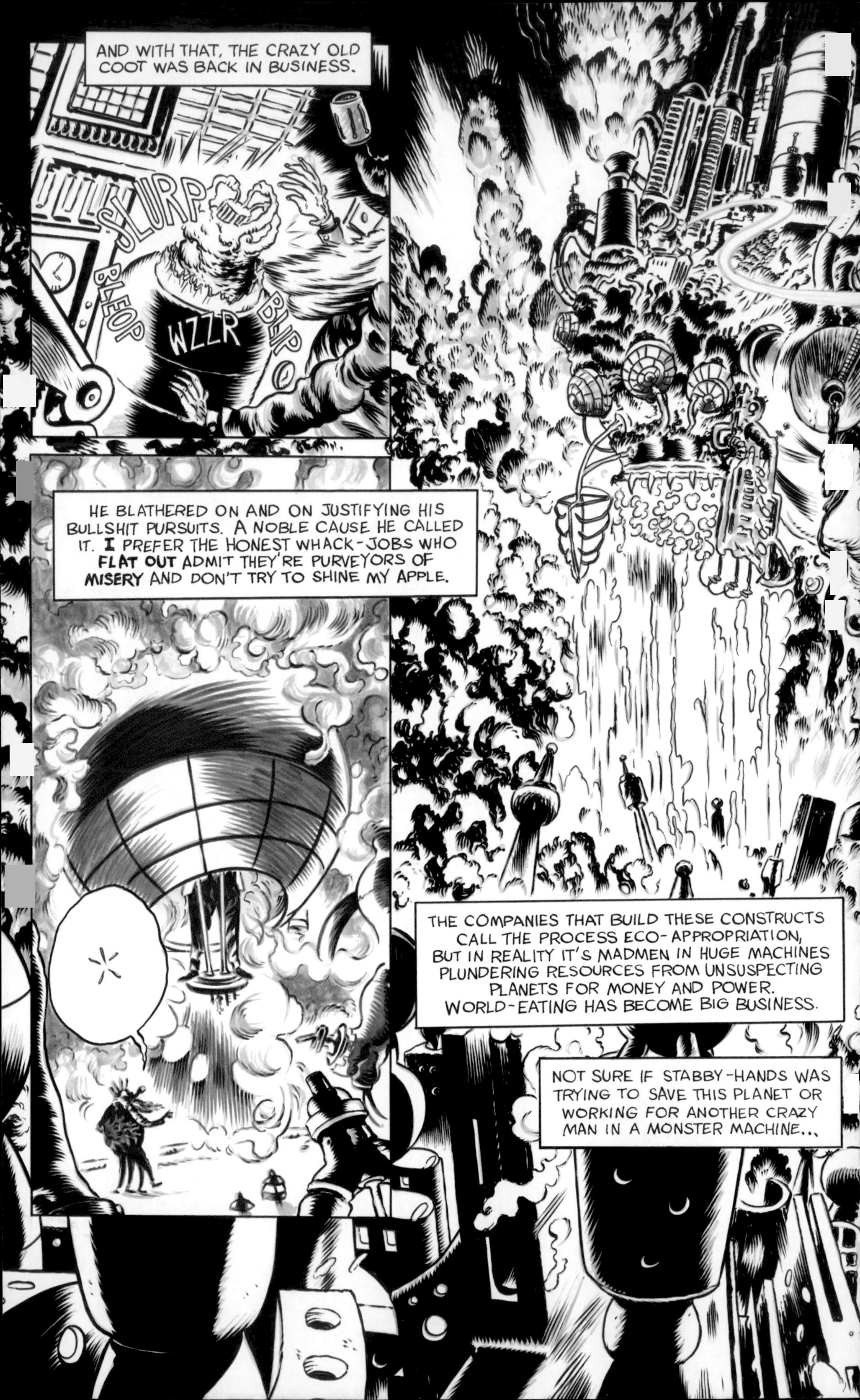
AND WITH THAT, THE CRAZY OLD COOT WAS BACK IN BUSINESS.
SLURP
BLEOP
WZZR
BLIP
HE BLATHERED ON AND ON JUSTIFYING HIS BULLSHIT PURSUITS. A NOBLE CAUSE HE CALLED IT. I PREFER THE HONEST WHACK-JOBS WHO FLAT OUT ADMIT THEY'RE PURVEYORS OF MISERY AND DON'T TRY TO SHINE MY APPLE.
THE COMPANIES THAT BUILD THESE CONSTRUCTS CALL THE PROCESS ECO-APPROPRIATION, BUT IN REALITY IT'S MADMEN IN HUGE MACHINES PLUNDERING RESOURCES FROM UNSUSPECTING PLANETS FOR MONEY AND POWER. WORLD-EATING HAS BECOME BIG BUSINESS.
NOT SURE IF STABBY-HANDS WAS TRYING TO SAVE THIS PLANET OR WORKING FOR ANOTHER CRAZY MAN IN A MONSTER MACHINE...

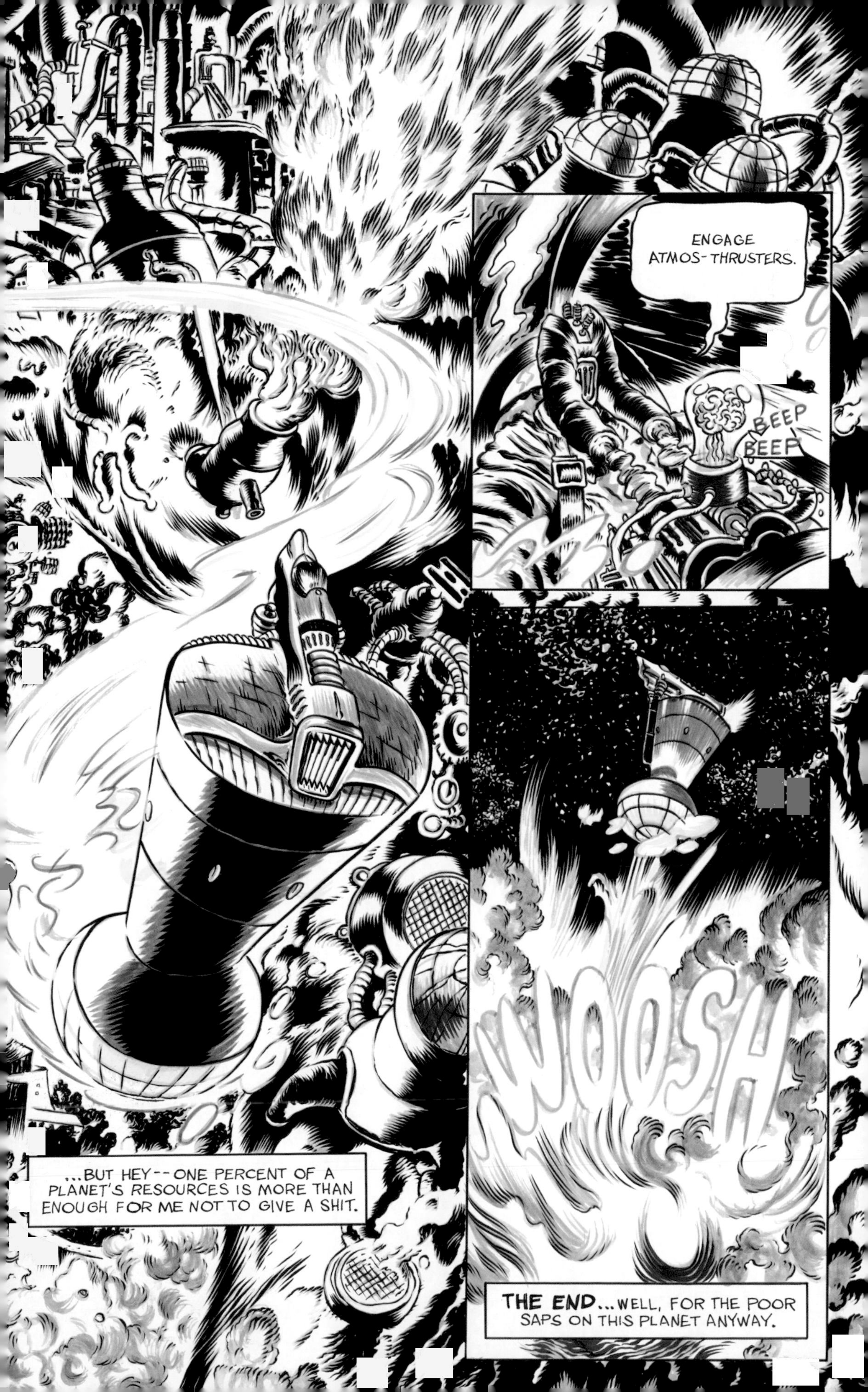
ENGAGE ATMOS-THRUSTERS.
BEEP BEEP
...BUT HEY--ONE PERCENT OF A PLANET'S RESOURCES IS MORE THAN ENOUGH FOR ME NOT TO GIVE A SHIT.
WOOSH
THE END...WELL, FOR THE POOR SAPS ON THIS PLANET ANYWAY.

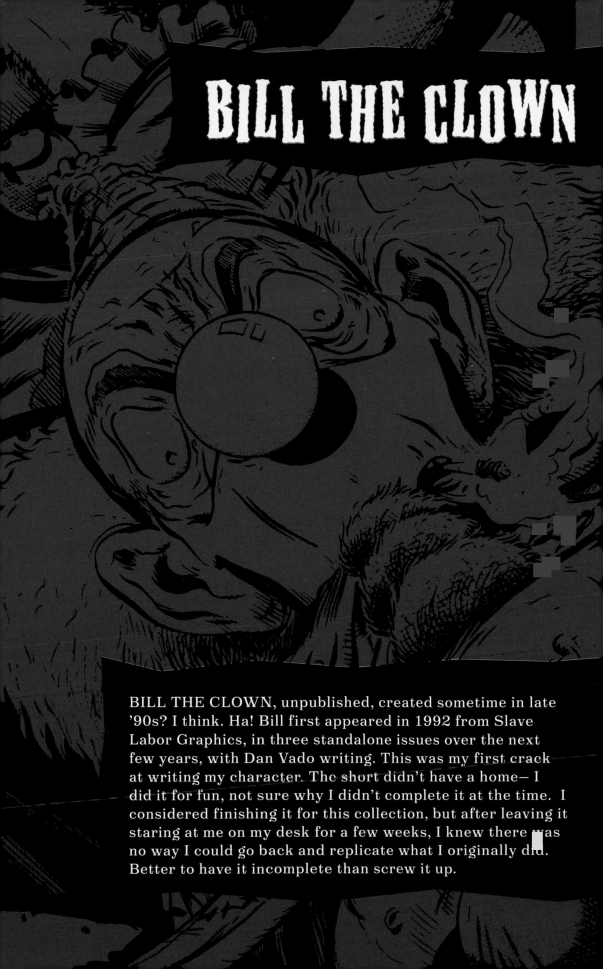

BILL THE CLOWN

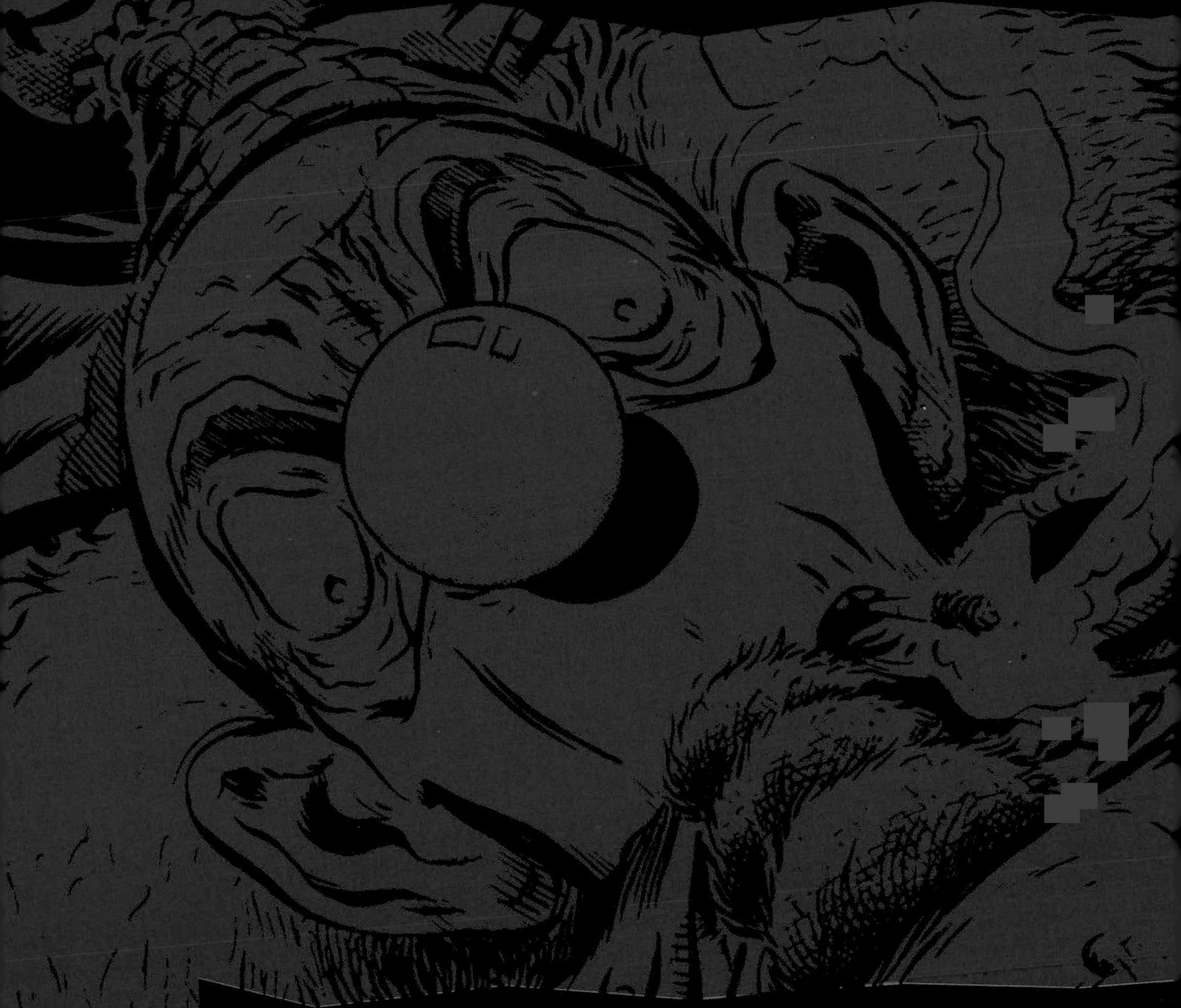

BILL THE CLOWN, unpublished, created sometime in late '90s? I think. Ha! Bill first appeared in 1992 from Slave Labor Graphics, in three standalone issues over the next few years, with Dan Vado writing. This was my first crack at writing my character. The short didn't have a home– I did it for fun, not sure why I didn't complete it at the time. I considered finishing it for this collection, but after leaving it staring at me on my desk for a few weeks, I knew there was no way I could go back and replicate what I originally did. Better to have it incomplete than screw it up.

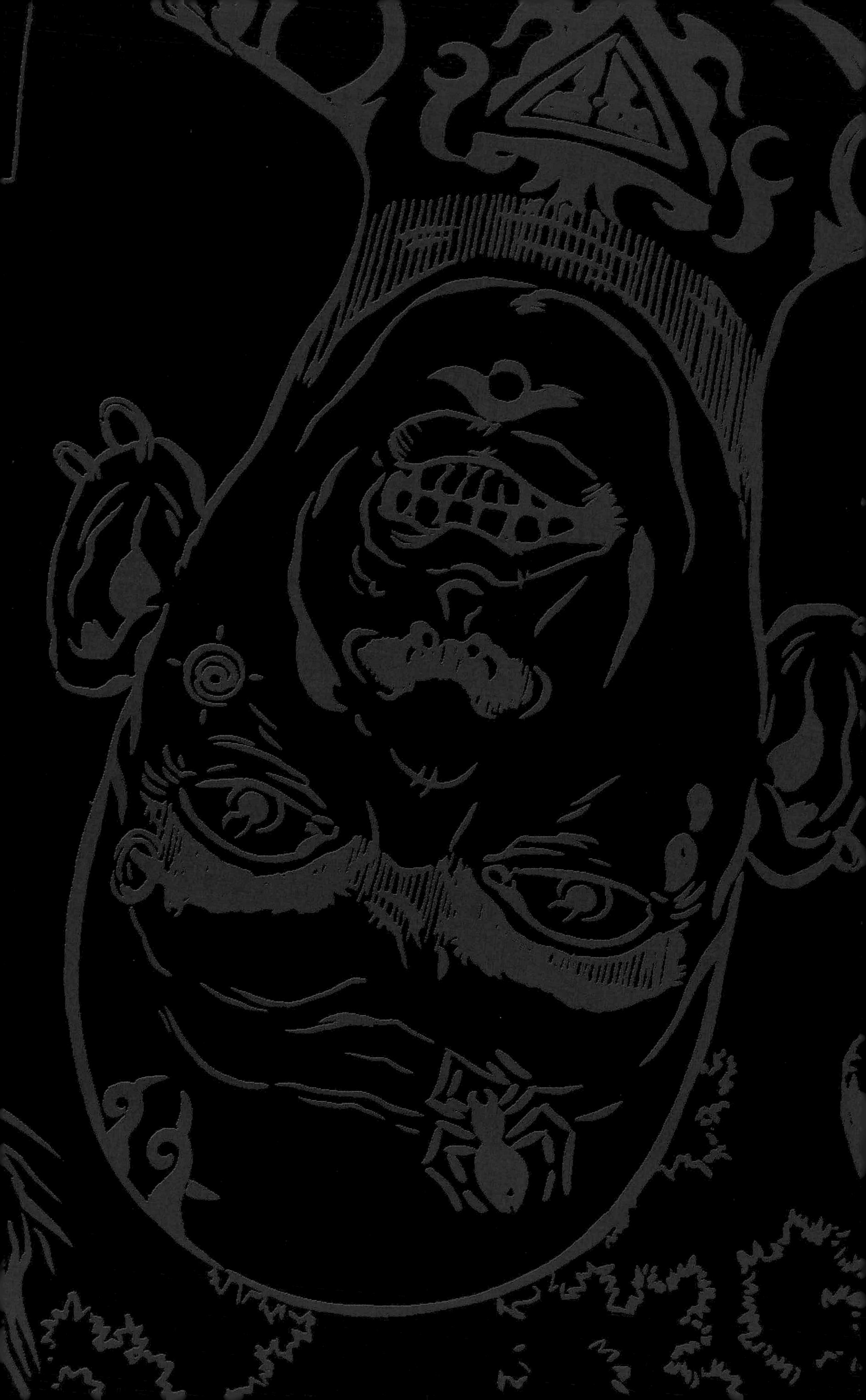

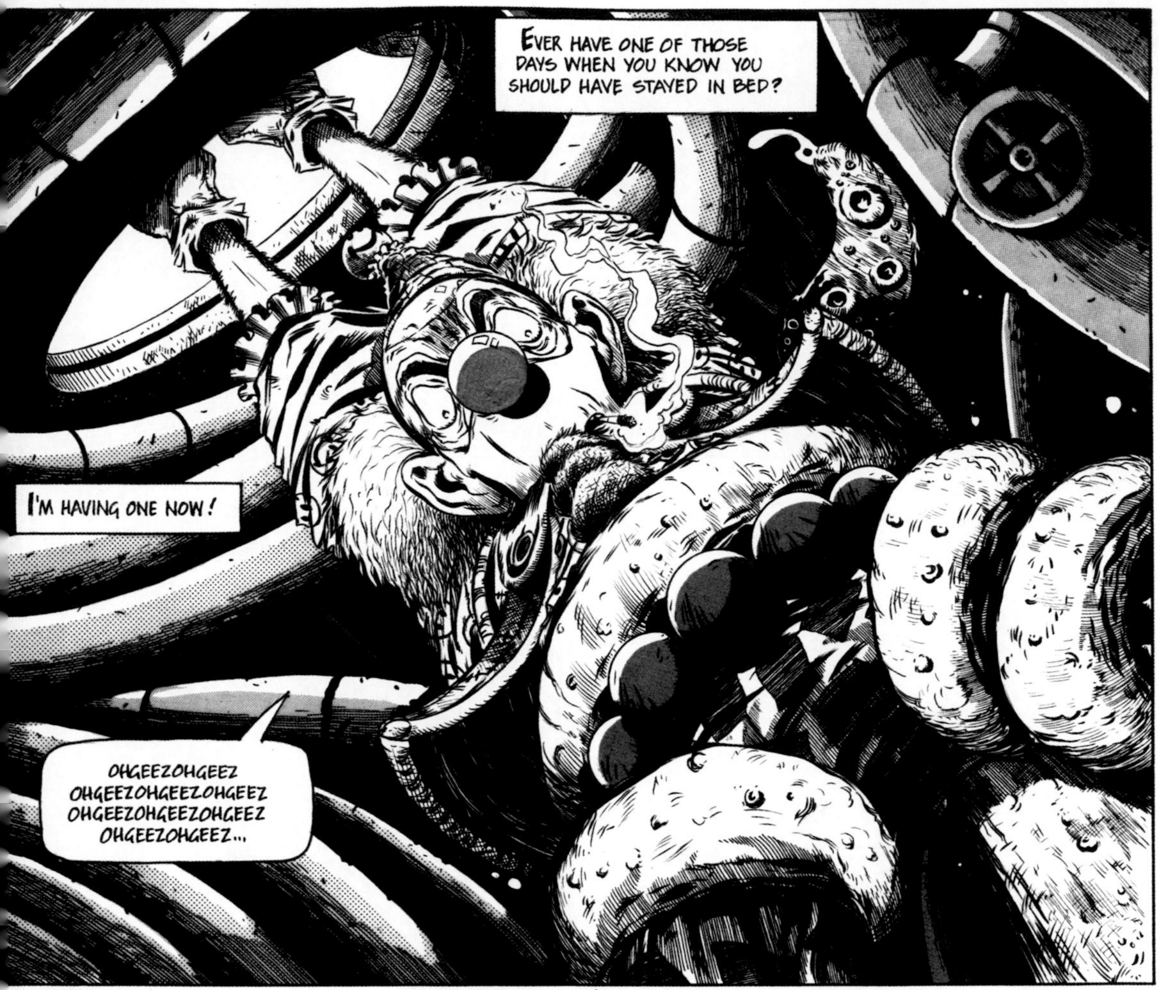
EVER HAVE ONE OF THOSE DAYS WHEN YOU KNOW YOU SHOULD HAVE STAYED IN BED?
I'M HAVING ONE NOW!
OHGEEZOHGEEZ OHGEEZOHGEEZOHGEEZ OHGEEZOHGEEZOHGEEZ OHGEEZOHGEEZ...

BILL THE CLOWN IN:

THE DAY THE ALIENS ATE MY BRAIN!!

CREATED · WRITTEN · DRAWN · INKED BY: TA DAH! TROY NIXEY   LETTERS BY: ROGER WILLIAMSON

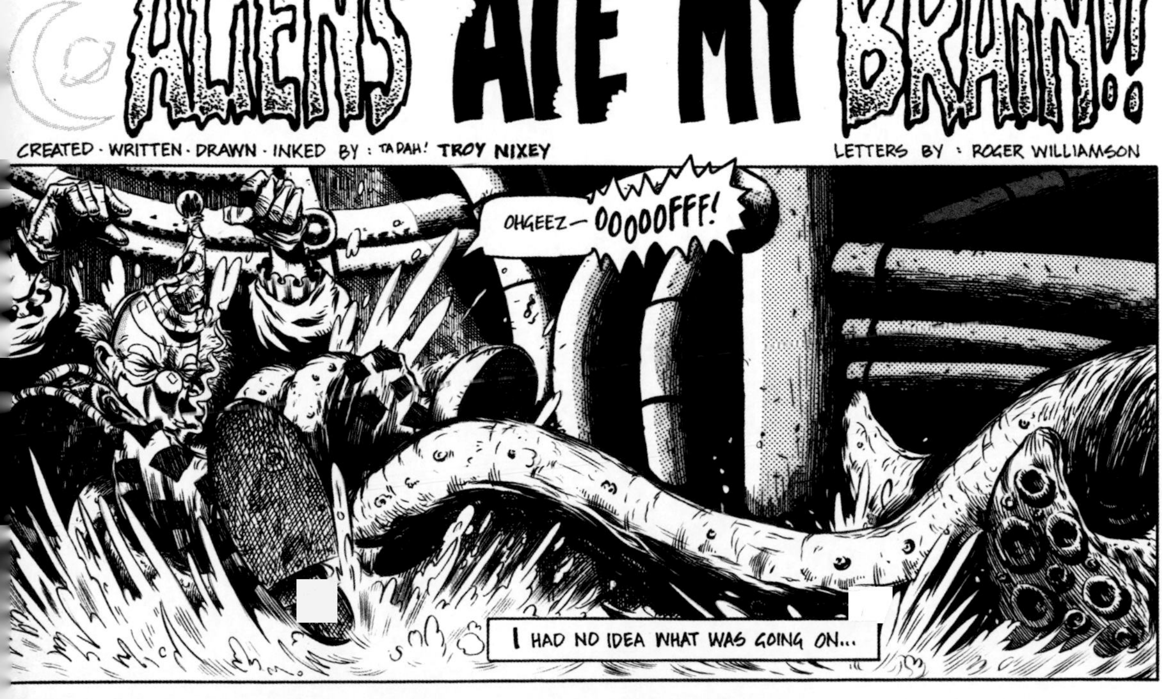
OHGEEZ— OOOOOFFF!
I HAD NO IDEA WHAT WAS GOING ON...

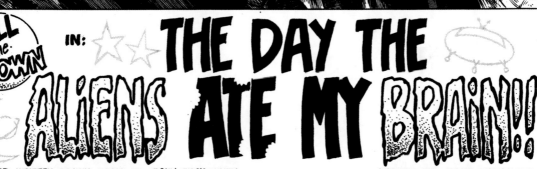

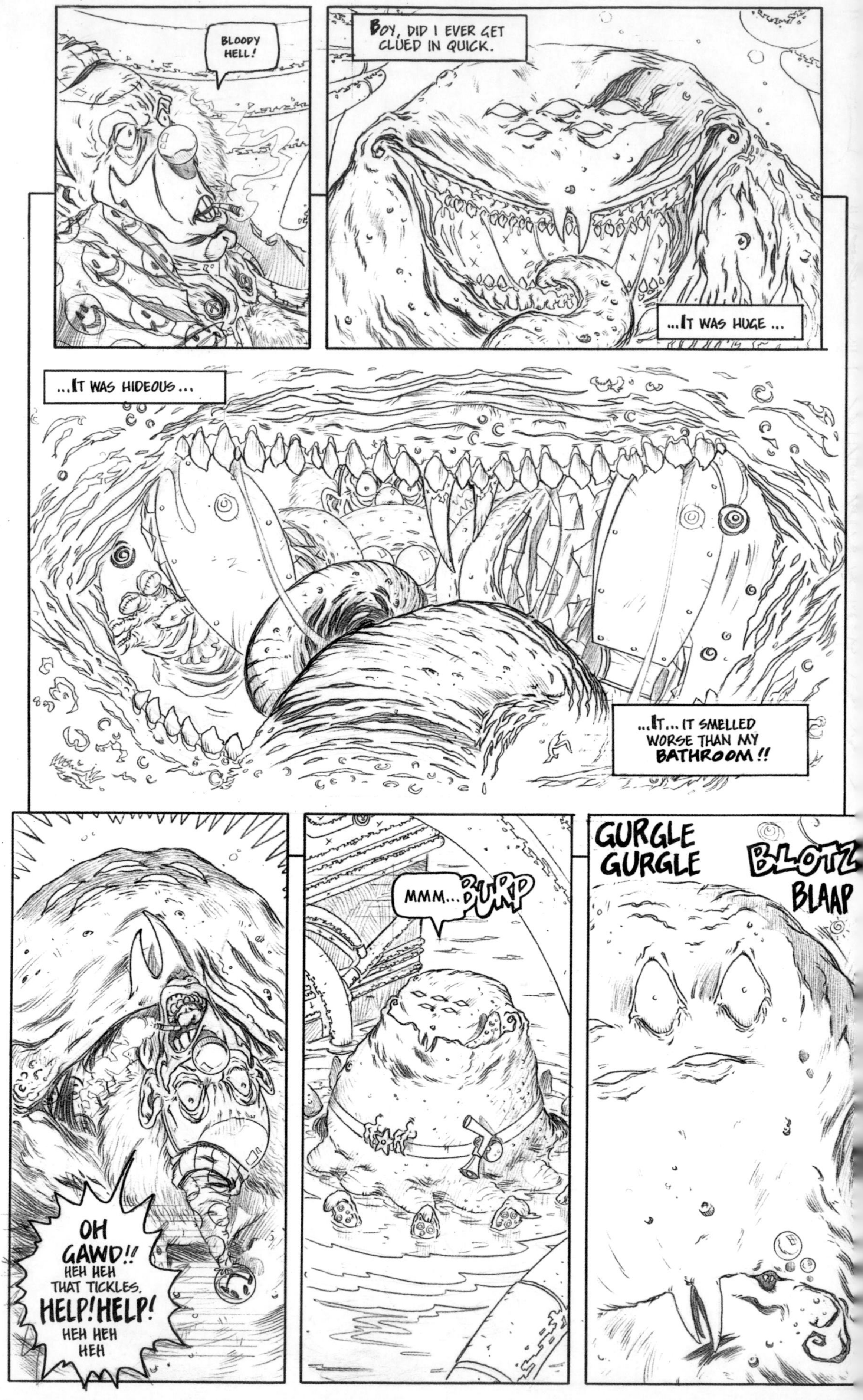
BLOODY HELL!
BOY, DID I EVER GET CLUED IN QUICK.
...IT WAS HUGE ...
...IT WAS HIDEOUS ...
...IT... IT SMELLED WORSE THAN MY BATHROOM!!
OH GAWD!! HEH HEH THAT TICKLES. HELP! HELP! HEH HEH HEH
MMM... BURP
GURGLE GURGLE
BLOTZ
BLAAP

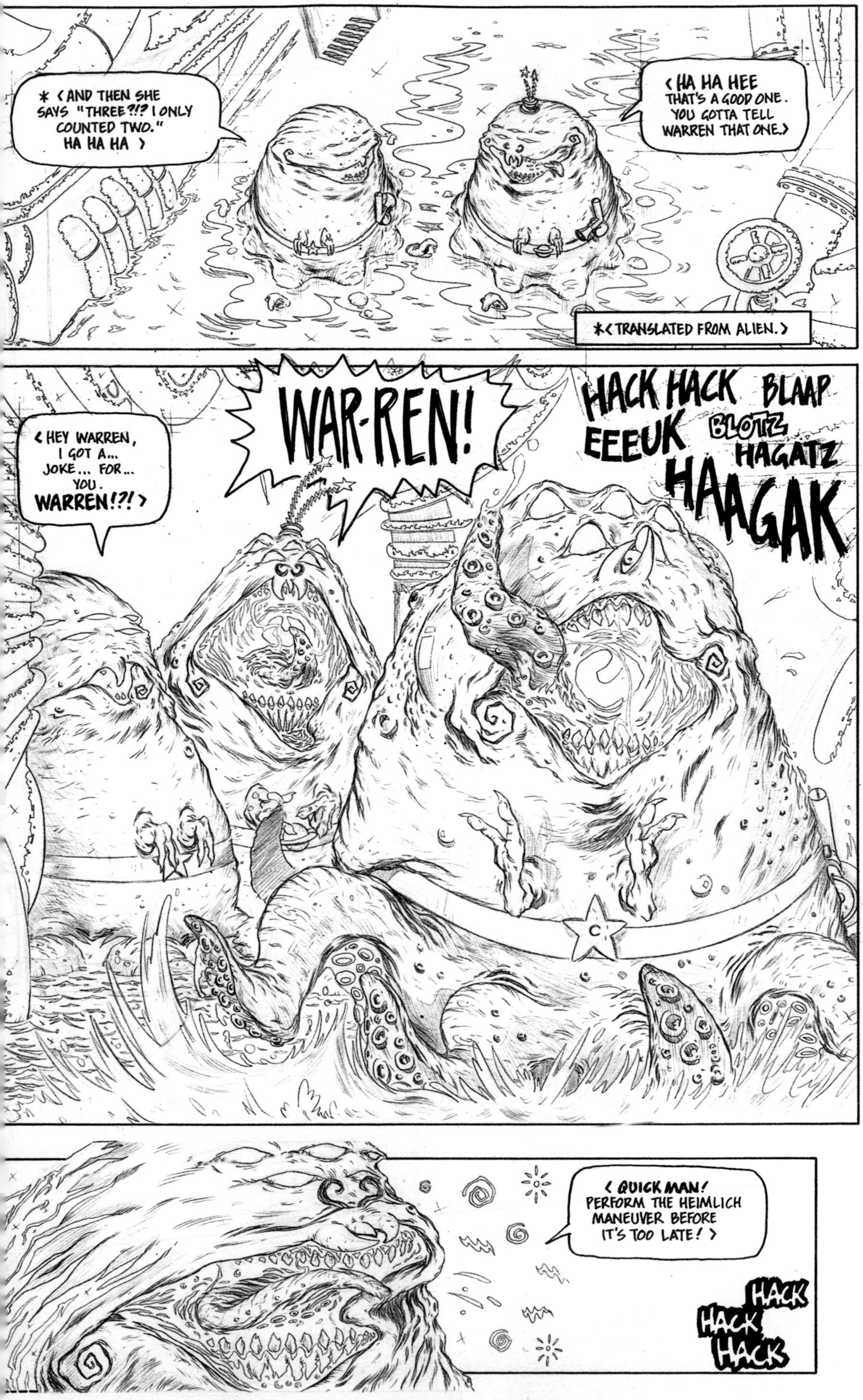
*‹AND THEN SHE SAYS "THREE?!? I ONLY COUNTED TWO." HA HA HA›
‹HA HA HEE THAT'S A GOOD ONE. YOU GOTTA TELL WARREN THAT ONE.›
*‹TRANSLATED FROM ALIEN.›
‹HEY WARREN, I GOT A... JOKE... FOR... YOU. WARREN!?!›
WAR-REN!
HACK HACK BLAAP
EEEUK BLOTZ HAGATZ
HAAGAK
‹QUICK MAN! PERFORM THE HEIMLICH MANEUVER BEFORE IT'S TOO LATE!›
HACK
HACK
HACK

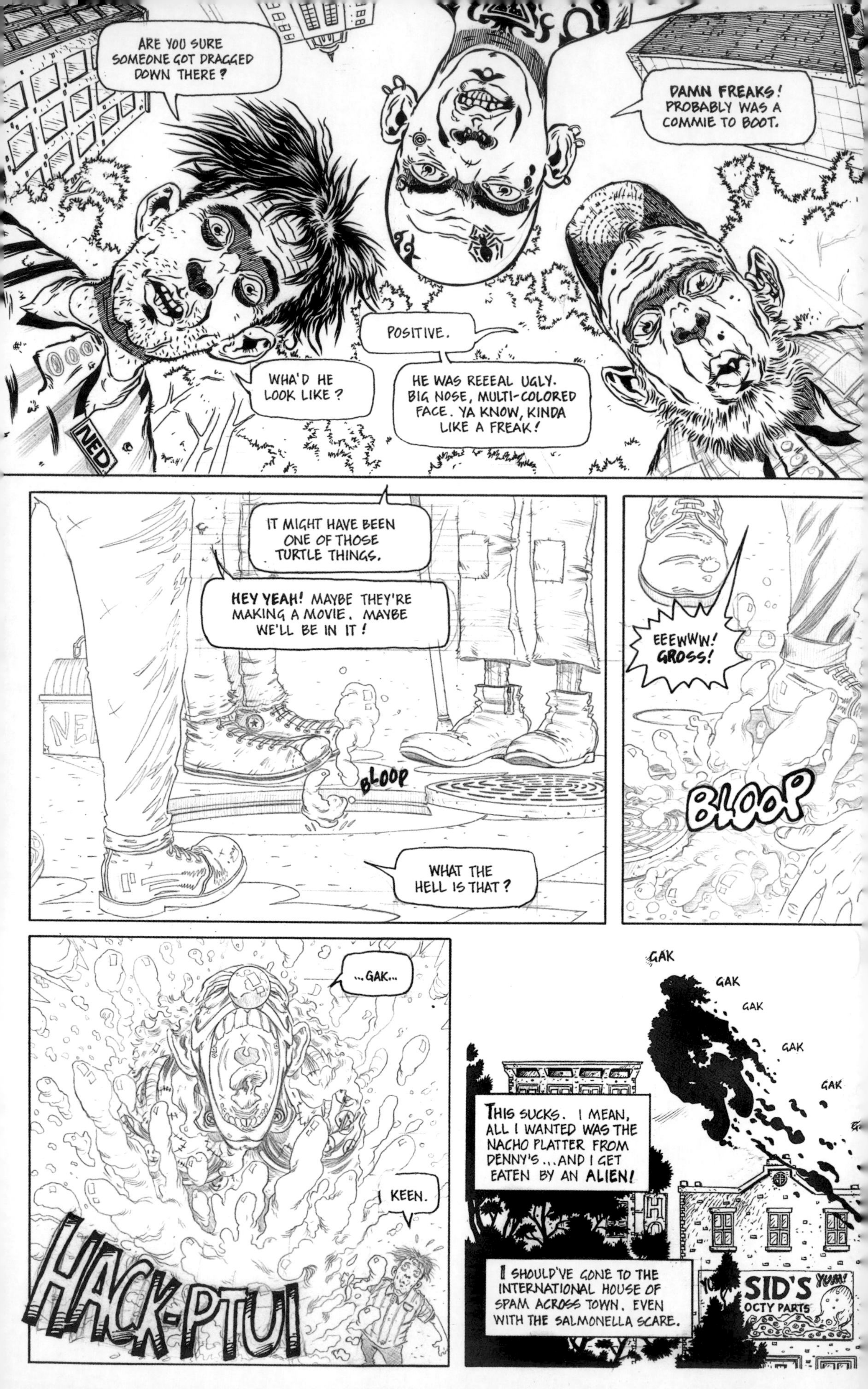

ARE YOU SURE SOMEONE GOT DRAGGED DOWN THERE?
DAMN FREAKS! PROBABLY WAS A COMMIE TO BOOT.
POSITIVE.
WHA'D HE LOOK LIKE?
HE WAS REEEAL UGLY. BIG NOSE, MULTI-COLORED FACE. YA KNOW, KINDA LIKE A FREAK!
NED
IT MIGHT HAVE BEEN ONE OF THOSE TURTLE THINGS.
HEY YEAH! MAYBE THEY'RE MAKING A MOVIE. MAYBE WE'LL BE IN IT!
BLOOP
WHAT THE HELL IS THAT?
EEEWWW! GROSS!
BLOOP
...GAK...
I KEEN.
HACK-PTUI
GAK
GAK
GAK
GAK
GAK
THIS SUCKS. I MEAN, ALL I WANTED WAS THE NACHO PLATTER FROM DENNY'S...AND I GET EATEN BY AN ALIEN!
I SHOULD'VE GONE TO THE INTERNATIONAL HOUSE OF SPAM ACROSS TOWN. EVEN WITH THE SALMONELLA SCARE.
SID'S
YUM!
OCTY PARTS

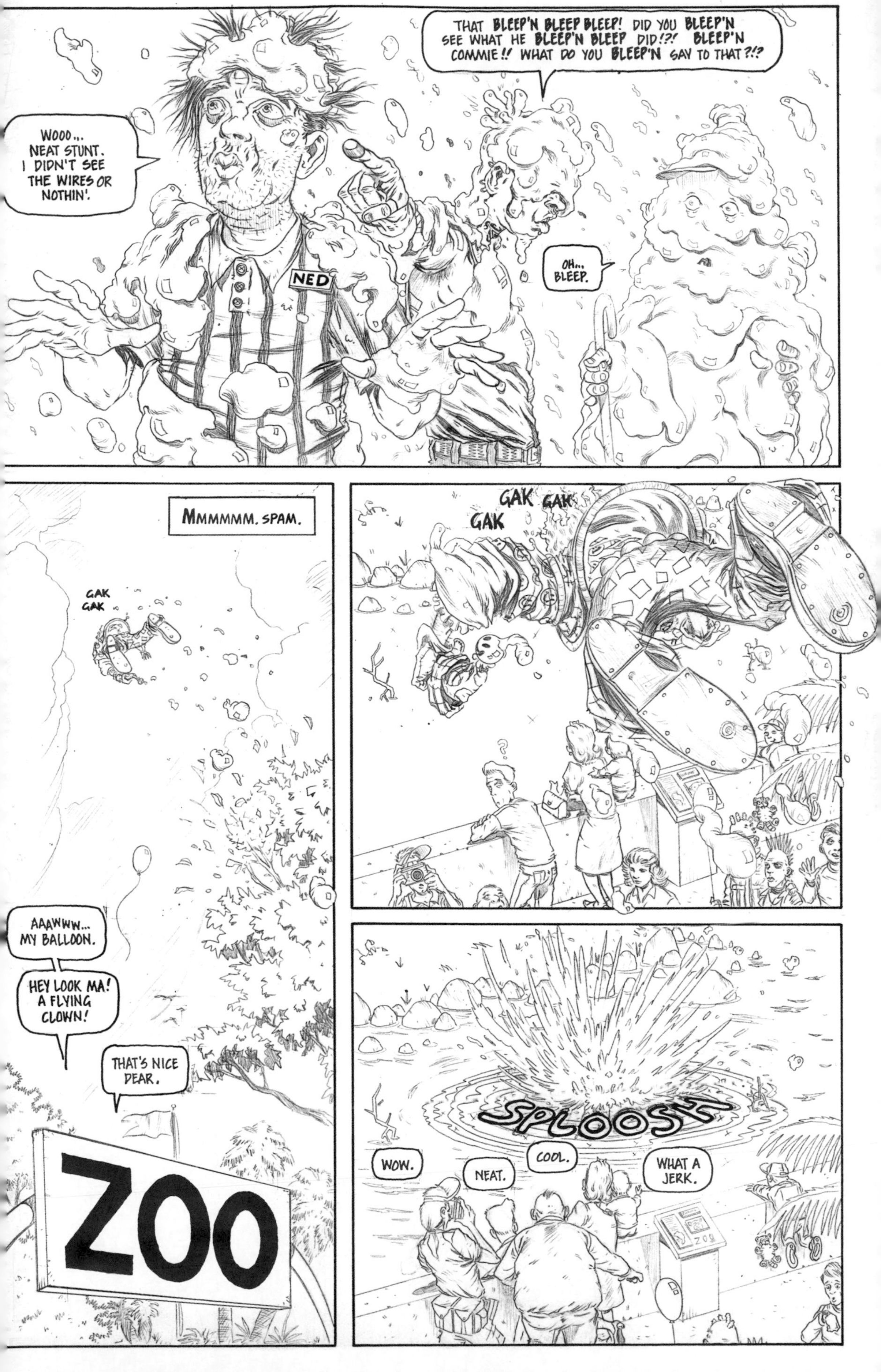
THAT BLEEP'N BLEEP BLEEP! DID YOU BLEEP'N SEE WHAT HE BLEEP'N BLEEP DID!?! BLEEP'N COMMIE!! WHAT DO YOU BLEEP'N SAY TO THAT?!?
WOOO... NEAT STUNT. I DIDN'T SEE THE WIRES OR NOTHIN'.
NED
OH... BLEEP.
MMMMMM. SPAM.
GAK GAK
GAK GAK GAK
AAAWWW... MY BALLOON.
HEY LOOK MA! A FLYING CLOWN!
THAT'S NICE DEAR.
ZOO
SPLOOSH
WOW.
NEAT.
COOL.
WHAT A JERK.

OOH OOH AHH AHH

OH MAN...

OOH OOH AHH AHH OOH OOH AHH AHH

I NEED A DRINK.

AHH

SPLUT

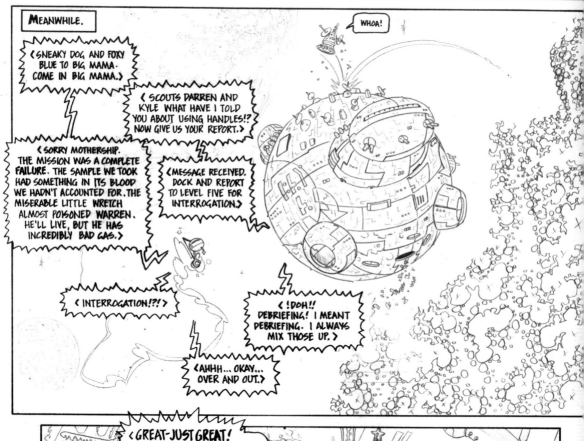

MEANWHILE.

‹SNEAKY DOG AND FOXY BLUE TO BIG MAMA. COME IN BIG MAMA.›

WHOA!

‹SCOUTS DARREN AND KYLE WHAT HAVE I TOLD YOU ABOUT USING HANDLES!? NOW GIVE US YOUR REPORT.›

‹SORRY MOTHERSHIP. THE MISSION WAS A COMPLETE FAILURE. THE SAMPLE WE TOOK HAD SOMETHING IN ITS BLOOD WE HADN'T ACCOUNTED FOR. THE MISERABLE LITTLE WRETCH ALMOST POISONED WARREN. HE'LL LIVE, BUT HE HAS INCREDIBLY BAD GAS.›

‹MESSAGE RECEIVED. DOCK AND REPORT TO LEVEL FIVE FOR INTERROGATION.›

‹INTERROGATION!?!›

‹!DOH!! DEBRIEFING! I MEANT DEBRIEFING. I ALWAYS MIX THOSE UP.›

‹AHHH... OKAY... OVER AND OUT.›

‹GREAT-JUST GREAT! EVERY PLANET IN THIS SOLAR SYSTEM HAS BEEN A DUD. NOTHING WORTH EATING ON ANY OF THEM.›

‹NEXT, SOMEONE'S GOING TO TELL ME THE SUN IS JUST A BIG BALL OF GAS AND THERE IS NOTHING WORTH EATING THERE EITHER! SHEESH!!›

COBWEB

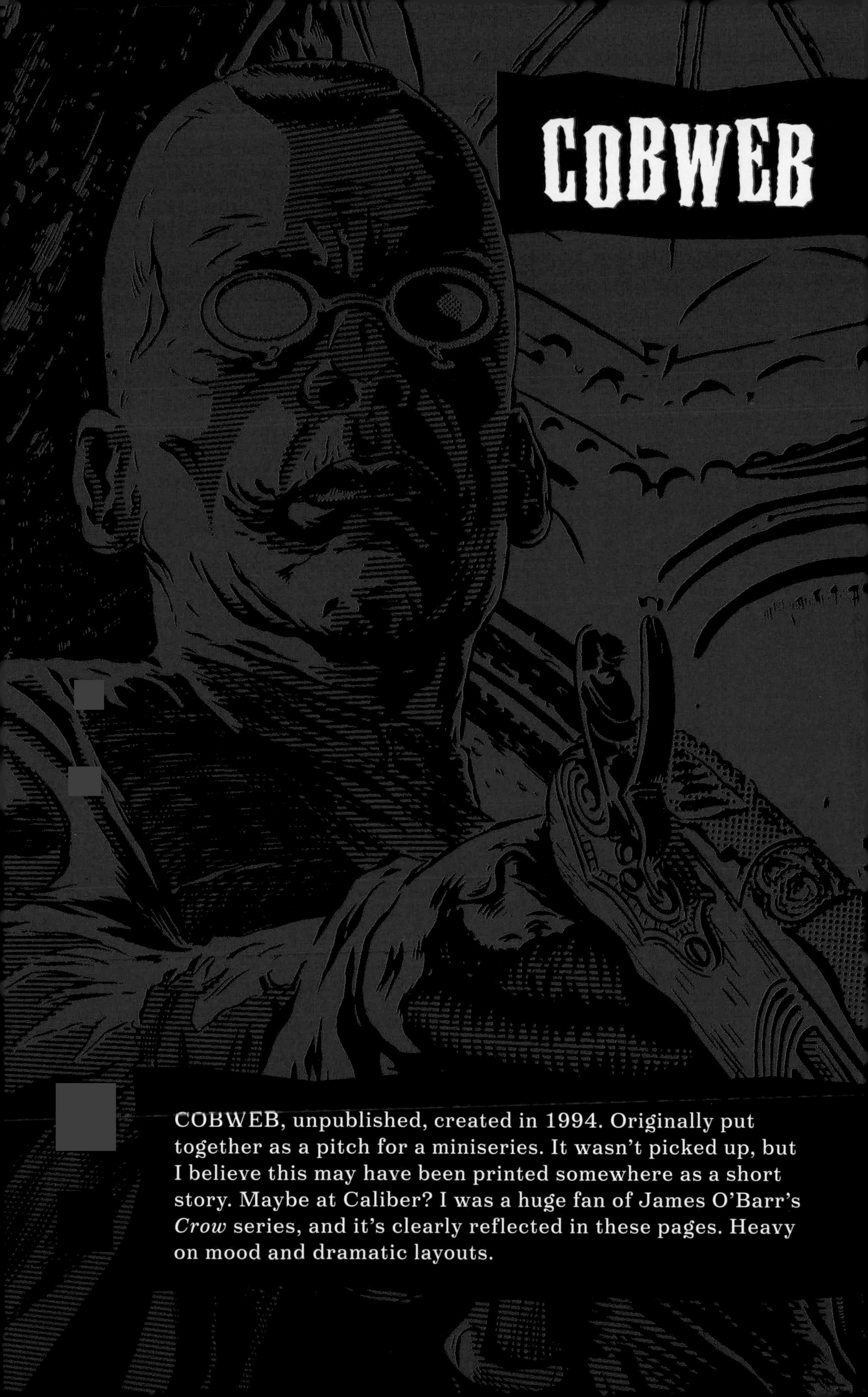

COBWEB, unpublished, created in 1994. Originally put together as a pitch for a miniseries. It wasn't picked up, but I believe this may have been printed somewhere as a short story. Maybe at Caliber? I was a huge fan of James O'Barr's *Crow* series, and it's clearly reflected in these pages. Heavy on mood and dramatic layouts.

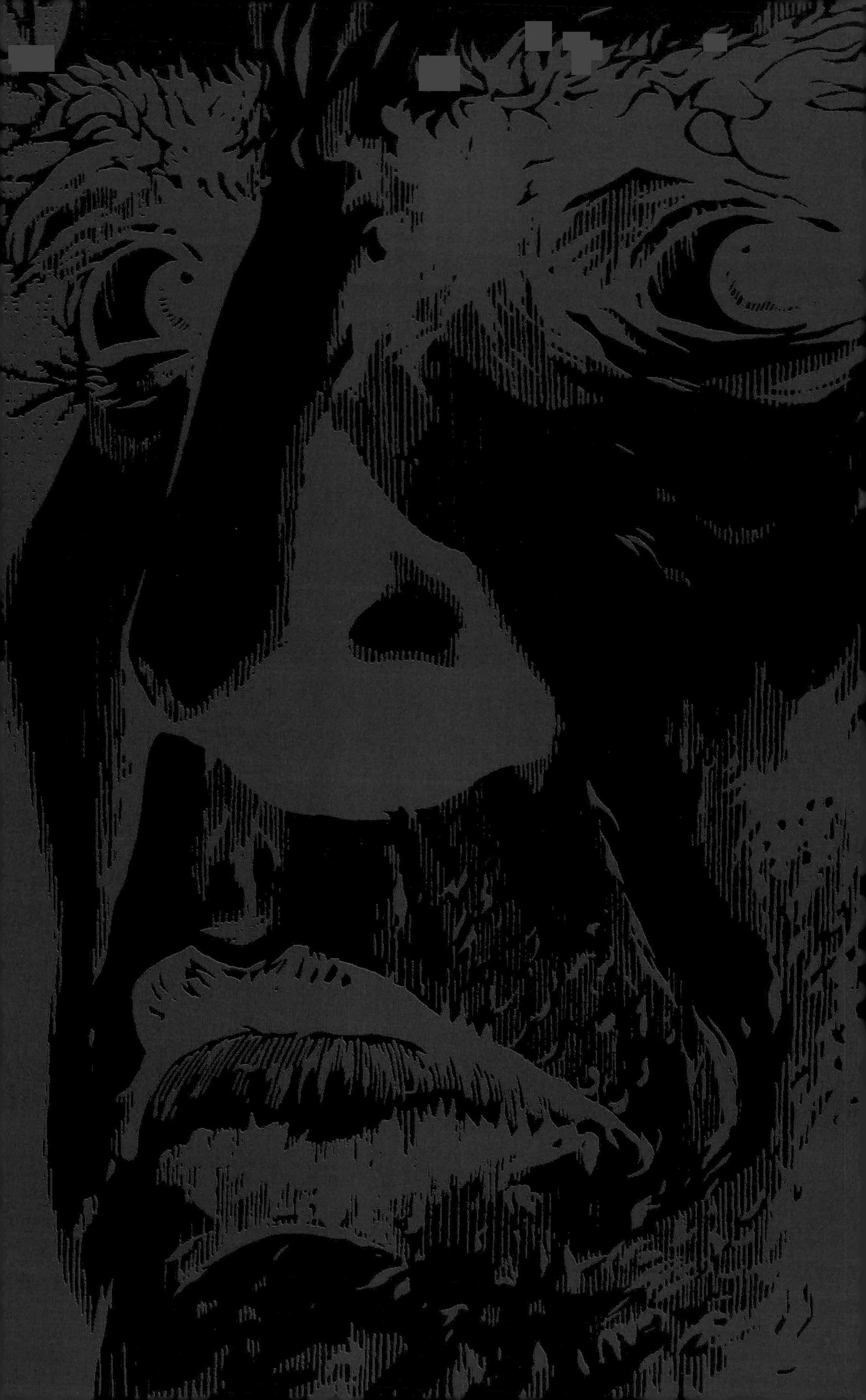

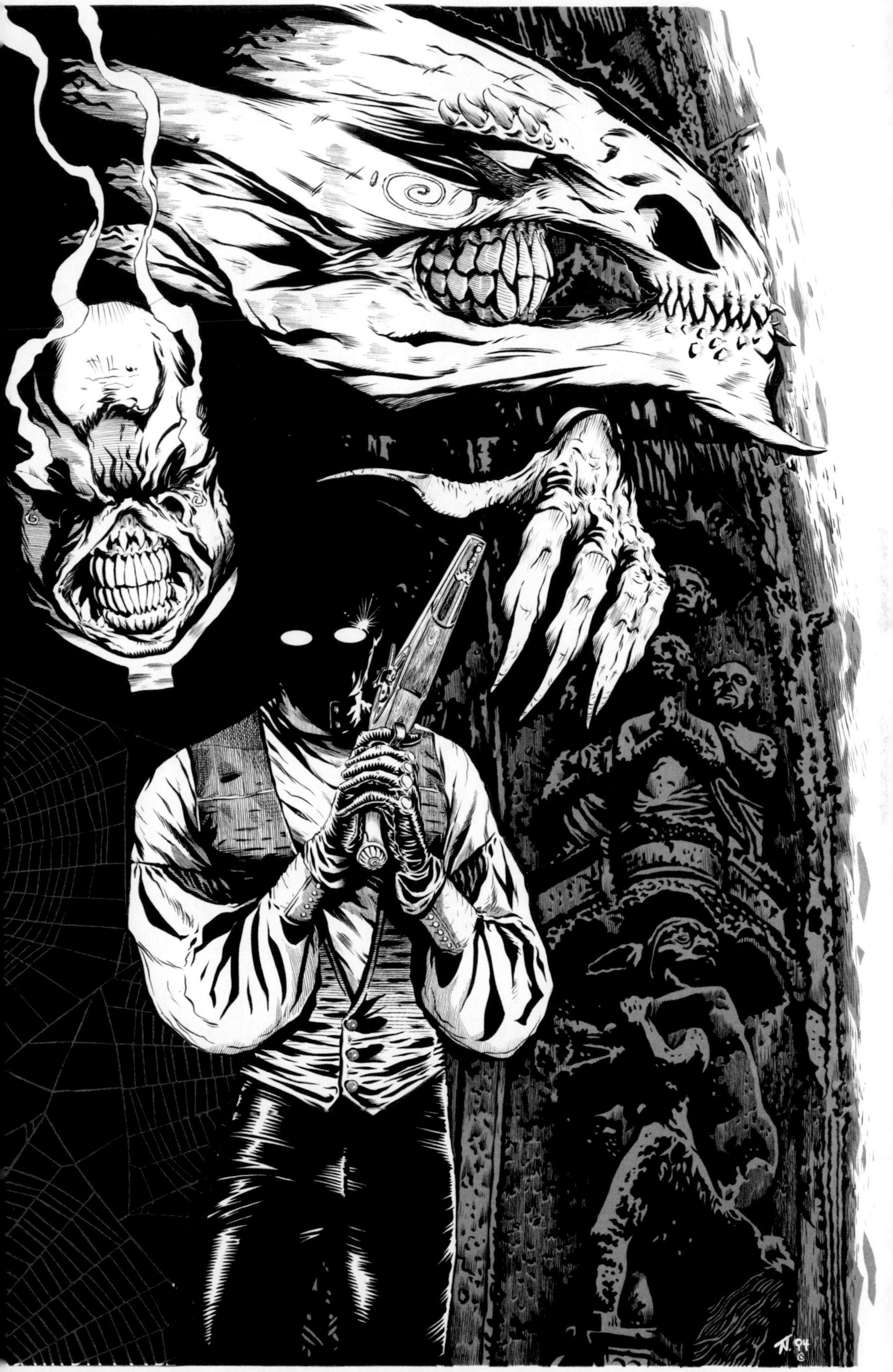

COBWEB
DIVINE REDEMPTION
by TROY NIXEY

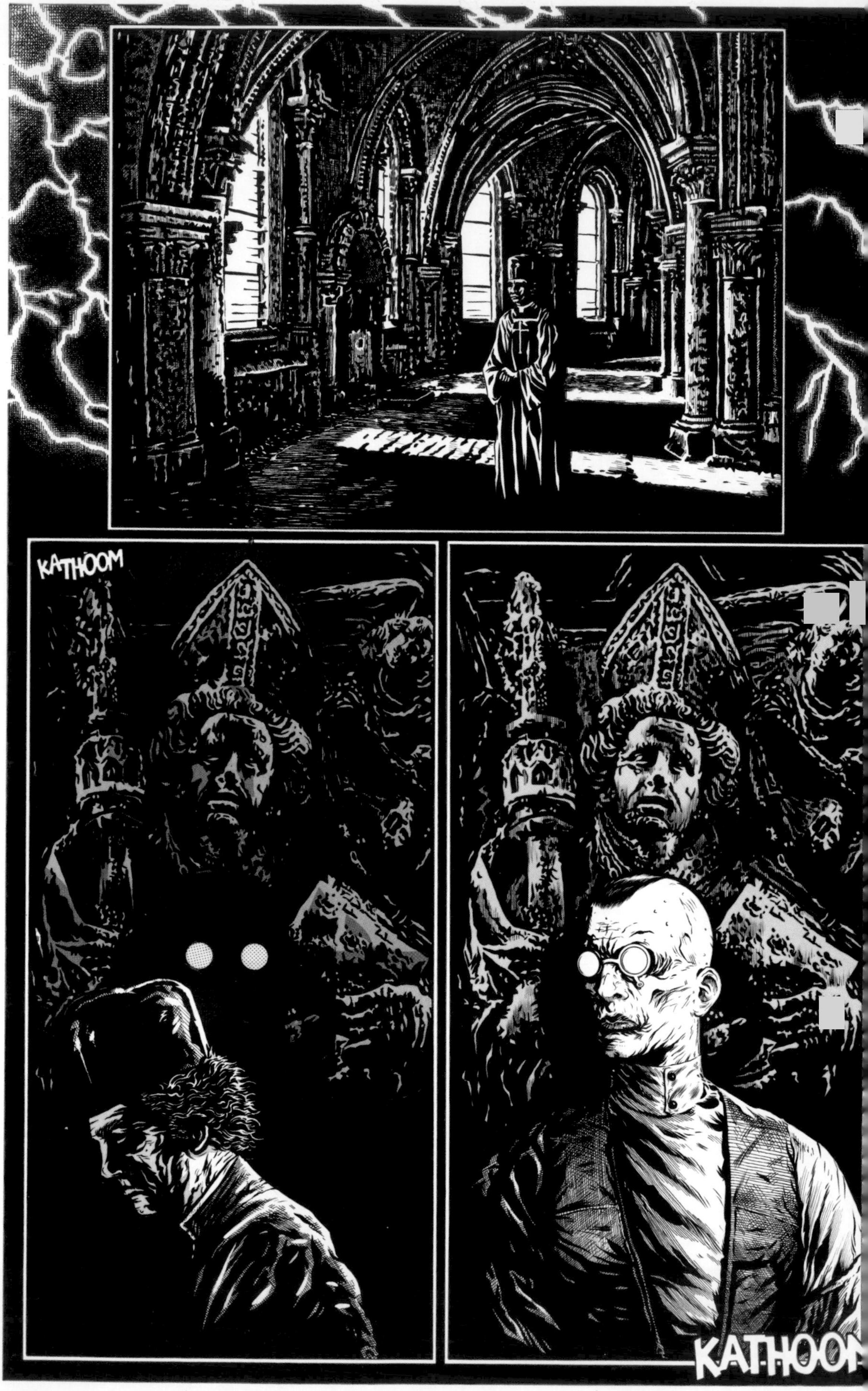
KATHOOM
KATHOOM

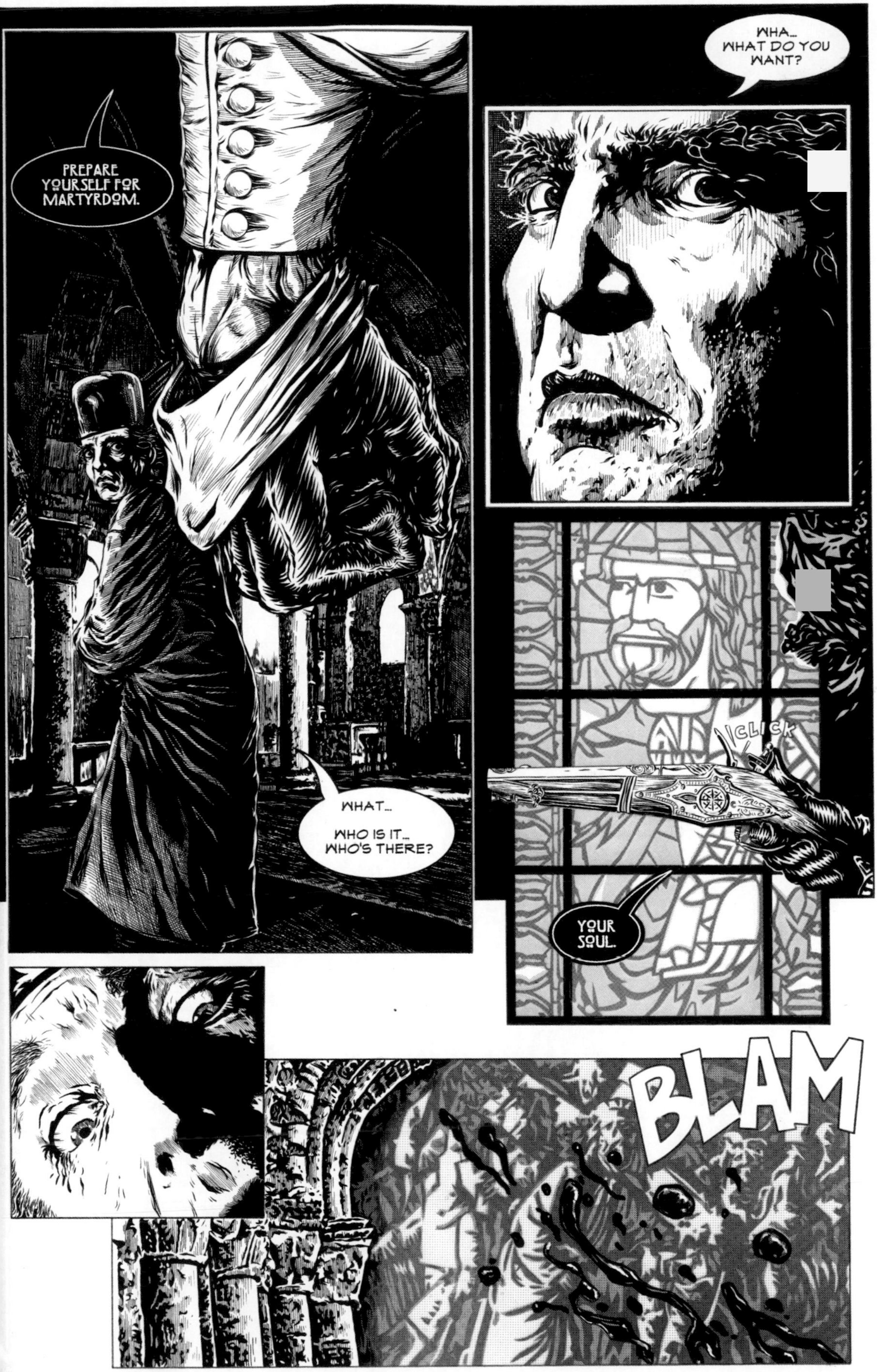
PREPARE YOURSELF FOR MARTYRDOM.
WHAT... WHO IS IT... WHO'S THERE?
WHA... WHAT DO YOU WANT?
CLICK
YOUR SOUL.
BLAM

SHOW YOURSELF.

NNNGG... UNH... UNH...

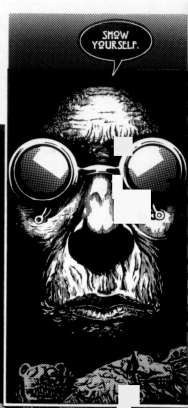

SHOW YOURSELF.

SOOO... CHOKE... THE SEEKER HAS COME, BUT THIS TIME TOO LATE.

THROUGHOUT THE CENTURIES YOU HAVE MANAGED TO WAYLAY OUR ASCENSION TO POWER...

...BUT THIS TIME... THIS TIME...CHOKE... OUR PATIENCE HAS BEEN REWARDED. WE ARE TOO DEEPLY ENTRENCHED... UNH...EVEN FOR YOU. OUR TIME HAS COME, AND FOR THAT I GLADLY GIVE OF MY LIFE.

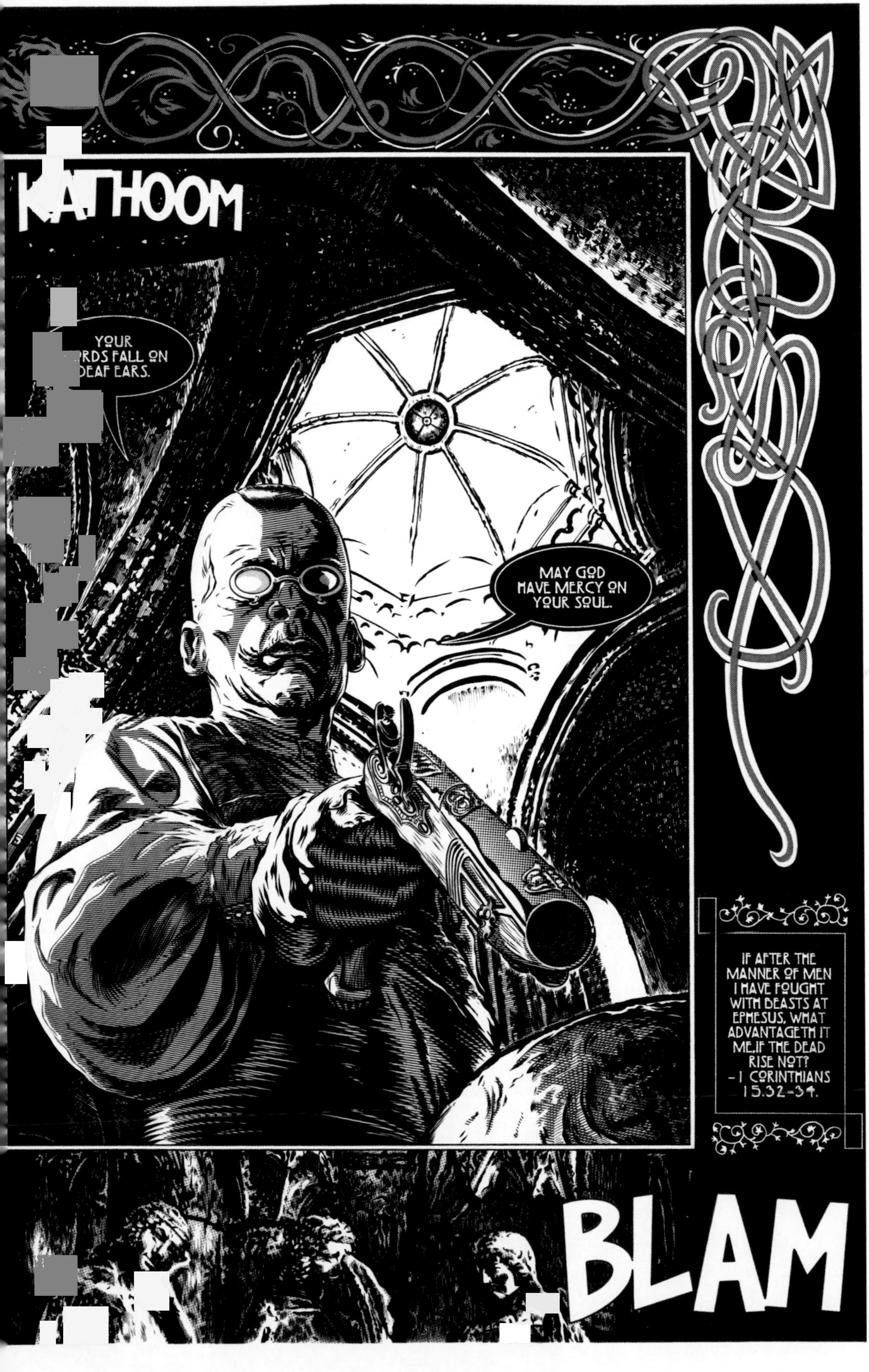
KATHOOM
YOUR RDS FALL ON DEAF EARS.
MAY GOD HAVE MERCY ON YOUR SOUL.
IF AFTER THE MANNER OF MEN I HAVE FOUGHT WITH BEASTS AT EPHESUS, WHAT ADVANTAGETH IT ME, IF THE DEAD RISE NOT? -1 CORINTHIANS 15.32-34.
BLAM

GUS, STAN & THE END OF BLOODY EVERYTHING

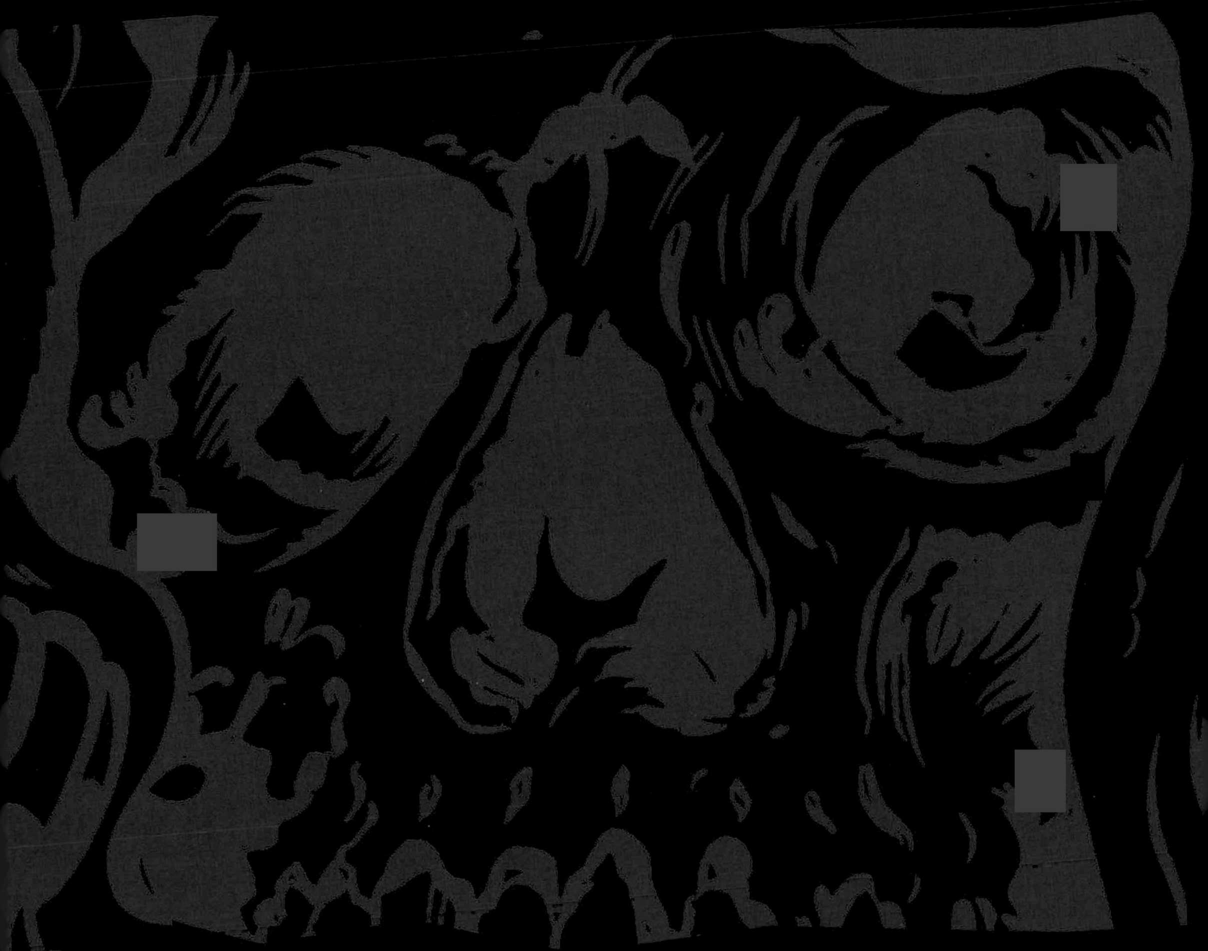

GUS, STAN & THE END OF BLOODY EVERYTHING, *Fangoria* magazine Vol. 2 #1-#4, 2018-19. I was thrille[redacted] be part of the relaunch of a magazine I loved as a kid. I [redacted] three years of stories planned before I started the first strip, but editorial decided to end all ongoing features after the first year. The series conclusion I originally created wouldn't have worked, so the ending of the fourth strip feels a tad abrupt. I love these characters, and they'll definitely be back somewhere, somehow . . . sometime.

BRAAIIINS

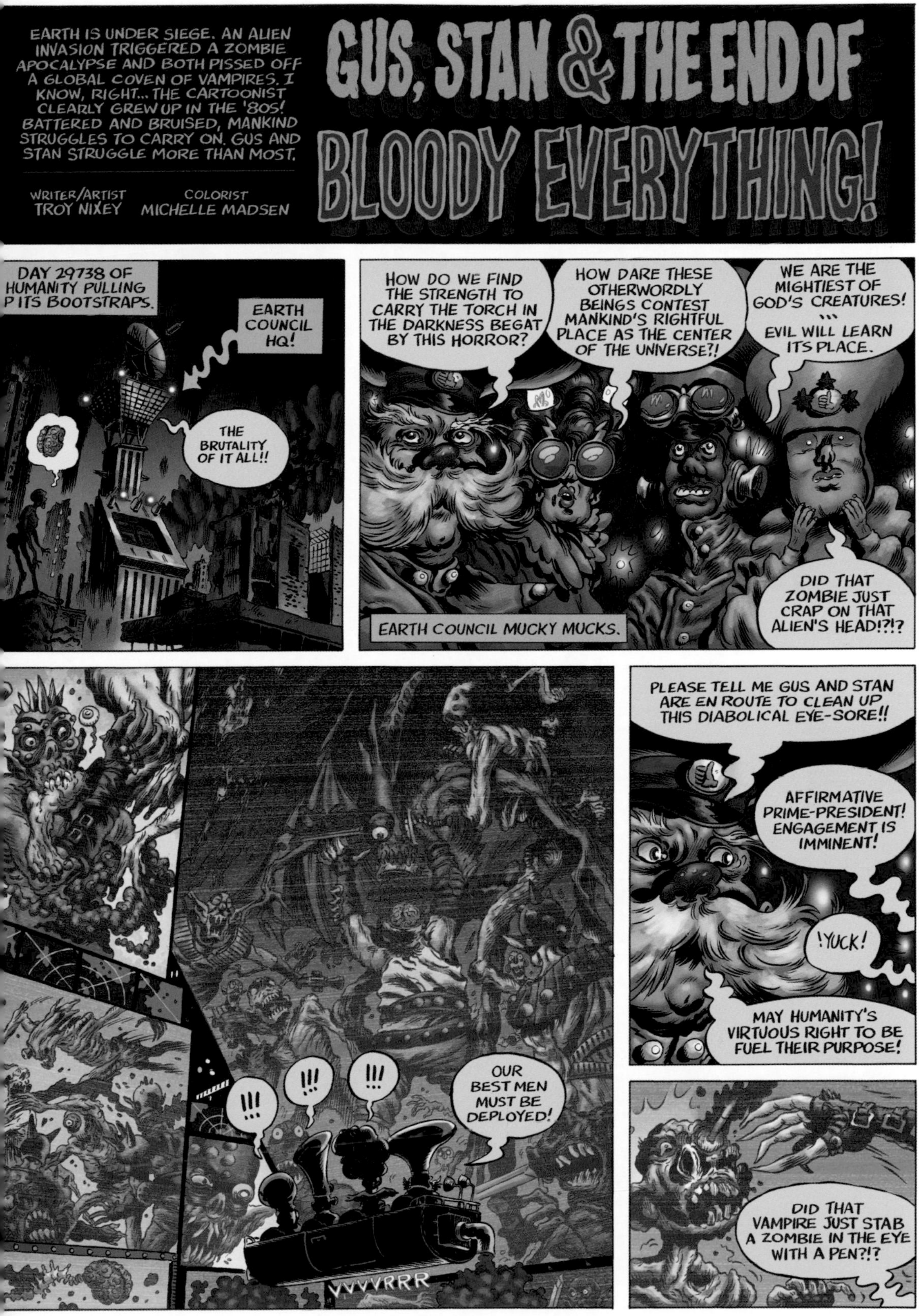

GUS, STAN & THE END OF BLOODY EVERYTHING!
EARTH IS UNDER SIEGE. AN ALIEN INVASION TRIGGERED A ZOMBIE APOCALYPSE AND BOTH PISSED OFF A GLOBAL COVEN OF VAMPIRES. I KNOW, RIGHT... THE CARTOONIST CLEARLY GREW UP IN THE '80S! BATTERED AND BRUISED, MANKIND STRUGGLES TO CARRY ON. GUS AND STAN STRUGGLE MORE THAN MOST.
WRITER/ARTIST TROY NIXEY
COLORIST MICHELLE MADSEN
DAY 29738 OF HUMANITY PULLING P ITS BOOTSTRAPS.
EARTH COUNCIL HQ!
THE BRUTALITY OF IT ALL!!
HOW DO WE FIND THE STRENGTH TO CARRY THE TORCH IN THE DARKNESS BEGAT BY THIS HORROR?
HOW DARE THESE OTHERWORDLY BEINGS CONTEST MANKIND'S RIGHTFUL PLACE AS THE CENTER OF THE UNIVERSE?!
WE ARE THE MIGHTIEST OF GOD'S CREATURES! ... EVIL WILL LEARN ITS PLACE.
EARTH COUNCIL MUCKY MUCKS.
DID THAT ZOMBIE JUST CRAP ON THAT ALIEN'S HEAD!?!?
!!!
!!!
!!!
OUR BEST MEN MUST BE DEPLOYED!
VVVVRRR
PLEASE TELL ME GUS AND STAN ARE EN ROUTE TO CLEAN UP THIS DIABOLICAL EYE-SORE!!
AFFIRMATIVE PRIME-PRESIDENT! ENGAGEMENT IS IMMINENT!
!YUCK!
MAY HUMANITY'S VIRTUOUS RIGHT TO BE FUEL THEIR PURPOSE!
DID THAT VAMPIRE JUST STAB A ZOMBIE IN THE EYE WITH A PEN?!?

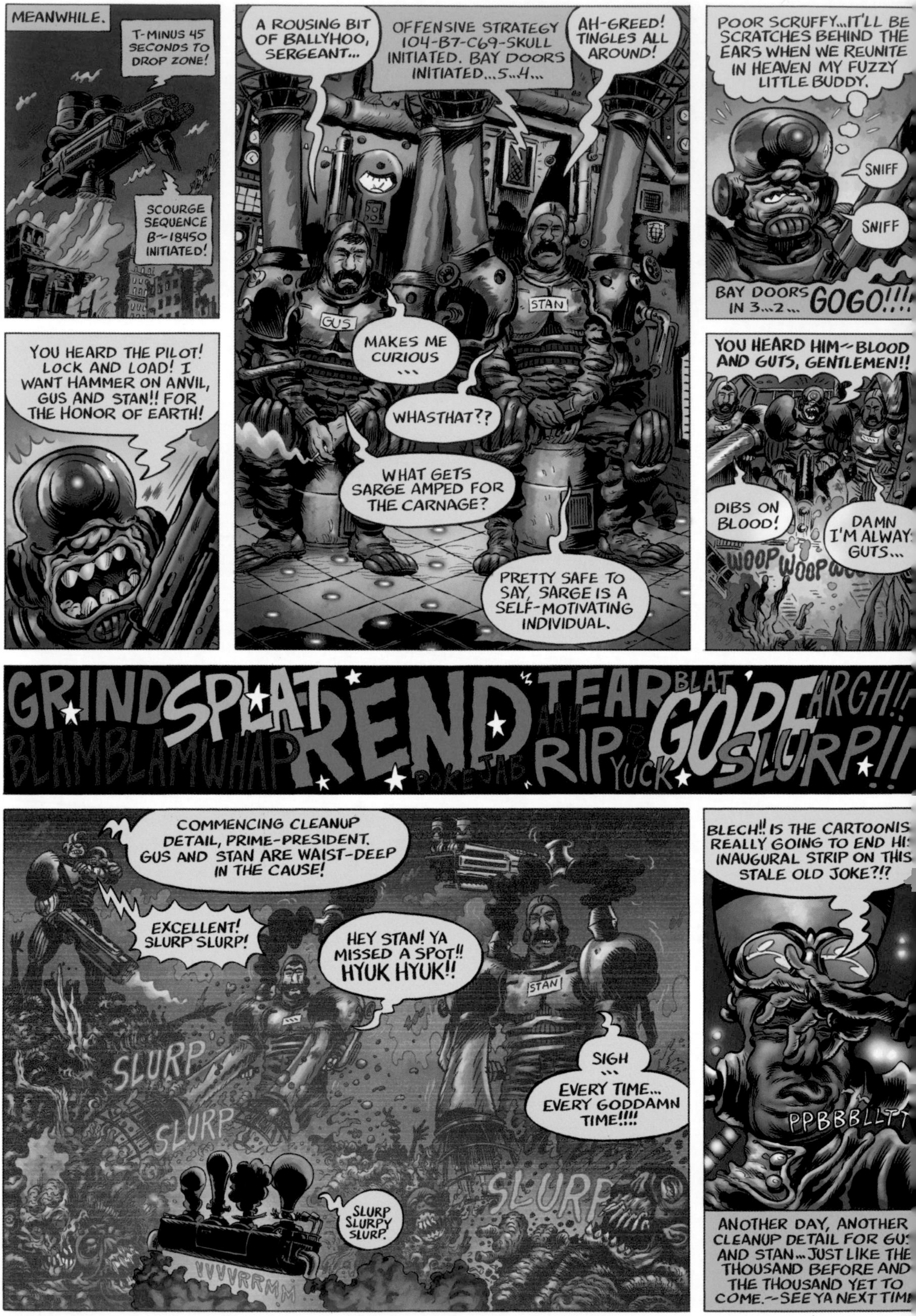
MEANWHILE.
T-MINUS 45 SECONDS TO DROP ZONE!
SCOURGE SEQUENCE B--18450 INITIATED!
A ROUSING BIT OF BALLYHOO, SERGEANT...
OFFENSIVE STRATEGY 104-B7-C69-SKULL INITIATED. BAY DOORS INITIATED...5...4...
AH-GREED! TINGLES ALL AROUND!
POOR SCRUFFY...IT'LL BE SCRATCHES BEHIND THE EARS WHEN WE REUNITE IN HEAVEN MY FUZZY LITTLE BUDDY.
SNIFF
SNIFF
BAY DOORS IN 3...2... GOGO!!!
YOU HEARD THE PILOT! LOCK AND LOAD! I WANT HAMMER ON ANVIL, GUS AND STAN!! FOR THE HONOR OF EARTH!
GUS
STAN
MAKES ME CURIOUS ...
WHASTHAT??
WHAT GETS SARGE AMPED FOR THE CARNAGE?
PRETTY SAFE TO SAY, SARGE IS A SELF-MOTIVATING INDIVIDUAL.
YOU HEARD HIM--BLOOD AND GUTS, GENTLEMEN!!
DIBS ON BLOOD!
DAMN I'M ALWAY GUTS...
WOOP WOOP
GRIND SPLAT REND TEAR BLAT ARGH!!
BLAMBLAMWHAP POKE JAB AAH RIP YUCK GORE SLURP!!
COMMENCING CLEANUP DETAIL, PRIME-PRESIDENT. GUS AND STAN ARE WAIST-DEEP IN THE CAUSE!
EXCELLENT! SLURP SLURP!
HEY STAN! YA MISSED A SPOT!! HYUK HYUK!!
STAN
SIGH ...
EVERY TIME... EVERY GODDAMN TIME!!!!
SLURP
SLURP
SLURP
SLURP SLURPY SLURP.
VVVVRRMM
BLECH!! IS THE CARTOONIS REALLY GOING TO END HI INAUGURAL STRIP ON THIS STALE OLD JOKE?!?
PPBBBLLTT
ANOTHER DAY, ANOTHER CLEANUP DETAIL FOR GU AND STAN... JUST LIKE THE THOUSAND BEFORE AND THE THOUSAND YET TO COME.--SEE YA NEXT TIM

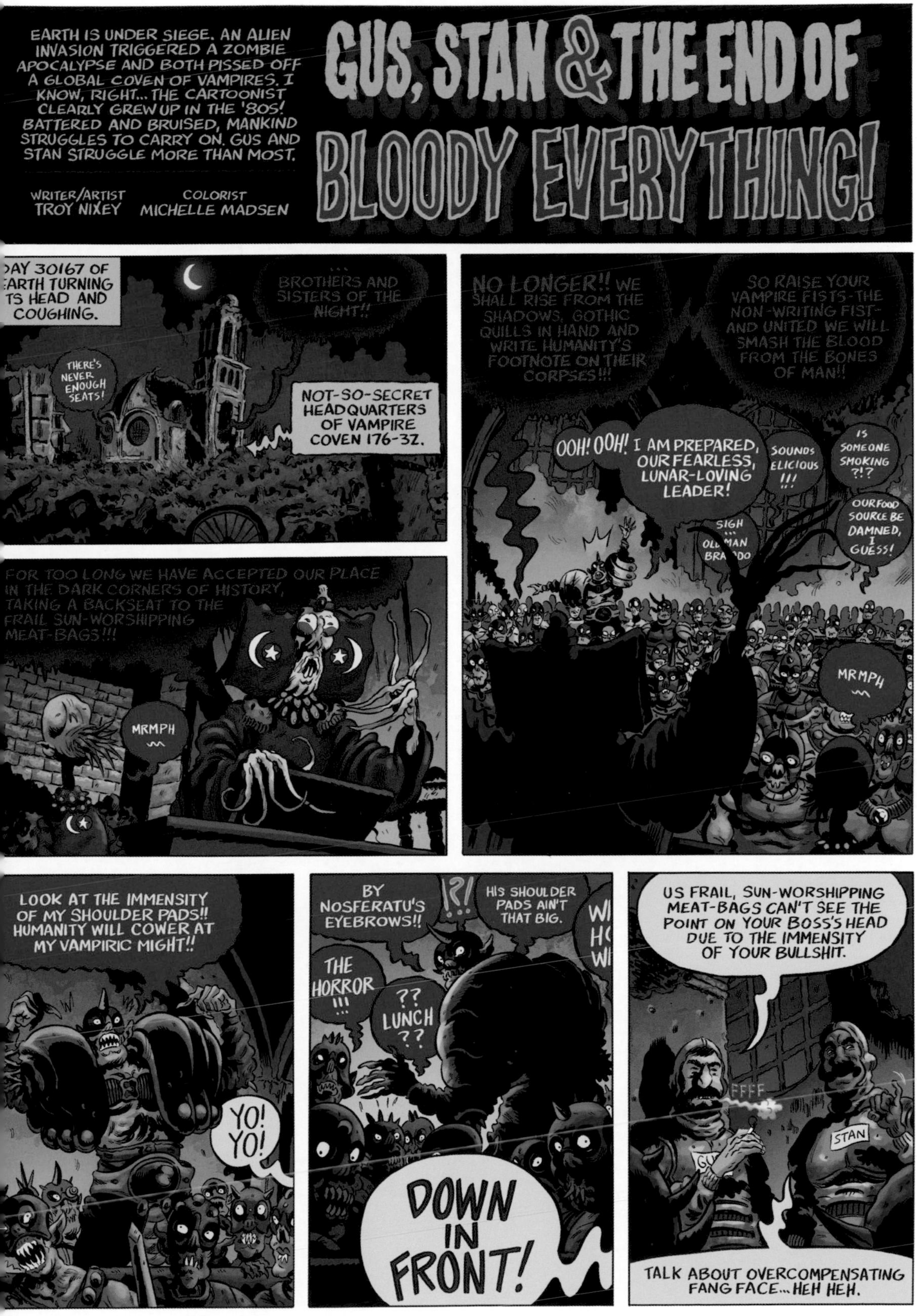
EARTH IS UNDER SIEGE. AN ALIEN INVASION TRIGGERED A ZOMBIE APOCALYPSE AND BOTH PISSED OFF A GLOBAL COVEN OF VAMPIRES. I KNOW, RIGHT... THE CARTOONIST CLEARLY GREW UP IN THE '80S! BATTERED AND BRUISED, MANKIND STRUGGLES TO CARRY ON. GUS AND STAN STRUGGLE MORE THAN MOST.
GUS, STAN & THE END OF BLOODY EVERYTHING!
WRITER/ARTIST TROY NIXEY
COLORIST MICHELLE MADSEN
DAY 30167 OF EARTH TURNING ITS HEAD AND COUGHING.
... BROTHERS AND SISTERS OF THE NIGHT!!
THERE'S NEVER ENOUGH SEATS!
NOT-SO-SECRET HEADQUARTERS OF VAMPIRE COVEN 176-3Z.
FOR TOO LONG WE HAVE ACCEPTED OUR PLACE IN THE DARK CORNERS OF HISTORY, TAKING A BACKSEAT TO THE FRAIL SUN-WORSHIPPING MEAT-BAGS!!!
MRMPH
NO LONGER!! WE SHALL RISE FROM THE SHADOWS, GOTHIC QUILLS IN HAND AND WRITE HUMANITY'S FOOTNOTE ON THEIR CORPSES!!!
SO RAISE YOUR VAMPIRE FISTS-THE NON-WRITING FIST- AND UNITED WE WILL SMASH THE BLOOD FROM THE BONES OF MAN!!
OOH! OOH! I AM PREPARED, OUR FEARLESS, LUNAR-LOVING LEADER!
SOUNDS ELICIOUS !!!
IS SOMEONE SMOKING ?!?
SIGH ...
OUR FOOD SOURCE BE DAMNED, I GUESS!
MRMPH
LOOK AT THE IMMENSITY OF MY SHOULDER PADS!! HUMANITY WILL COWER AT MY VAMPIRIC MIGHT!!
YO! YO!
BY NOSFERATU'S EYEBROWS!!
!?!
HIS SHOULDER PADS AIN'T THAT BIG.
THE HORROR !!!
?? LUNCH ??
DOWN IN FRONT!
US FRAIL, SUN-WORSHIPPING MEAT-BAGS CAN'T SEE THE POINT ON YOUR BOSS'S HEAD DUE TO THE IMMENSITY OF YOUR BULLSHIT.
FFFF
STAN
TALK ABOUT OVERCOMPENSATING FANG FACE... HEH HEH.

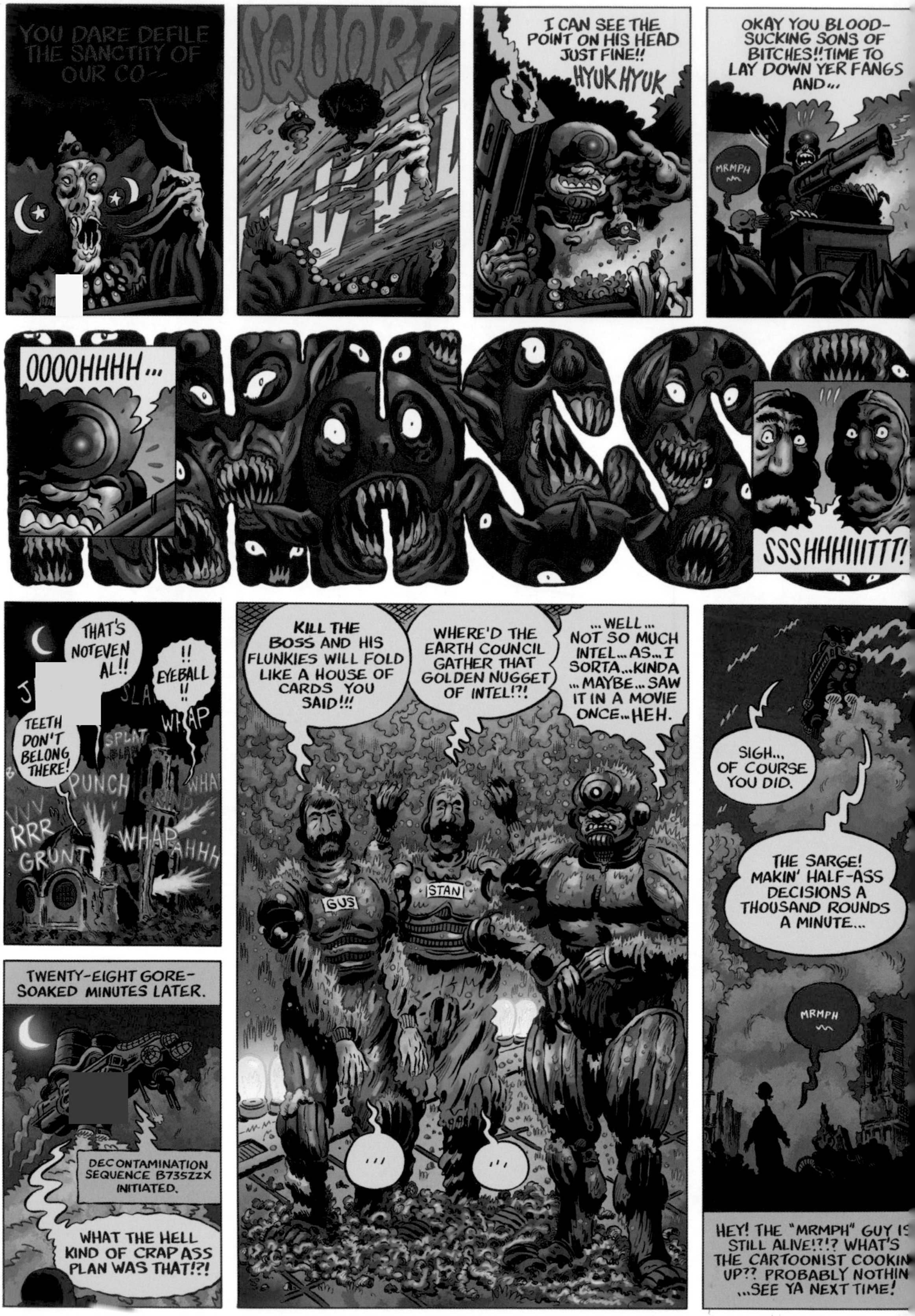

YOU DARE DEFILE THE SANCTITY OF OUR CO--
SQUORT
I CAN SEE THE POINT ON HIS HEAD JUST FINE!!
HYUK HYUK
OKAY YOU BLOOD-SUCKING SONS OF BITCHES!! TIME TO LAY DOWN YER FANGS AND...
MRMPH
OOOOHHHH...
SSSHHHIIIITTT!
THAT'S NOTEVEN AL!!
!! EYEBALL !!
TEETH DON'T BELONG THERE!
WHAP
PUNCH
KRR
GRUNT
WHAP
AHHH
TWENTY-EIGHT GORE-SOAKED MINUTES LATER.
DECONTAMINATION SEQUENCE B735ZZX INITIATED.
WHAT THE HELL KIND OF CRAP ASS PLAN WAS THAT!?!
KILL THE BOSS AND HIS FLUNKIES WILL FOLD LIKE A HOUSE OF CARDS YOU SAID!!!
WHERE'D THE EARTH COUNCIL GATHER THAT GOLDEN NUGGET OF INTEL!?!
...WELL... NOT SO MUCH INTEL...AS...I SORTA...KINDA ...MAYBE...SAW IT IN A MOVIE ONCE...HEH.
GUS
STAN
SIGH... OF COURSE YOU DID.
THE SARGE! MAKIN' HALF-ASS DECISIONS A THOUSAND ROUNDS A MINUTE...
MRMPH
HEY! THE "MRMPH" GUY I STILL ALIVE!?!? WHAT'S THE CARTOONIST COOKIN UP?? PROBABLY NOTHIN ...SEE YA NEXT TIME!

GUS, STAN & THE END OF BLOODY EVERYTHING!

EARTH IS UNDER SIEGE. AN ALIEN INVASION TRIGGERED A ZOMBIE APOCALYPSE AND BOTH PISSED OFF A GLOBAL COVEN OF VAMPIRES. I KNOW, RIGHT... THE CARTOONIST CLEARLY GREW UP IN THE '80S! BATTERED AND BRUISED, MANKIND STRUGGLES TO CARRY ON. GUS AND STAN STRUGGLE MORE THAN MOST.

WRITER/ARTIST
TROY NIXEY

COLORIST
MICHELLE MADSEN

DAY 30673 OF HUMANITY SITTING ON A HEMORRHOID DONUT.

SLEEP!!! ...PLEASE... WHY CAN'T I SLEEP?!?!

JUST ONE GODDAMN HOUR!!!

ANYTHING FOR A REPRIEVE FROM THE BUZZING IN MY HEAD!

AAAAGH!!! IF NOT SLEEP, AT LEAST LET ME CONTROL MY LIMBS...

BLOODY LEGS!! DO ME A FAVOR AND WALK OFF A BRIDGE OR CLIFF WHY DON'TCHA!

OH!!

B B B B B...

LOOK AT THEM. IT'S ALWAYS THE SAME...

B B B B B R R R ...

...LIKE FLIES BUZZING AROUND SHIT.

ARE THEIR MINDS LIKE MINE?! SCREAMING FOR SWEET RELIEF?!?!

B B B B

WHY DOES MY HAND STILL HURT?!?! IT FELL OFF MONTHS AGO!!

OH MY SWEET SOPHIE, I MISS YOU SO. WOULD YOU RECOGNIZE ME IN THIS STATE?!

PLEASE GOD, IF YOU'RE REAL... LET ME FEEL HAPPINESS! YOU KNOW WHAT I'M TALKIN' ABOUT. HEH.

B B B

B B B

B B B

INTERNATIO BRAIN RE CENT

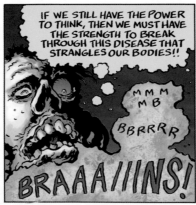

IF WE STILL HAVE THE POWER TO THINK, THEN WE MUST HAVE THE STRENGTH TO BREAK THROUGH THIS DISEASE THAT STRANGLES OUR BODIES!!

M M M M B

B B R R R R

BRAAA//INS!

BRAAA//INS!

INTERNATIO BRAIN RE CENT

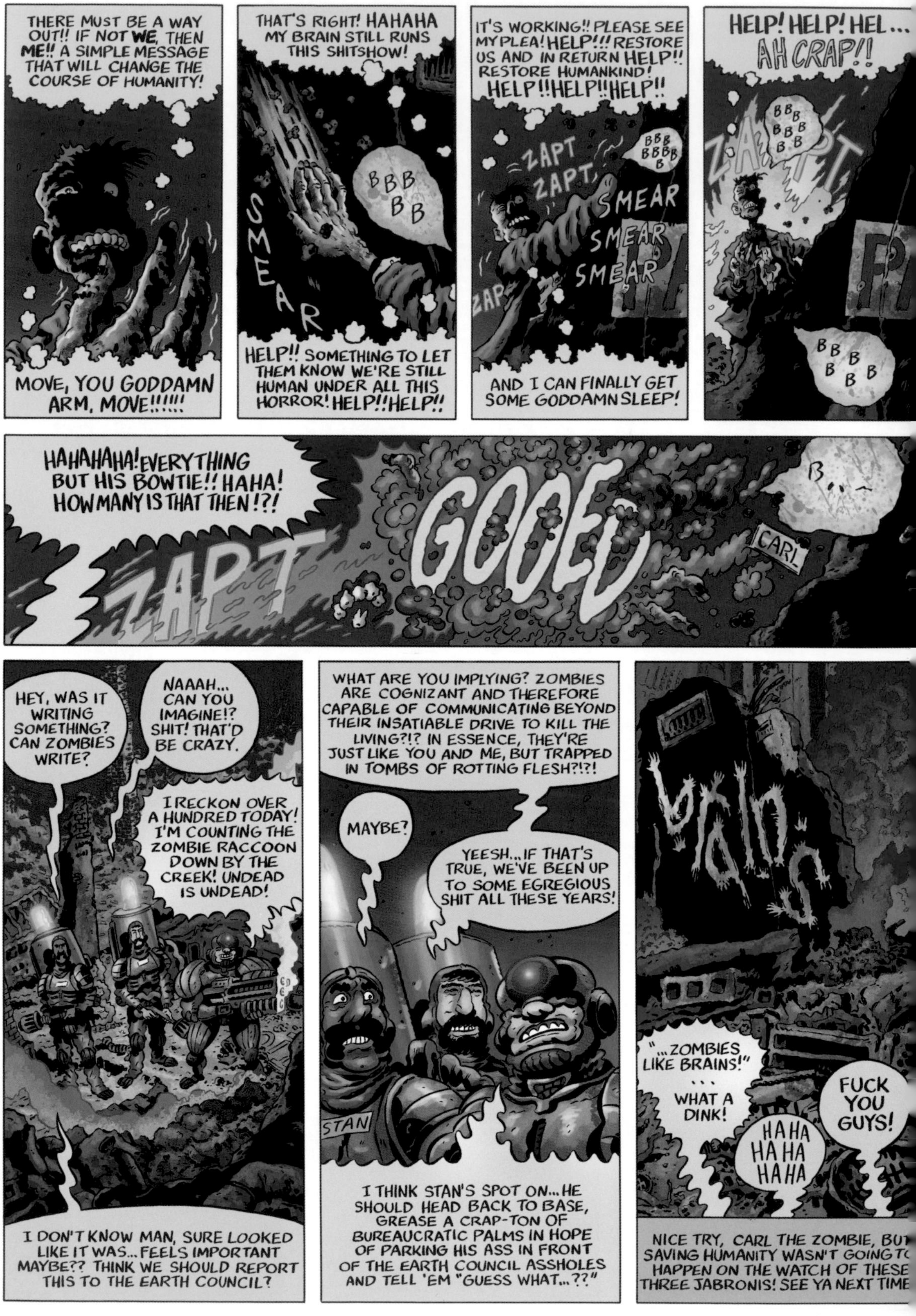
THERE MUST BE A WAY OUT!! IF NOT WE, THEN ME!! A SIMPLE MESSAGE THAT WILL CHANGE THE COURSE OF HUMANITY!
MOVE, YOU GODDAMN ARM, MOVE!!!!!!
THAT'S RIGHT! HAHAHA MY BRAIN STILL RUNS THIS SHITSHOW!
BBB BB
SMEAR
HELP!! SOMETHING TO LET THEM KNOW WE'RE STILL HUMAN UNDER ALL THIS HORROR! HELP!! HELP!!
IT'S WORKING!! PLEASE SEE MY PLEA! HELP!!! RESTORE US AND IN RETURN HELP!! RESTORE HUMANKIND! HELP!! HELP!! HELP!!
ZAPT ZAPT
BBB BBBB B
SMEAR SMEAR SMEAR
ZAP
AND I CAN FINALLY GET SOME GODDAMN SLEEP!
HELP! HELP! HEL... AH CRAP!!
BBB BBB BB
ZAPT
BB B B B B
HAHAHAHA! EVERYTHING BUT HIS BOWTIE!! HAHA! HOW MANY IS THAT THEN!?!
ZAPT
GOOED
CARL
HEY, WAS IT WRITING SOMETHING? CAN ZOMBIES WRITE?
NAAAH... CAN YOU IMAGINE!? SHIT! THAT'D BE CRAZY.
I RECKON OVER A HUNDRED TODAY! I'M COUNTING THE ZOMBIE RACCOON DOWN BY THE CREEK! UNDEAD IS UNDEAD!
I DON'T KNOW MAN, SURE LOOKED LIKE IT WAS... FEELS IMPORTANT MAYBE?? THINK WE SHOULD REPORT THIS TO THE EARTH COUNCIL?
WHAT ARE YOU IMPLYING? ZOMBIES ARE COGNIZANT AND THEREFORE CAPABLE OF COMMUNICATING BEYOND THEIR INSATIABLE DRIVE TO KILL THE LIVING?!? IN ESSENCE, THEY'RE JUST LIKE YOU AND ME, BUT TRAPPED IN TOMBS OF ROTTING FLESH?!?!
MAYBE?
YEESH... IF THAT'S TRUE, WE'VE BEEN UP TO SOME EGREGIOUS SHIT ALL THESE YEARS!
STAN
I THINK STAN'S SPOT ON... HE SHOULD HEAD BACK TO BASE, GREASE A CRAP-TON OF BUREAUCRATIC PALMS IN HOPE OF PARKING HIS ASS IN FRONT OF THE EARTH COUNCIL ASSHOLES AND TELL 'EM "GUESS WHAT...??"
"...ZOMBIES LIKE BRAINS!" . . . WHAT A DINK!
FUCK YOU GUYS!
HA HA HA HA HA HA
NICE TRY, CARL THE ZOMBIE, BUT SAVING HUMANITY WASN'T GOING TO HAPPEN ON THE WATCH OF THESE THREE JABRONIS! SEE YA NEXT TIME

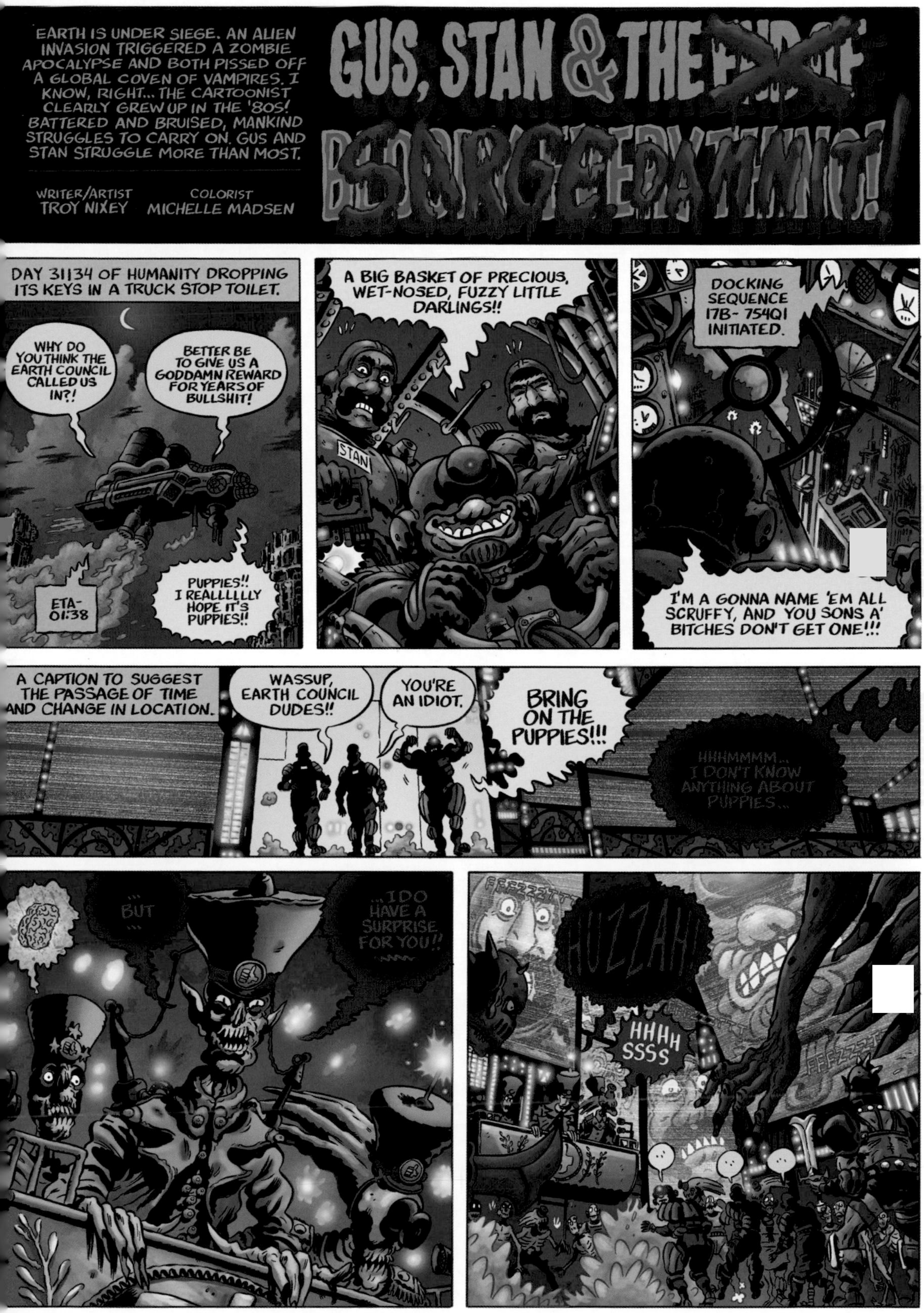
EARTH IS UNDER SIEGE. AN ALIEN INVASION TRIGGERED A ZOMBIE APOCALYPSE AND BOTH PISSED OFF A GLOBAL COVEN OF VAMPIRES. I KNOW, RIGHT... THE CARTOONIST CLEARLY GREW UP IN THE '80S! BATTERED AND BRUISED, MANKIND STRUGGLES TO CARRY ON. GUS AND STAN STRUGGLE MORE THAN MOST.
WRITER/ARTIST TROY NIXEY
COLORIST MICHELLE MADSEN
GUS, STAN & THE
DAY 31134 OF HUMANITY DROPPING ITS KEYS IN A TRUCK STOP TOILET.
WHY DO YOU THINK THE EARTH COUNCIL CALLED US IN?!
BETTER BE TO GIVE US A GODDAMN REWARD FOR YEARS OF BULLSHIT!
ETA- 01:38
PUPPIES!! I REALLLLLLY HOPE IT'S PUPPIES!!
A BIG BASKET OF PRECIOUS, WET-NOSED, FUZZY LITTLE DARLINGS!!
STAN
DOCKING SEQUENCE 17B- 754Q1 INITIATED.
I'M A GONNA NAME 'EM ALL SCRUFFY, AND YOU SONS A' BITCHES DON'T GET ONE!!!
A CAPTION TO SUGGEST THE PASSAGE OF TIME AND CHANGE IN LOCATION.
WASSUP, EARTH COUNCIL DUDES!!
YOU'RE AN IDIOT.
BRING ON THE PUPPIES!!!
HHHMMMM... I DON'T KNOW ANYTHING ABOUT PUPPIES...
...BUT...
...I DO HAVE A SURPRISE FOR YOU!!
HUZZAH!
HHHH SSSS

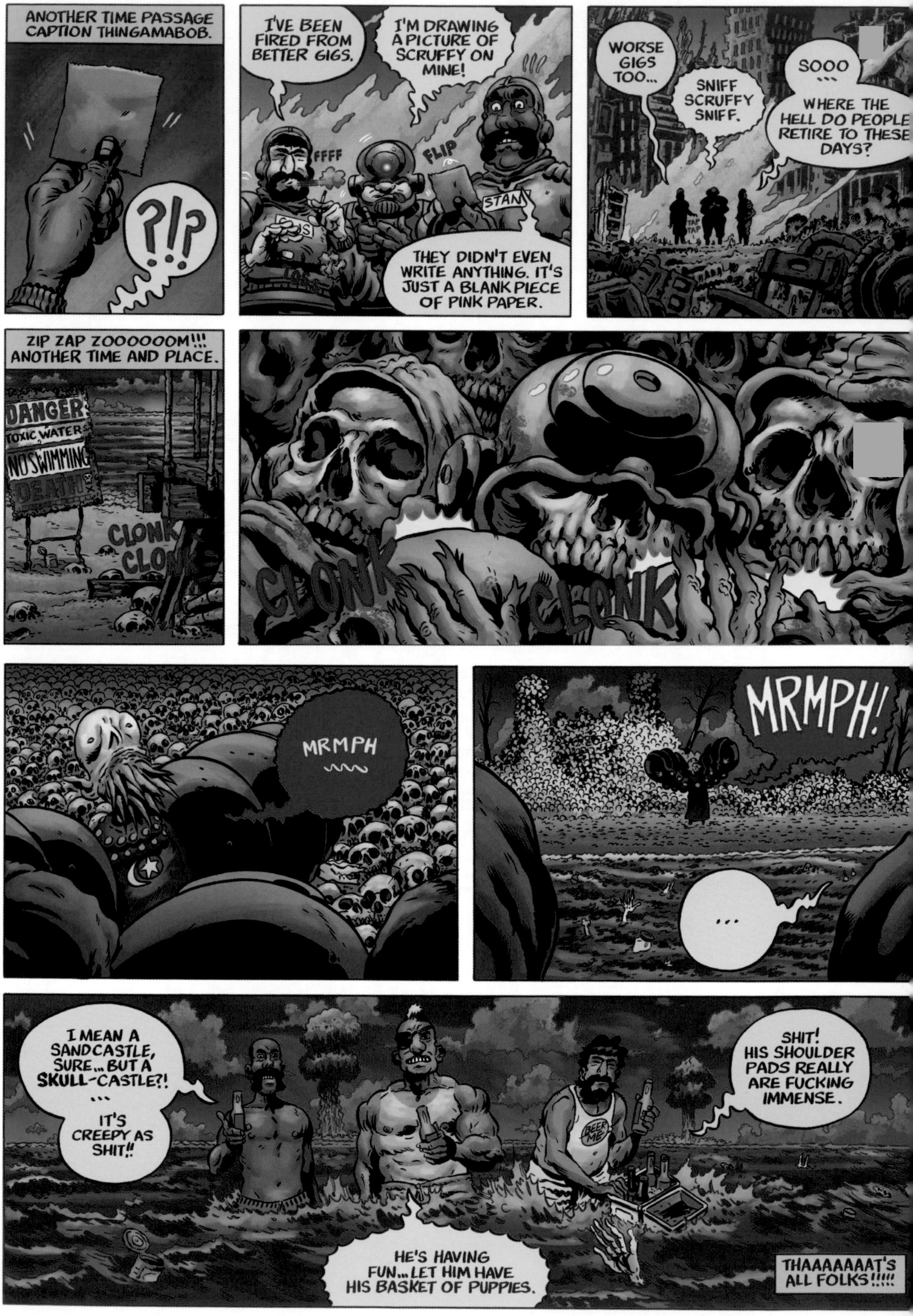
ANOTHER TIME PASSAGE CAPTION THINGAMABOB.
?!?
I'VE BEEN FIRED FROM BETTER GIGS.
I'M DRAWING A PICTURE OF SCRUFFY ON MINE!
FFFF
FLIP
STAN
THEY DIDN'T EVEN WRITE ANYTHING. IT'S JUST A BLANK PIECE OF PINK PAPER.
WORSE GIGS TOO...
SNIFF SCRUFFY SNIFF.
SOOO ...
WHERE THE HELL DO PEOPLE RETIRE TO THESE DAYS?
TAP TAP
ZIP ZAP ZOOOOOOM!!! ANOTHER TIME AND PLACE.
DANGER
TOXIC WATER
NO SWIMMING
DEATH
CLONK
CLONK
CLONK
CLONK
MRMPH
MRMPH!
...
I MEAN A SANDCASTLE, SURE... BUT A SKULL-CASTLE?!
...
IT'S CREEPY AS SHIT!!
SHIT! HIS SHOULDER PADS REALLY ARE FUCKING IMMENSE.
BEER ME!
HE'S HAVING FUN... LET HIM HAVE HIS BASKET OF PUPPIES.
THAAAAAAAT'S ALL FOLKS!!!!!

BACON

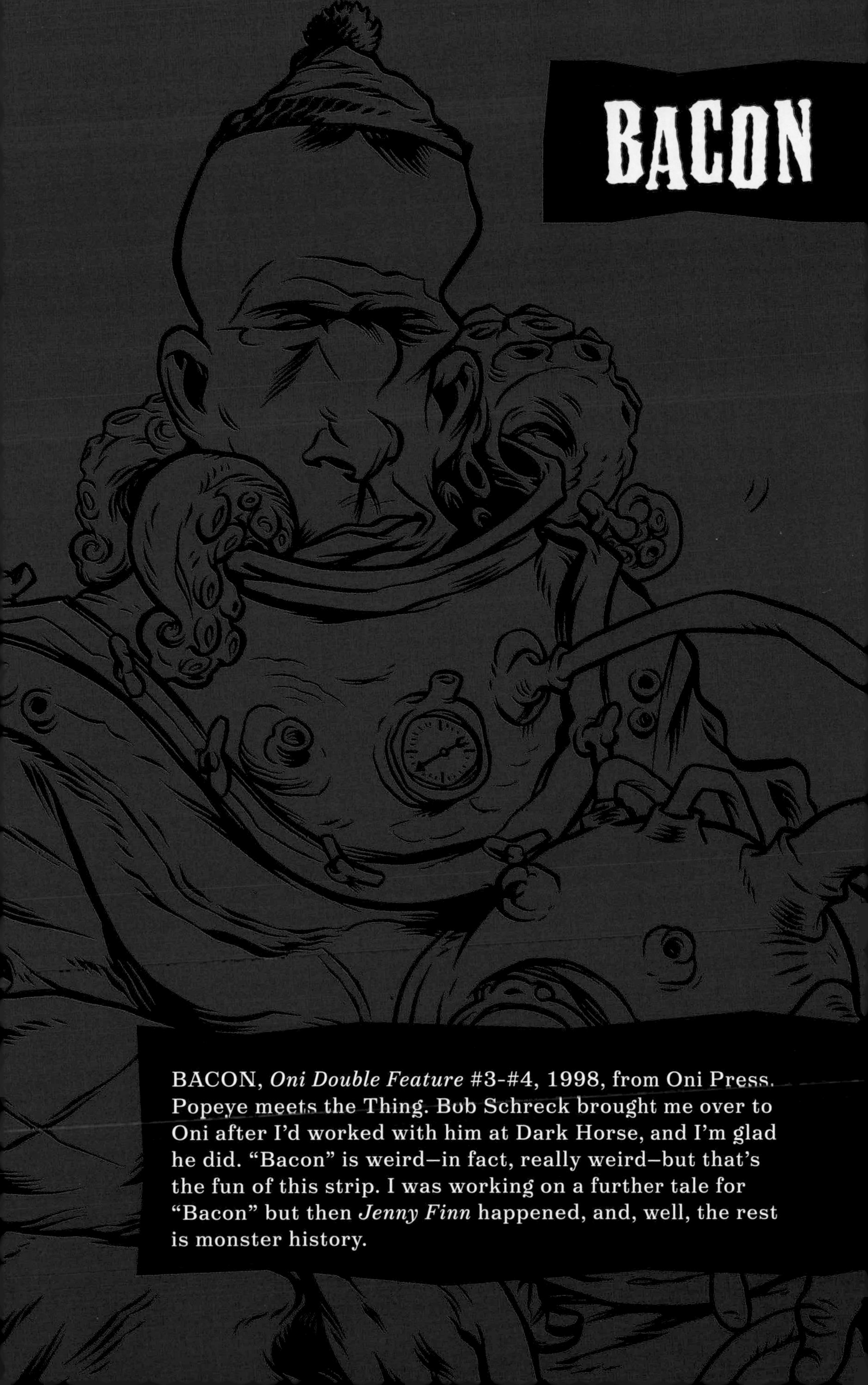

BACON, *Oni Double Feature* #3-#4, 1998, from Oni Press. Popeye meets the Thing. Bob Schreck brought me over to Oni after I'd worked with him at Dark Horse, and I'm glad he did. "Bacon" is weird—in fact, really weird—but that's the fun of this strip. I was working on a further tale for "Bacon" but then *Jenny Finn* happened, and, well, the rest is monster history.

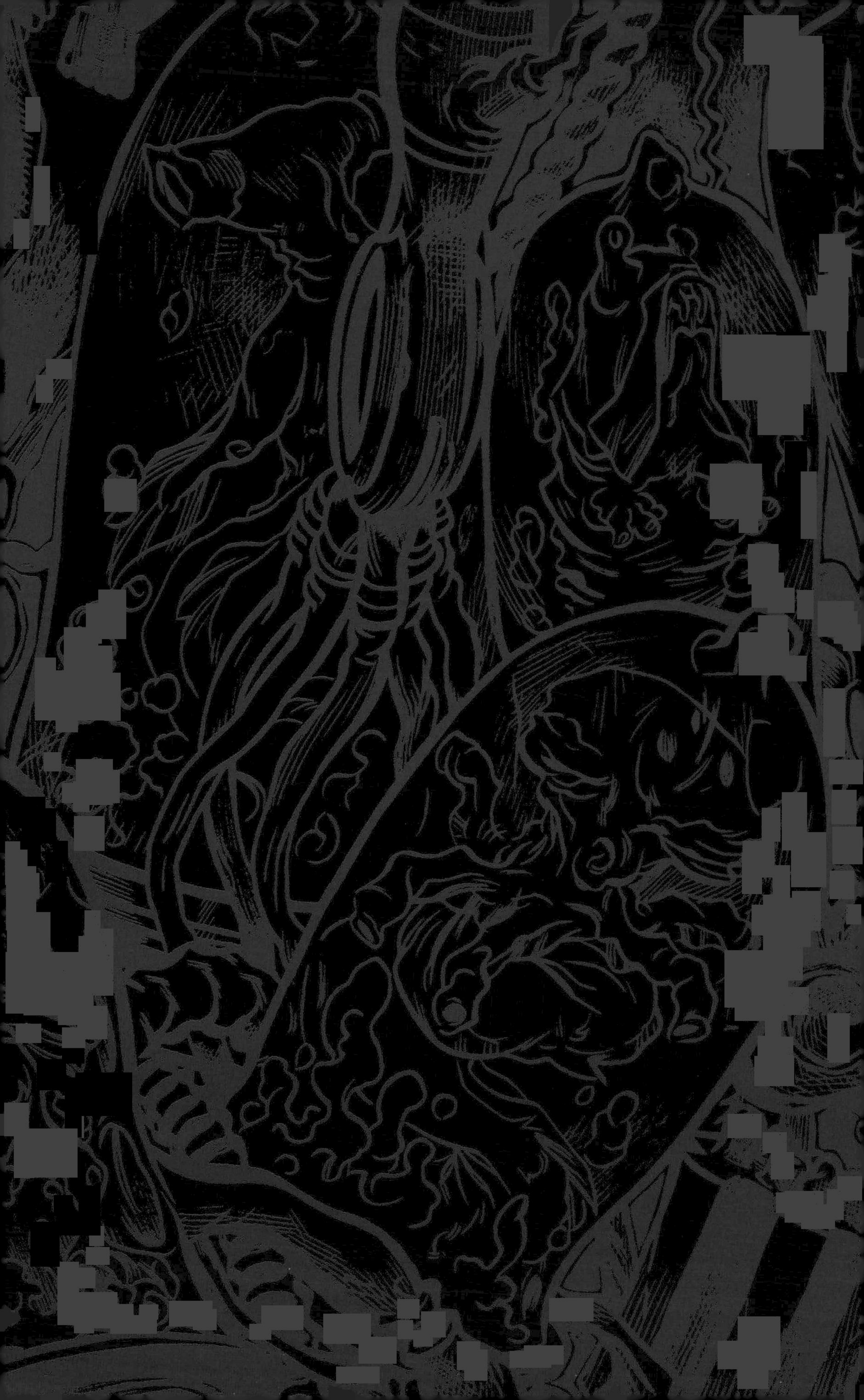

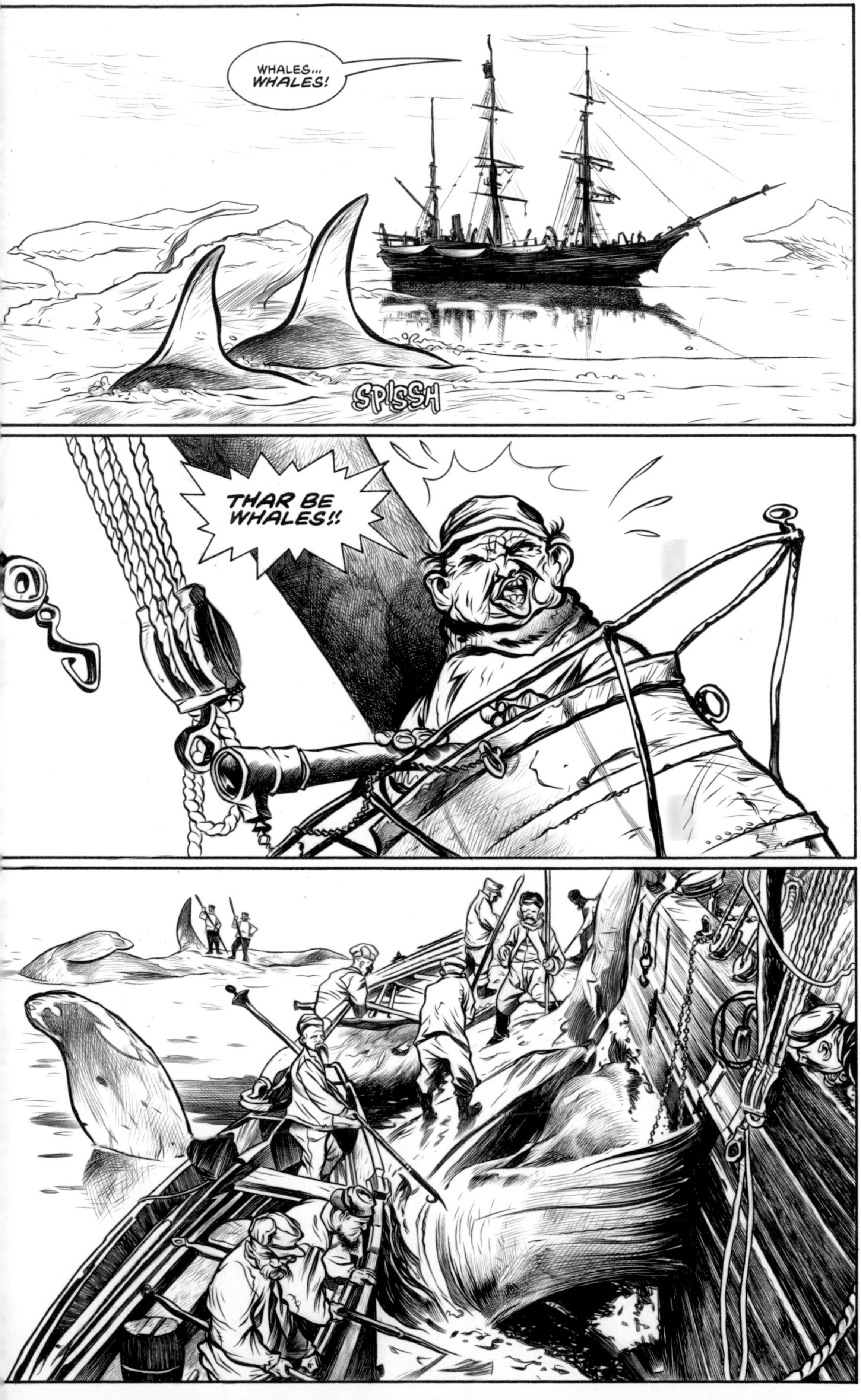
WHALES... WHALES!
SPISSH
THAR BE WHALES!!

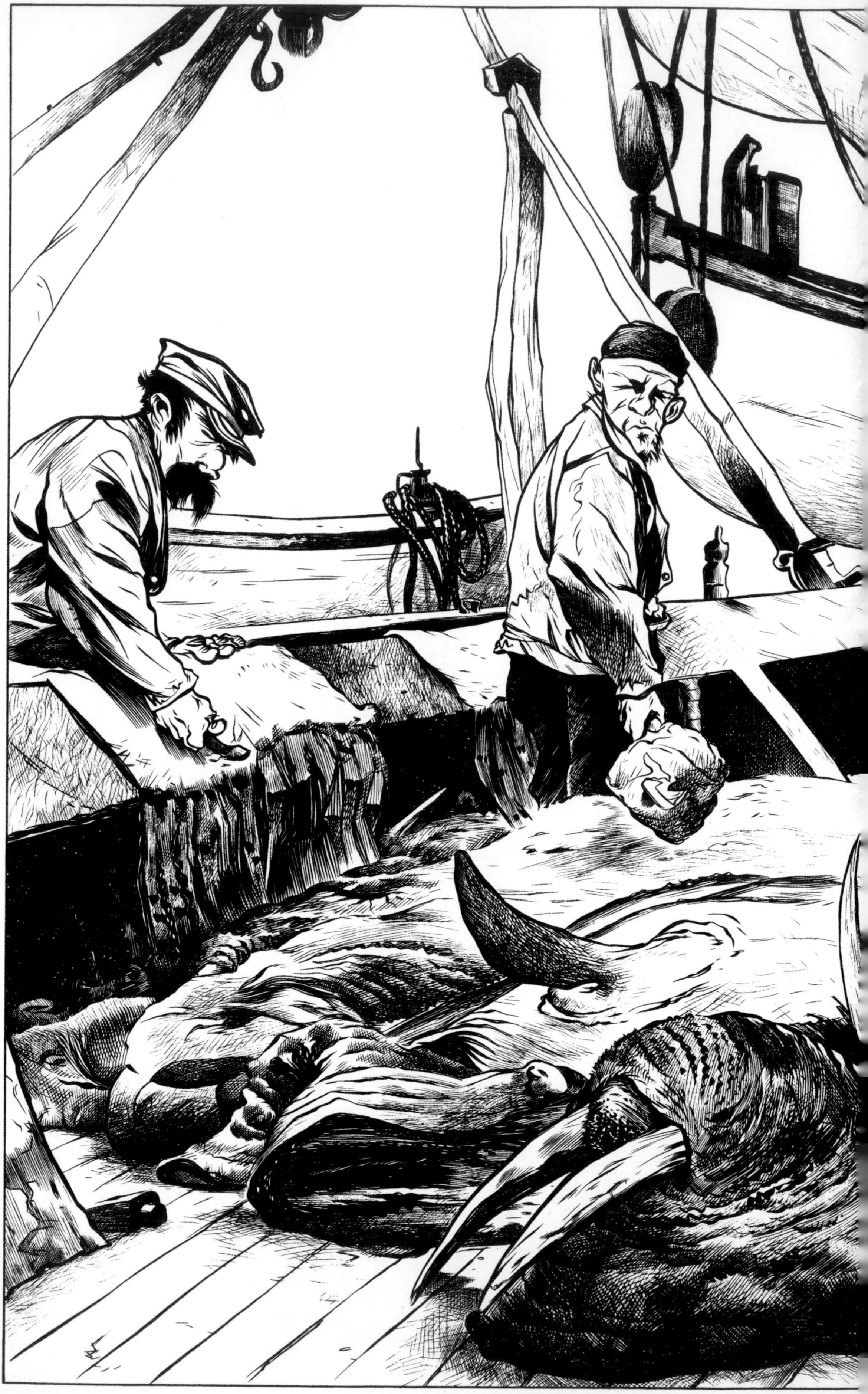

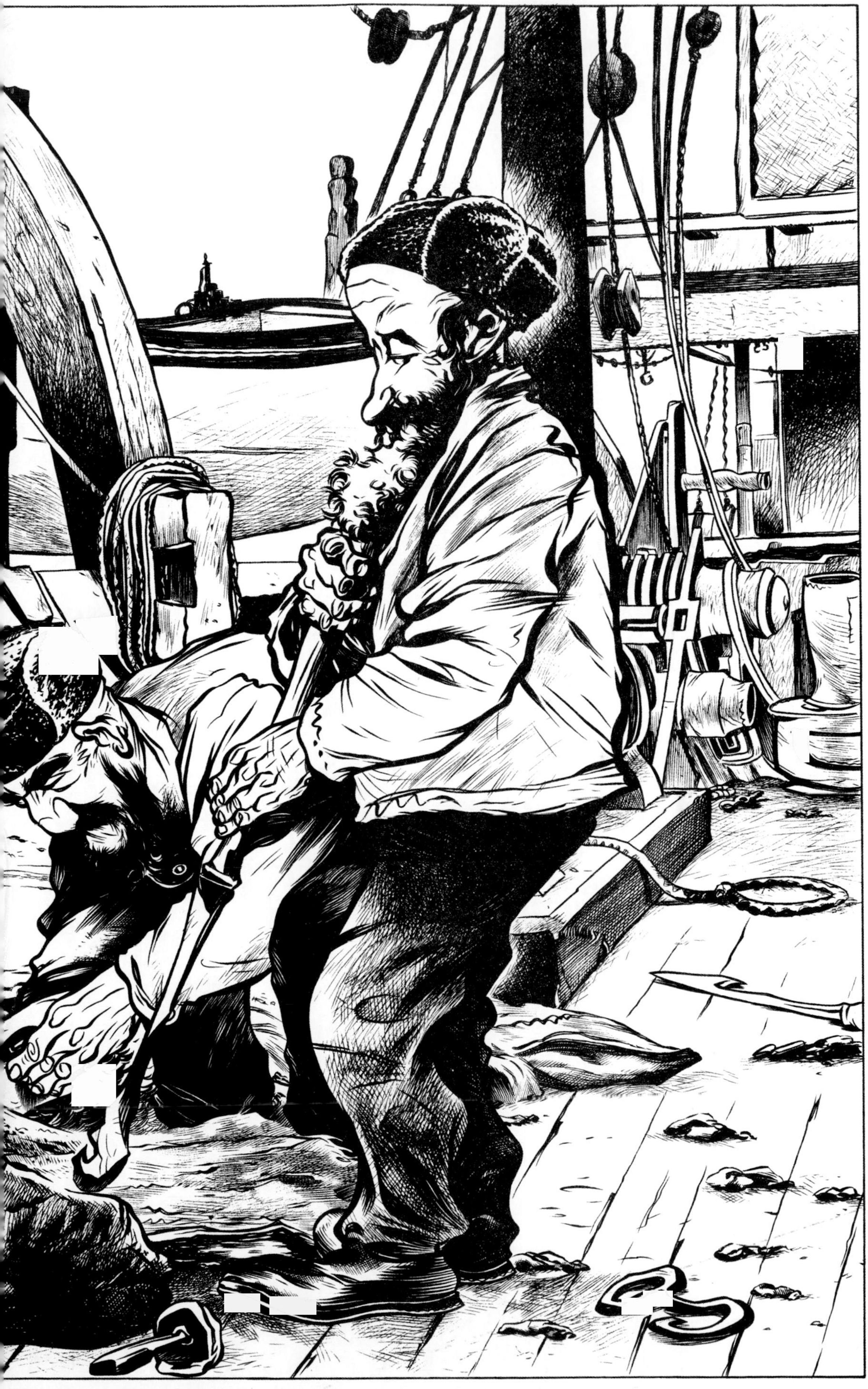

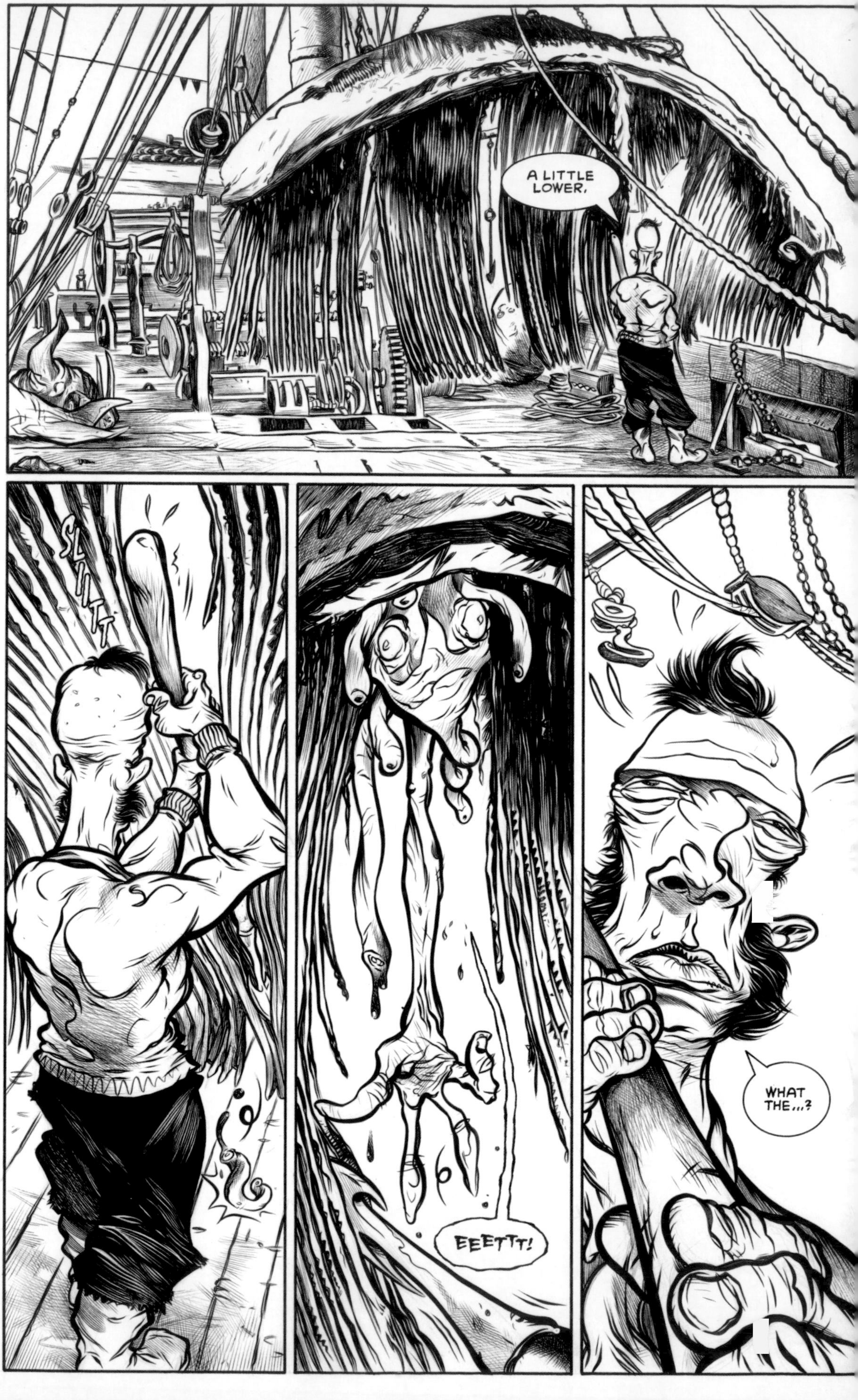
A LITTLE LOWER.
SLIIITT
EEETTT!
WHAT THE...?

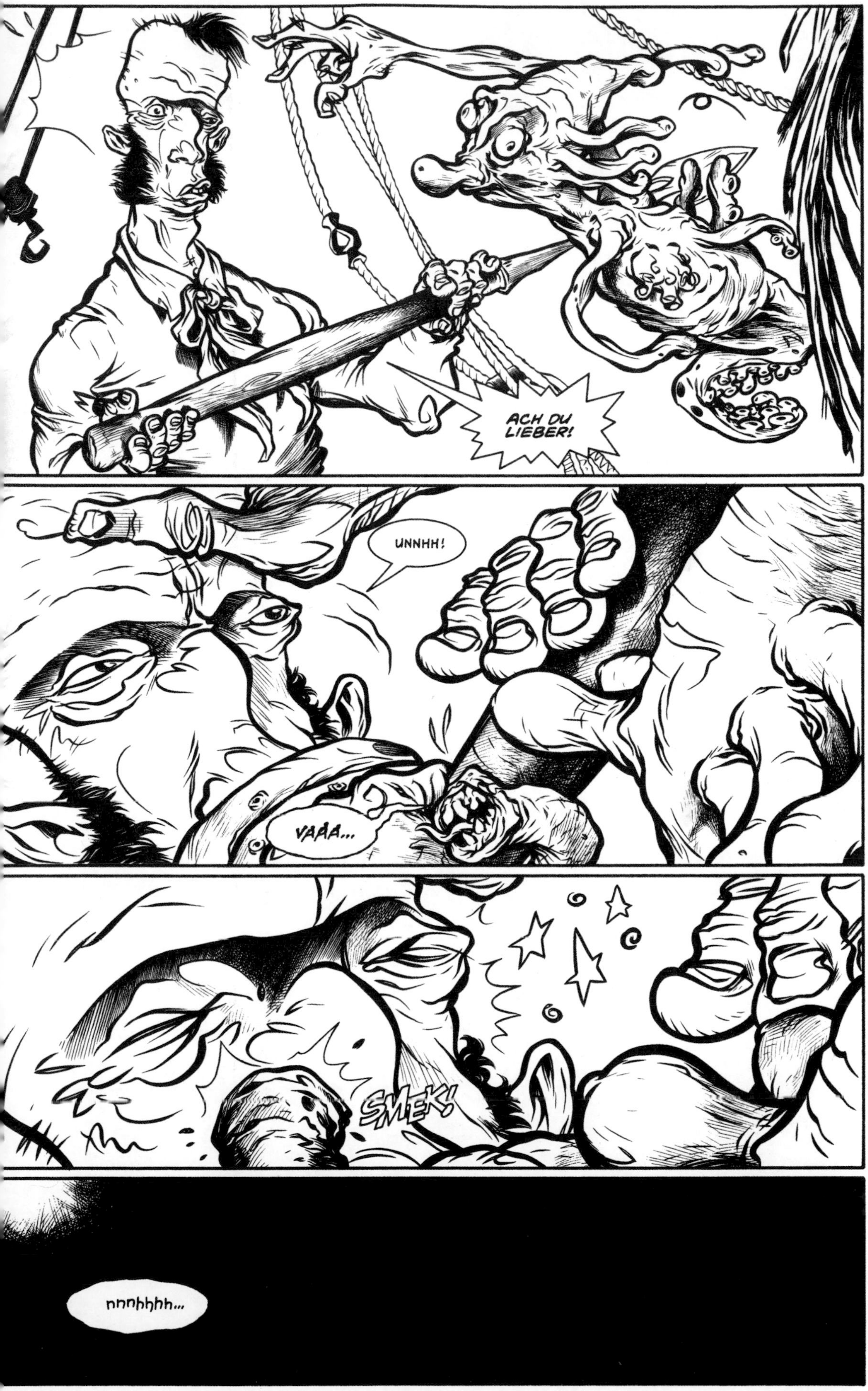
ACH DU LIEBER!
UNNHH!
VAAA...
SMEK!
nnnhhhh...

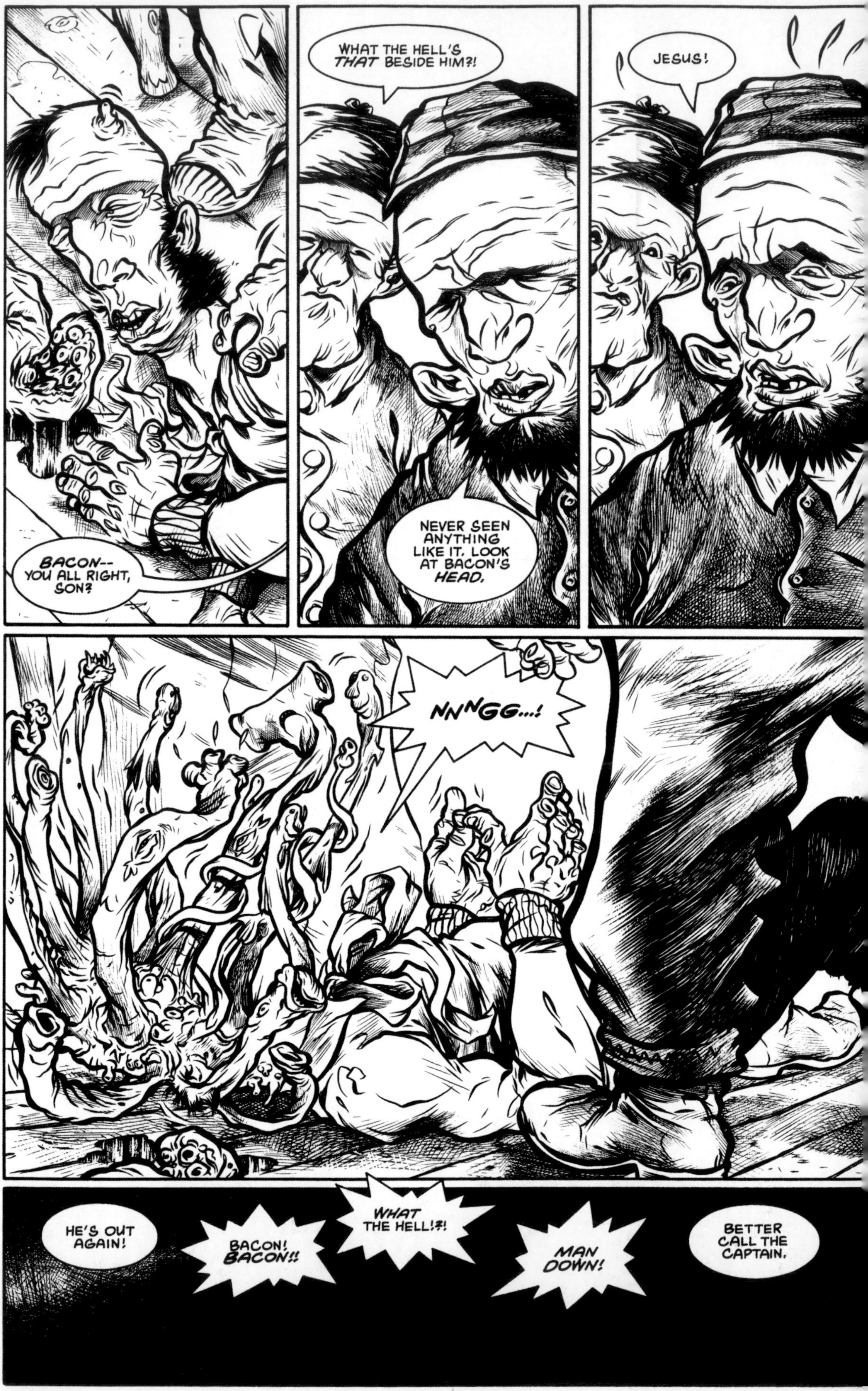
BACON-- YOU ALL RIGHT, SON?
WHAT THE HELL'S THAT BESIDE HIM?!
NEVER SEEN ANYTHING LIKE IT. LOOK AT BACON'S HEAD.
JESUS!
NNNGG...!
HE'S OUT AGAIN!
BACON! BACON!!
WHAT THE HELL!?!
MAN DOWN!
BETTER CALL THE CAPTAIN.

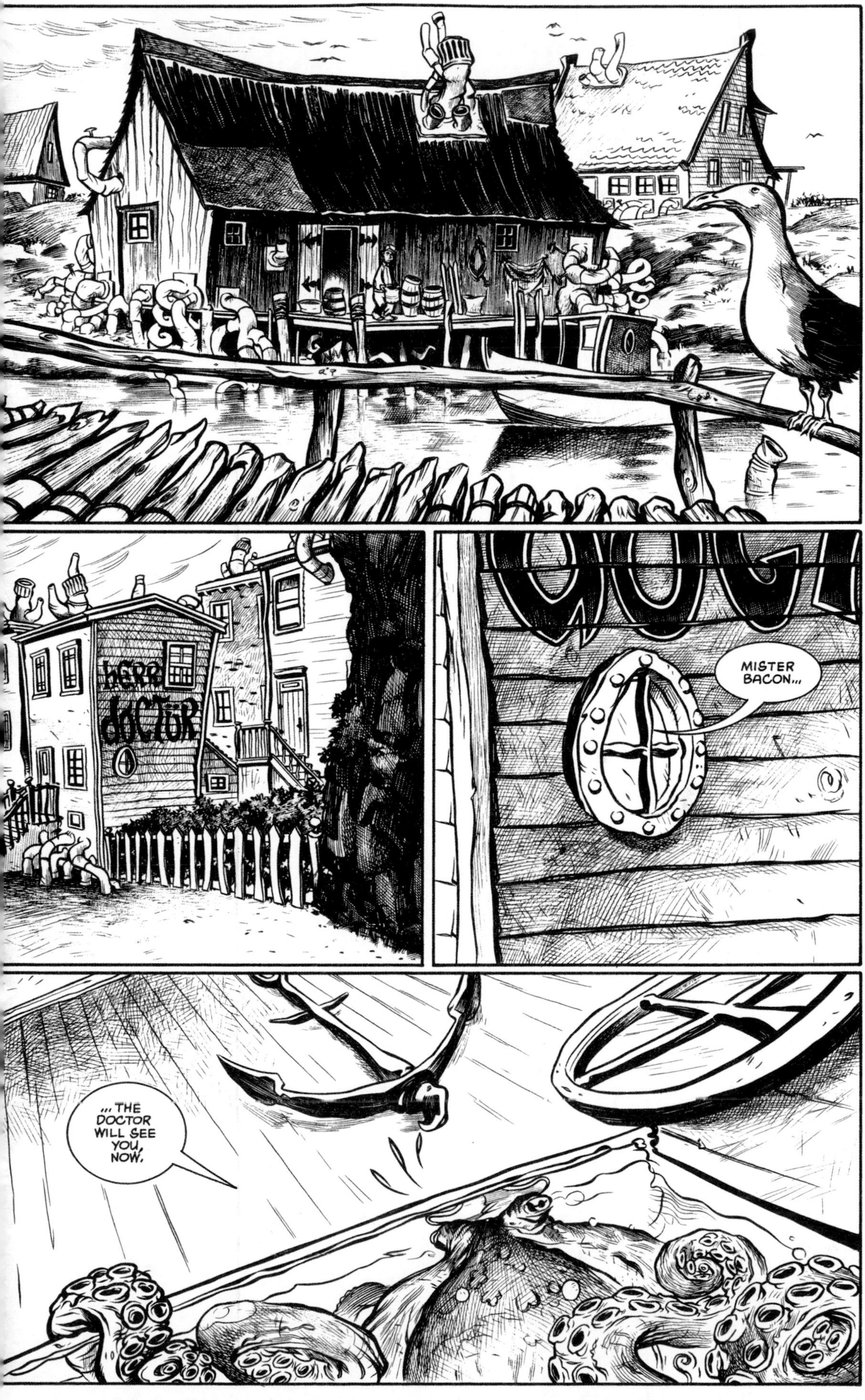
herr doctör
MISTER BACON...
...THE DOCTOR WILL SEE YOU, NOW.

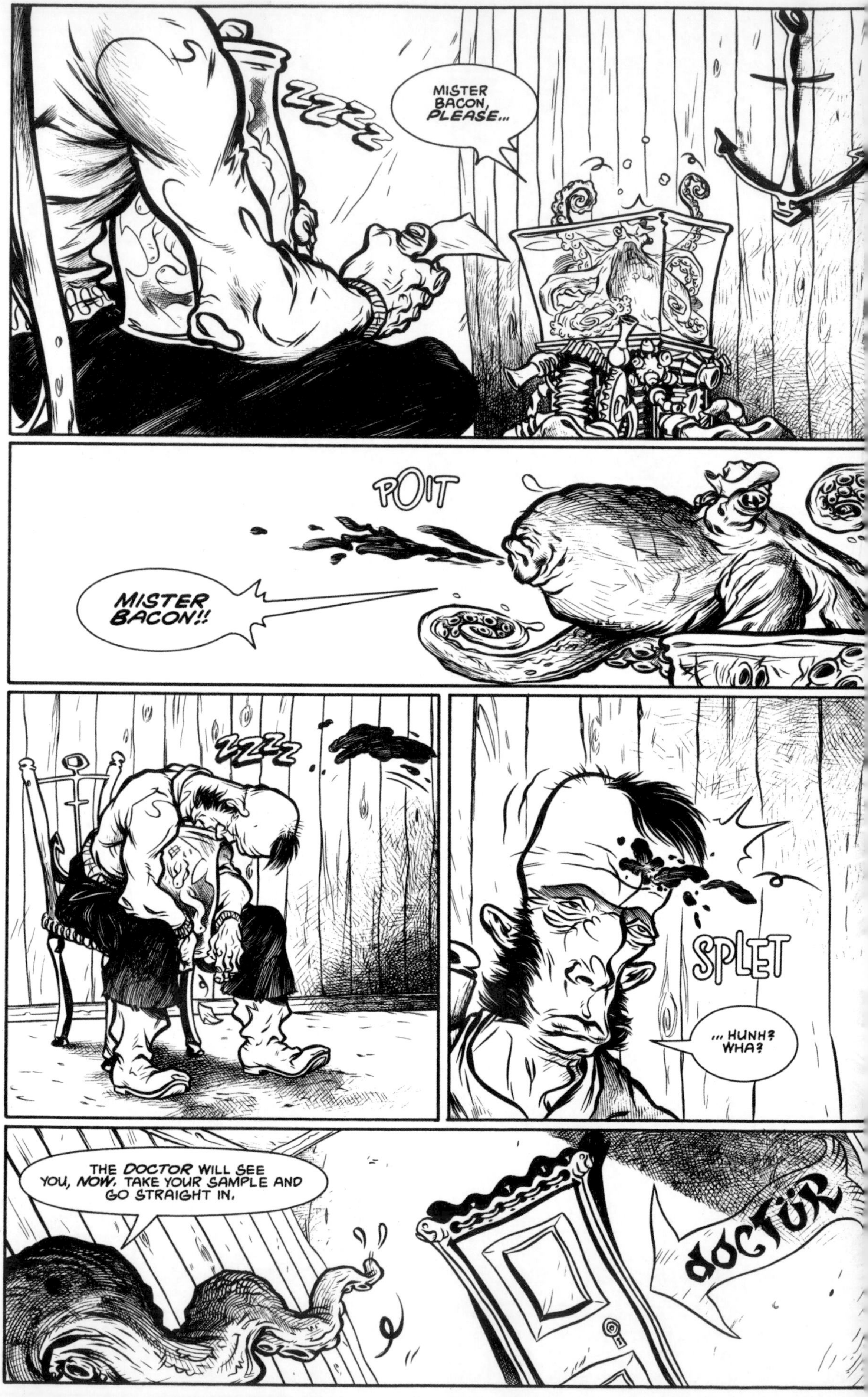
ZZZZZ
MISTER BACON, PLEASE...
POIT
MISTER BACON!!
ZZZZZ
SPLET
... HUNH? WHA?
THE DOCTOR WILL SEE YOU, NOW. TAKE YOUR SAMPLE AND GO STRAIGHT IN.
DOCTÜR

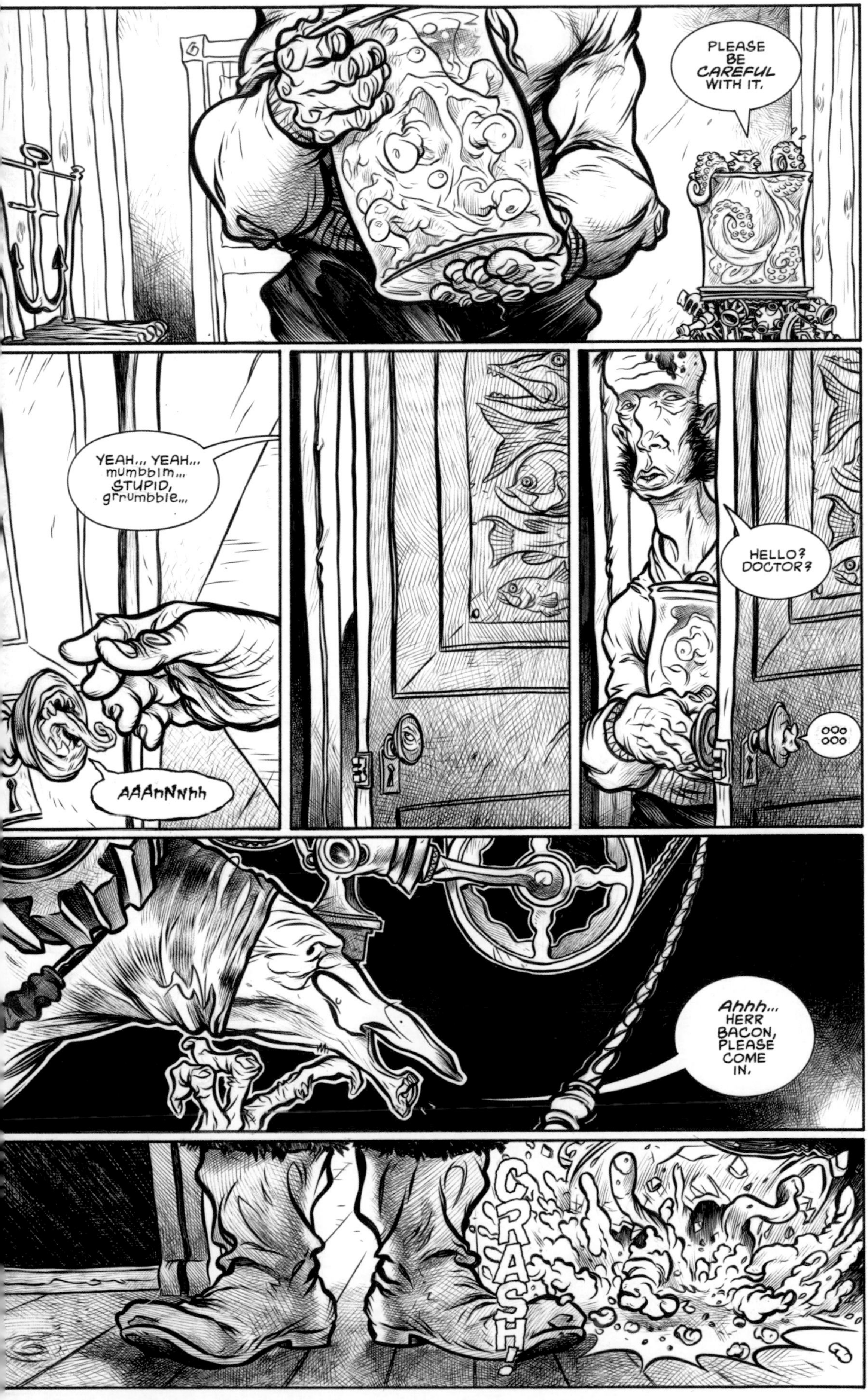
PLEASE BE CAREFUL WITH IT.
YEAH... YEAH... mumbblm... STUPID, grrumbble...
AAAnNhh
HELLO? DOCTOR?
OOO OOO
Ahhh... HERR BACON, PLEASE COME IN.
CRASH!

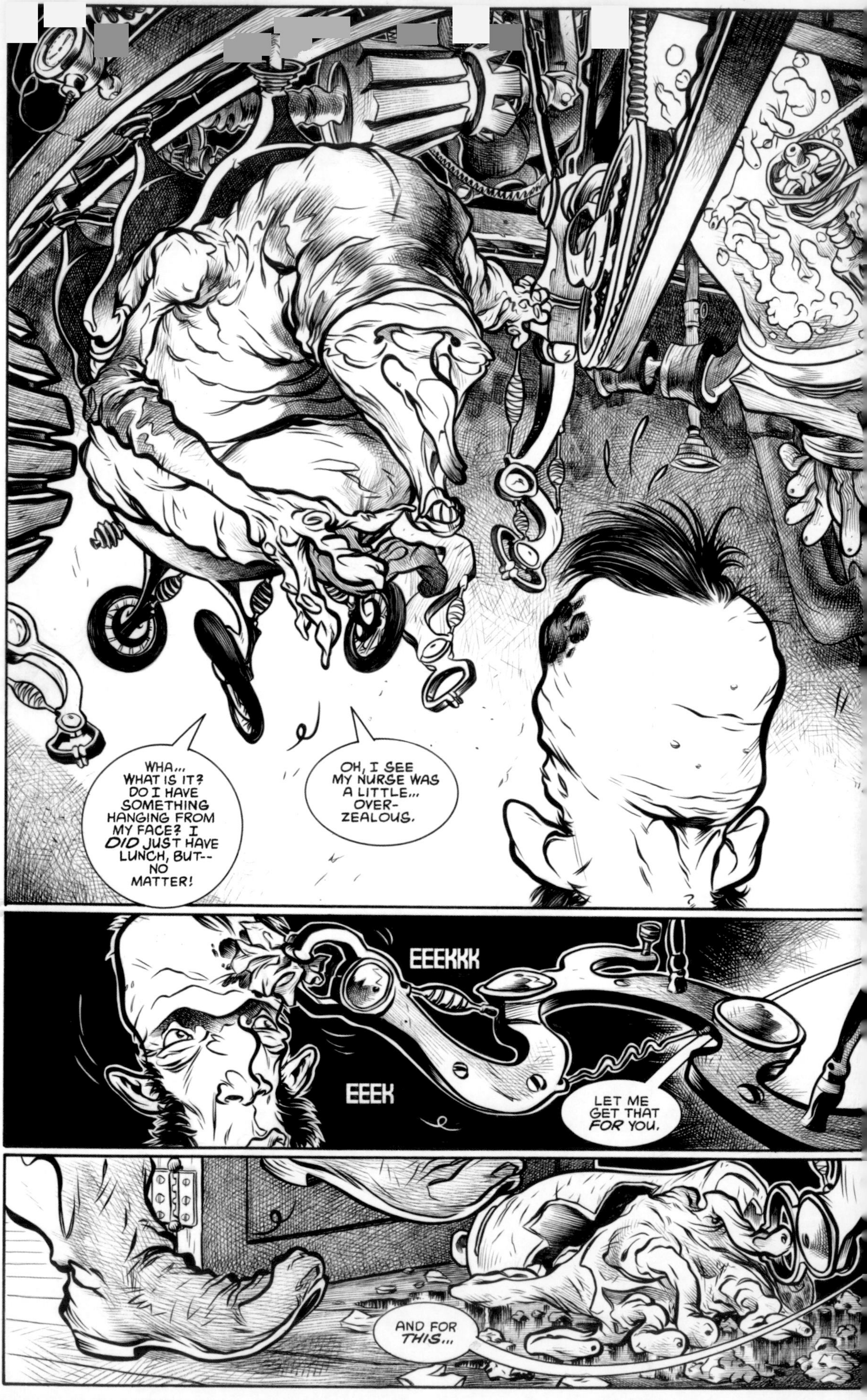
WHA... WHAT IS IT? DO I HAVE SOMETHING HANGING FROM MY FACE? I *DID* JUST HAVE LUNCH, BUT-- NO MATTER!
OH, I SEE MY NURSE WAS A LITTLE... OVER-ZEALOUS.
EEEKKK
EEEK
LET ME GET THAT *FOR* YOU.
AND FOR *THIS*...

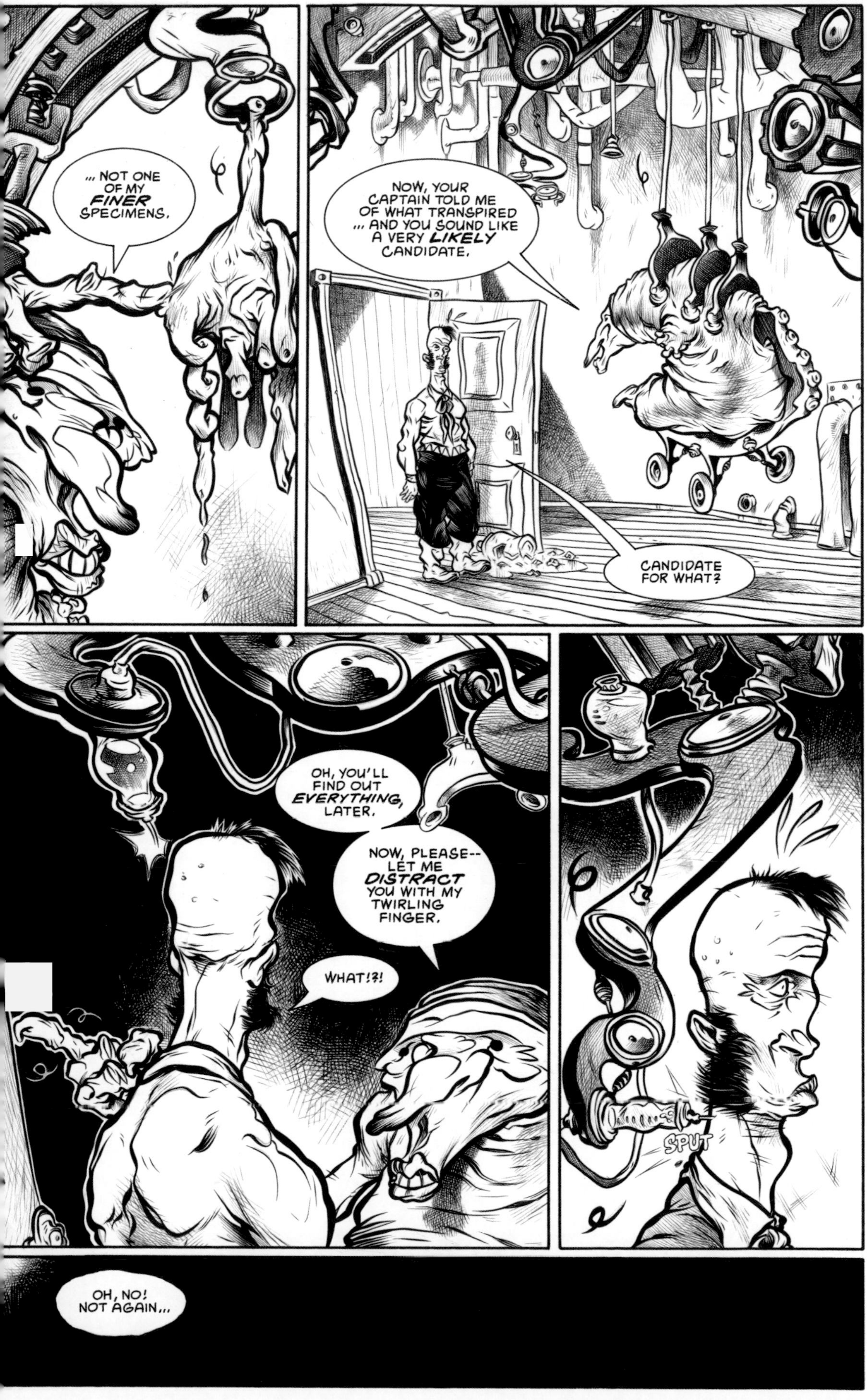
... NOT ONE OF MY FINER SPECIMENS.
NOW, YOUR CAPTAIN TOLD ME OF WHAT TRANSPIRED ... AND YOU SOUND LIKE A VERY LIKELY CANDIDATE.
CANDIDATE FOR WHAT?
OH, YOU'LL FIND OUT EVERYTHING, LATER.
NOW, PLEASE-- LET ME DISTRACT YOU WITH MY TWIRLING FINGER.
WHAT!?!
SPUT
OH, NO! NOT AGAIN...

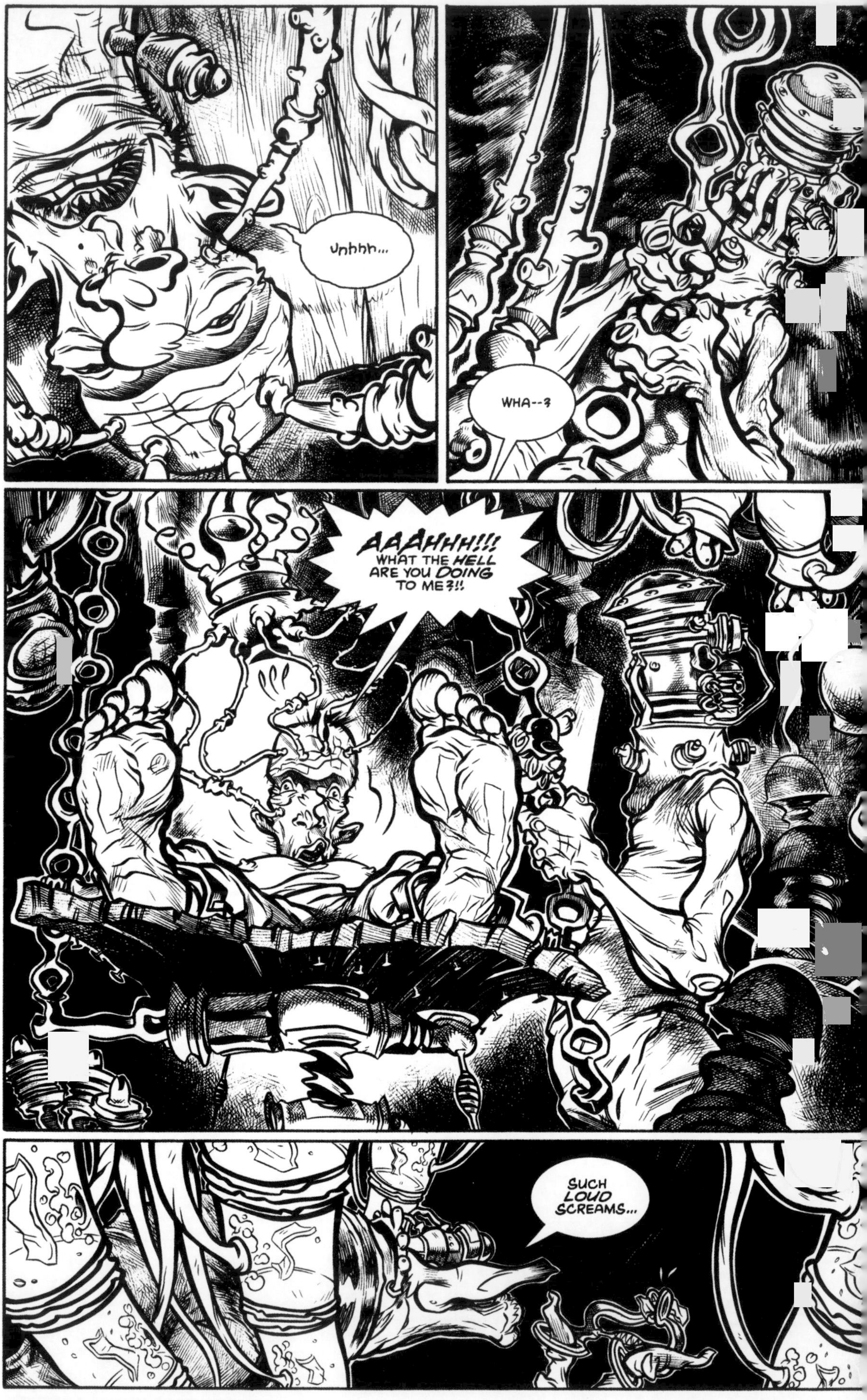
Unhhh...
WHA--?
AAAHHH!!! WHAT THE HELL ARE YOU DOING TO ME?!!
SUCH LOUD SCREAMS...

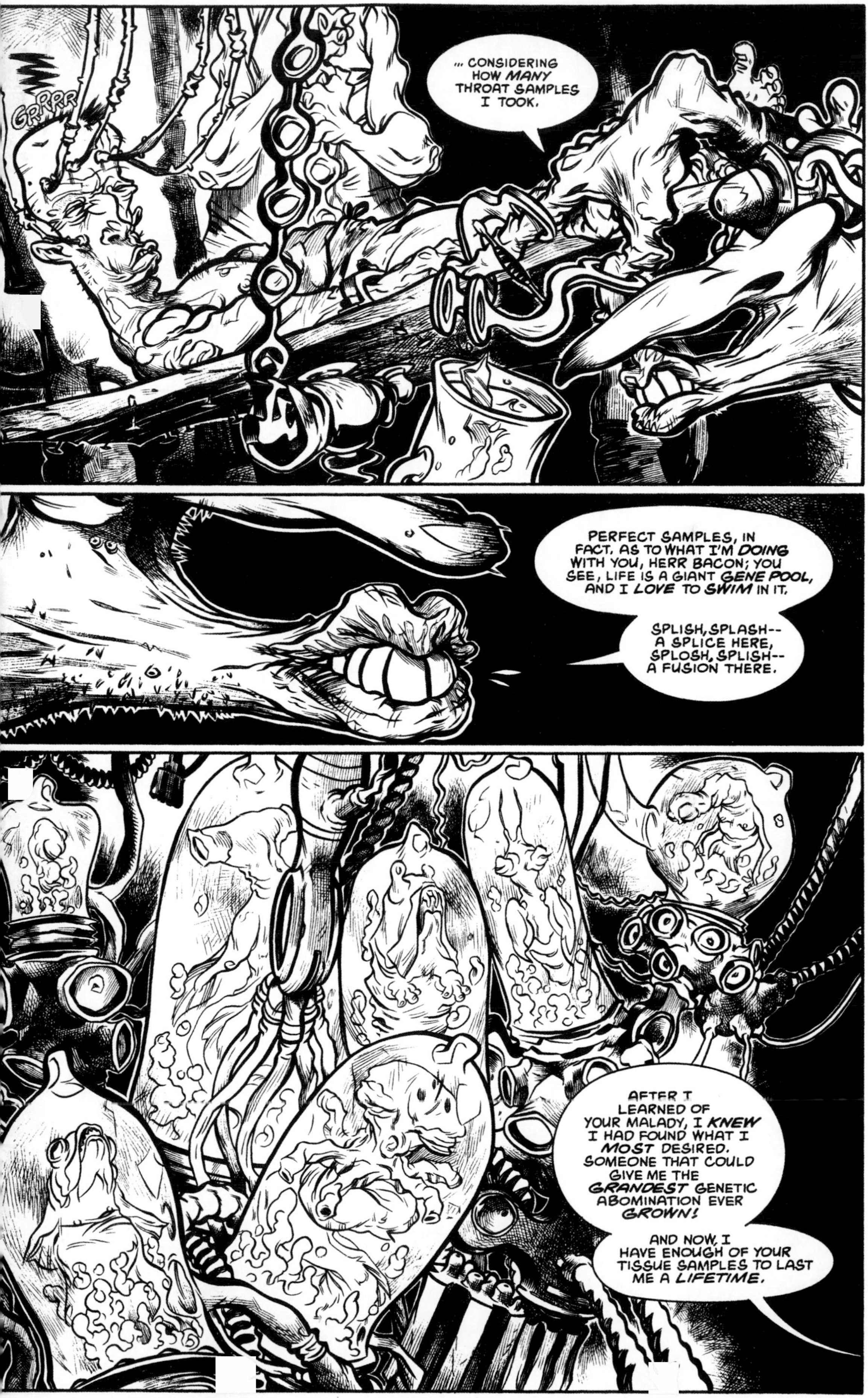
GRRRR
... CONSIDERING HOW MANY THROAT SAMPLES I TOOK.
PERFECT SAMPLES, IN FACT, AS TO WHAT I'M DOING WITH YOU, HERR BACON; YOU SEE, LIFE IS A GIANT GENE POOL, AND I LOVE TO SWIM IN IT.
SPLISH, SPLASH-- A SPLICE HERE, SPLOSH, SPLISH-- A FUSION THERE.
AFTER I LEARNED OF YOUR MALADY, I KNEW I HAD FOUND WHAT I MOST DESIRED. SOMEONE THAT COULD GIVE ME THE GRANDEST GENETIC ABOMINATION EVER GROWN!
AND NOW, I HAVE ENOUGH OF YOUR TISSUE SAMPLES TO LAST ME A LIFETIME.

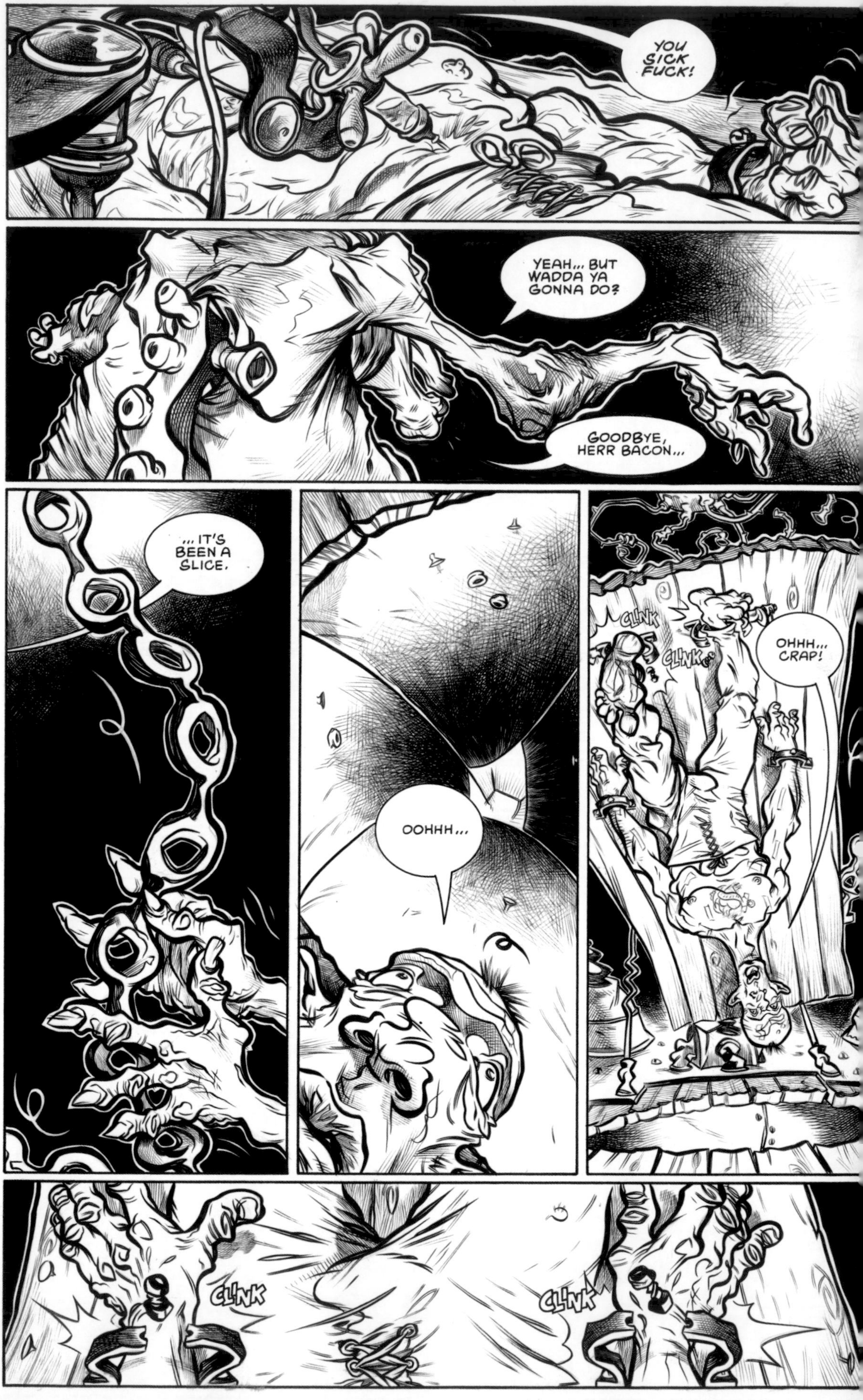
YOU SICK FUCK!
YEAH,,, BUT WADDA YA GONNA DO?
GOODBYE, HERR BACON,,,
,,, IT'S BEEN A SLICE.
OOHHH,,,
CLINK
CLINK
OHHH,,, CRAP!
CLINK
CLINK

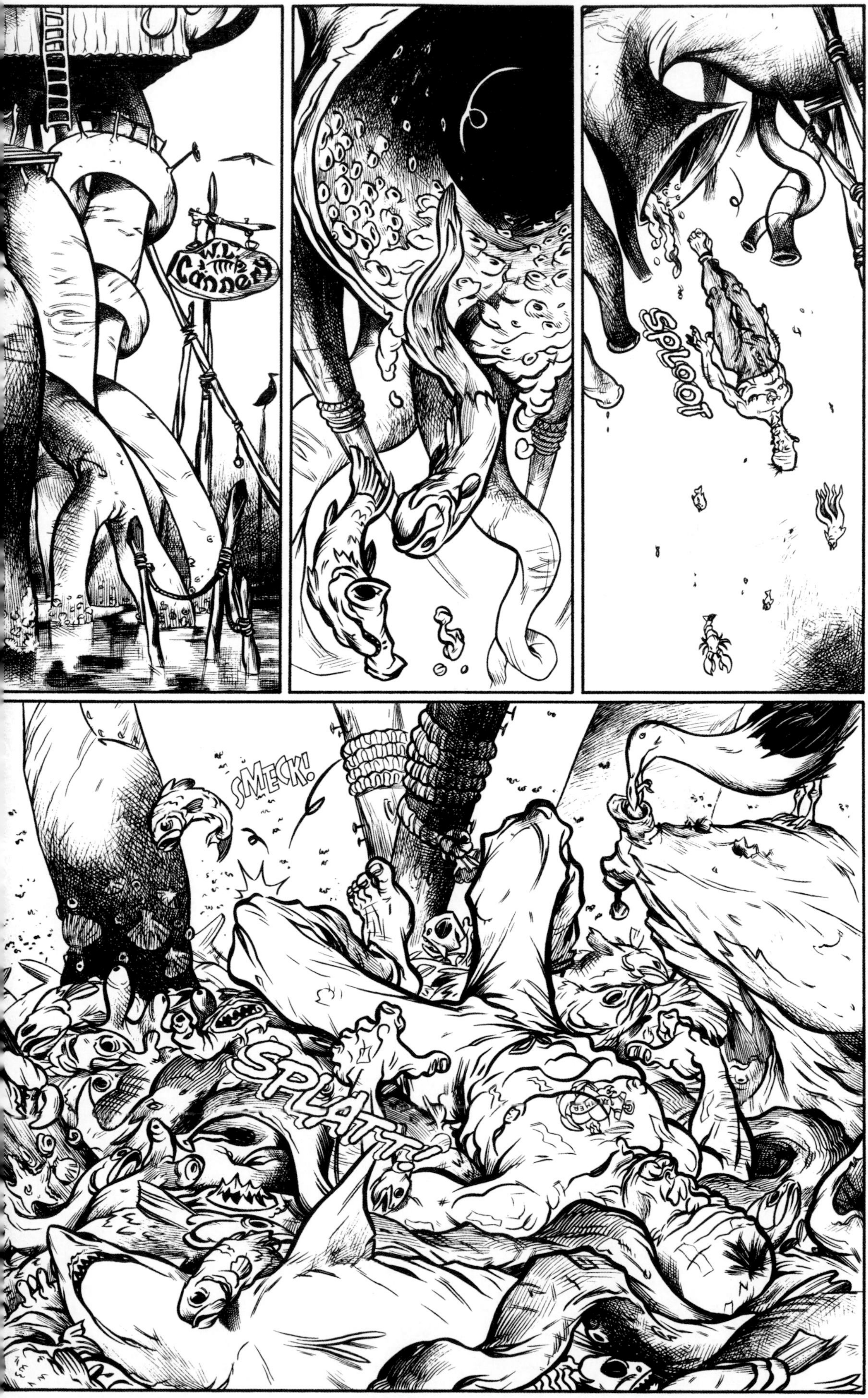
W.L.
Cannery
SPLOOT
SMECK!
SPLATT!

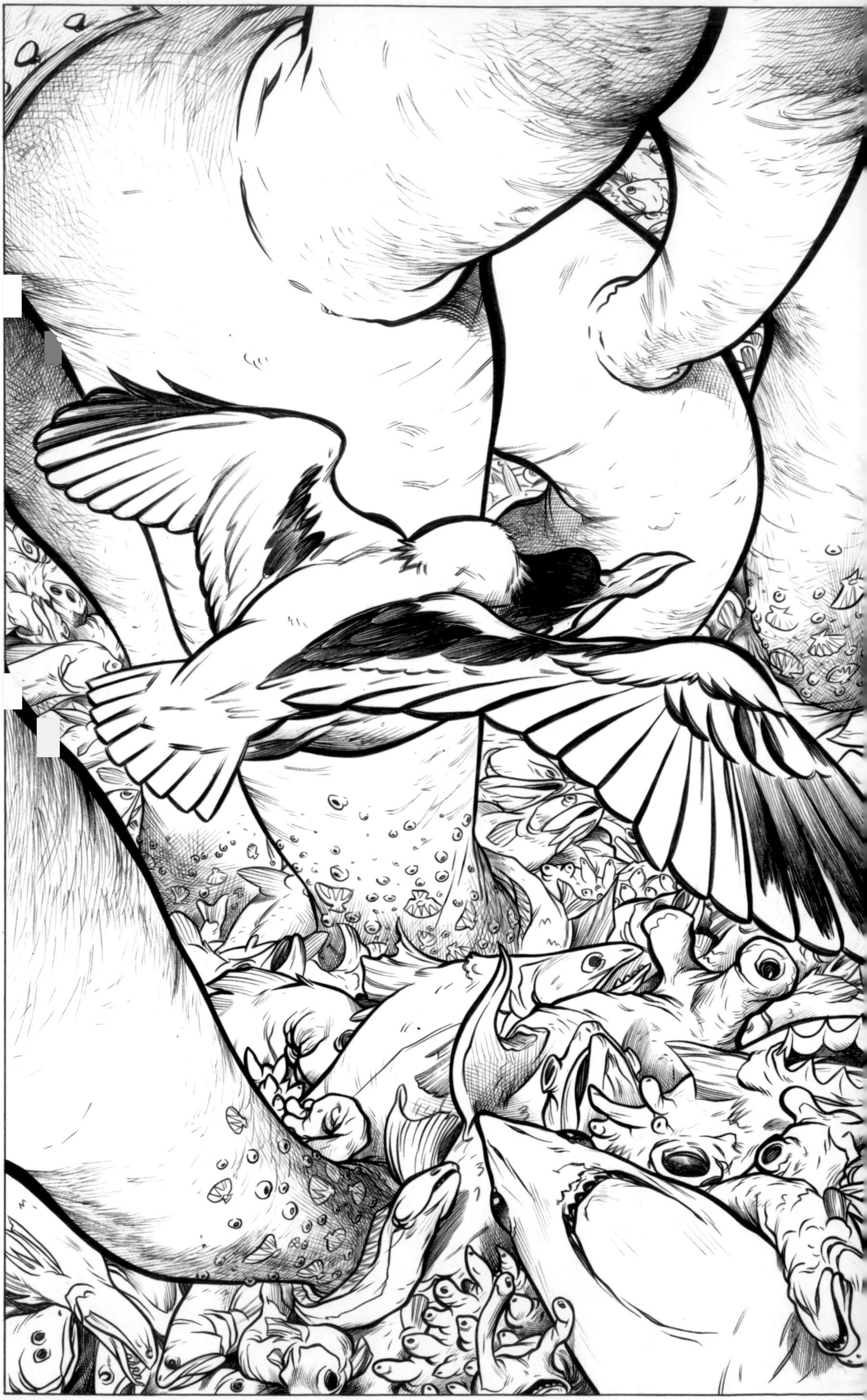

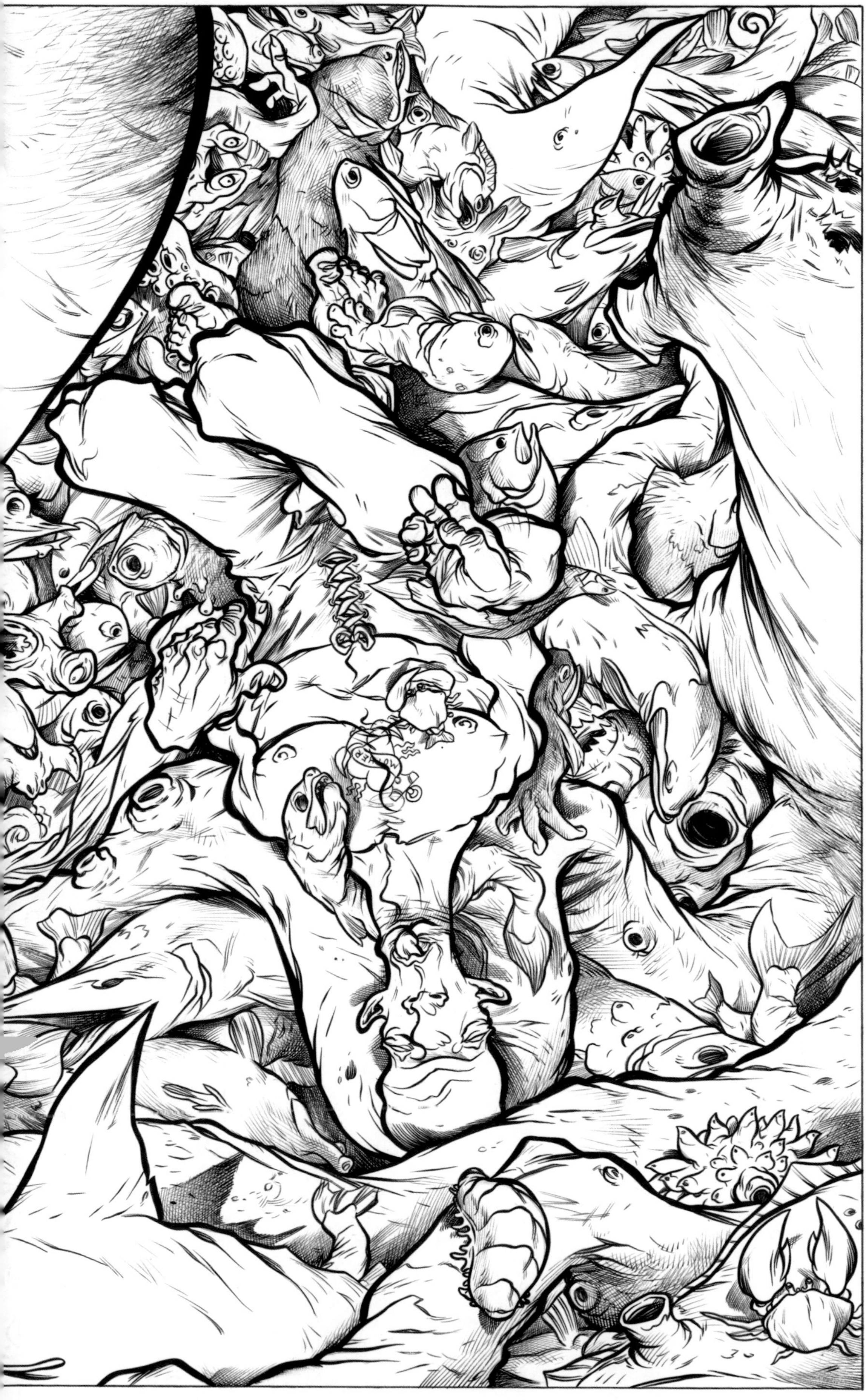

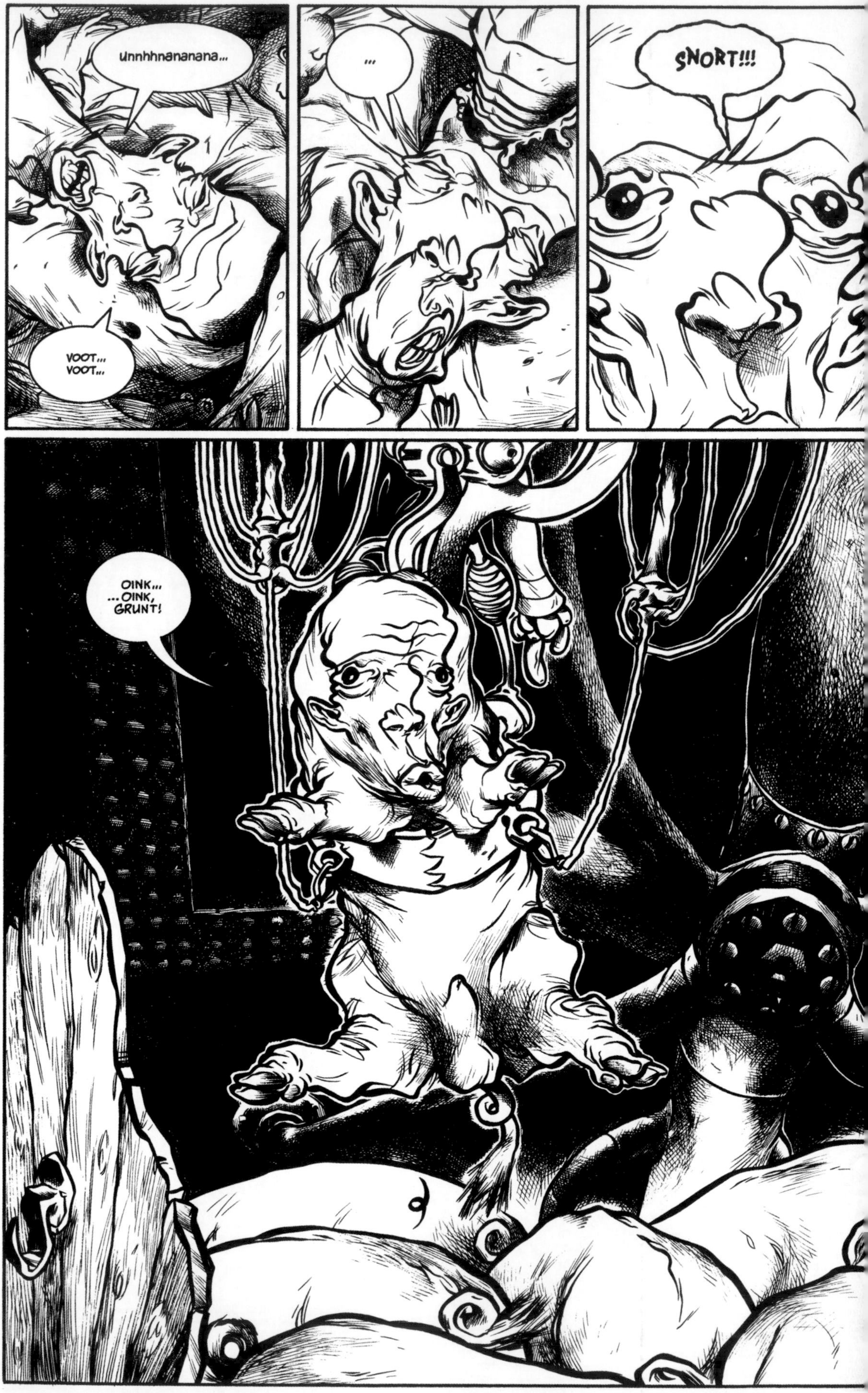
Unnhhnananana...
VOOT... VOOT...
...
SNORT!!!
OINK... ...OINK, GRUNT!

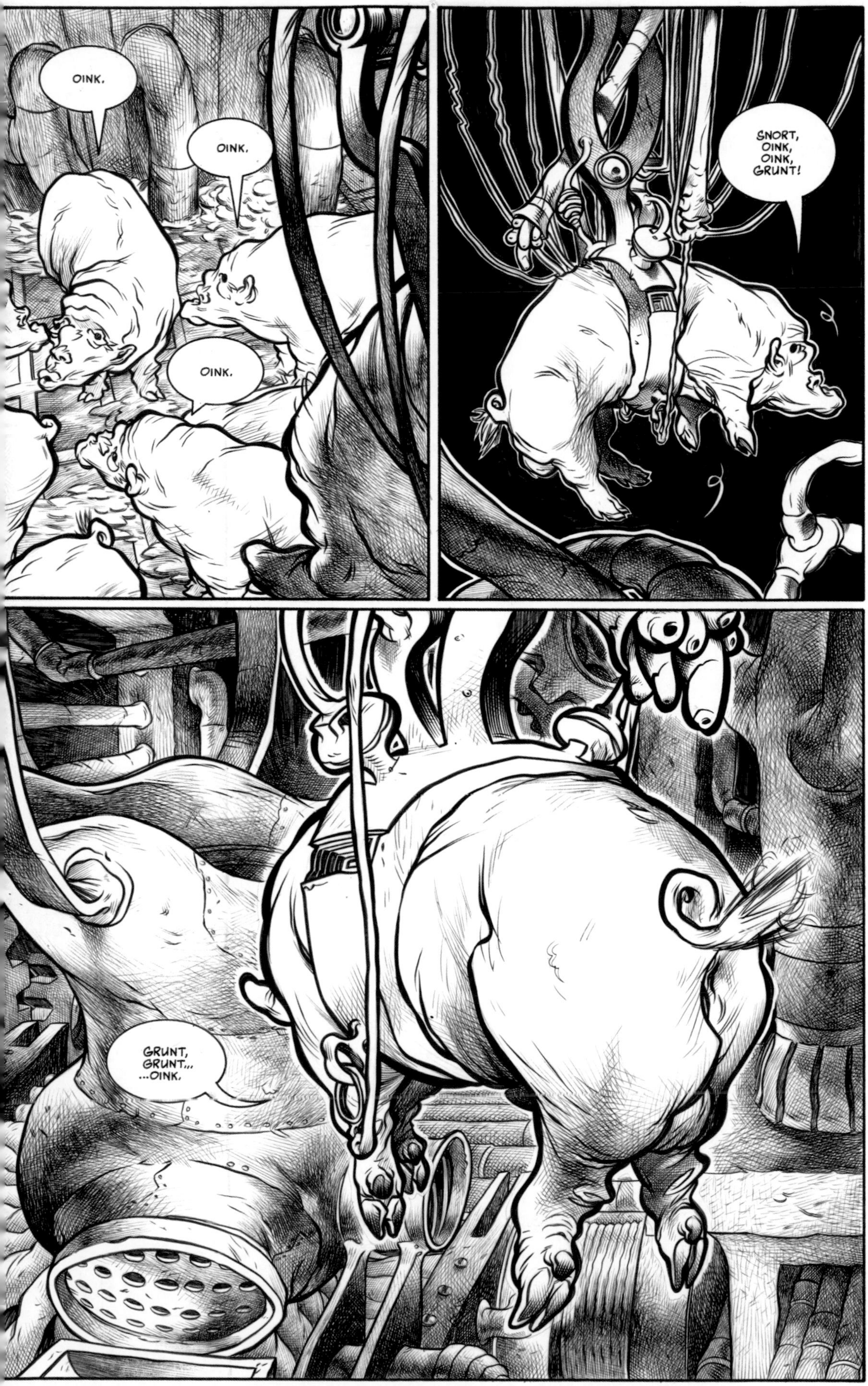
OINK.
OINK.
OINK.
SNORT, OINK, OINK, GRUNT!
GRUNT, GRUNT... ...OINK.

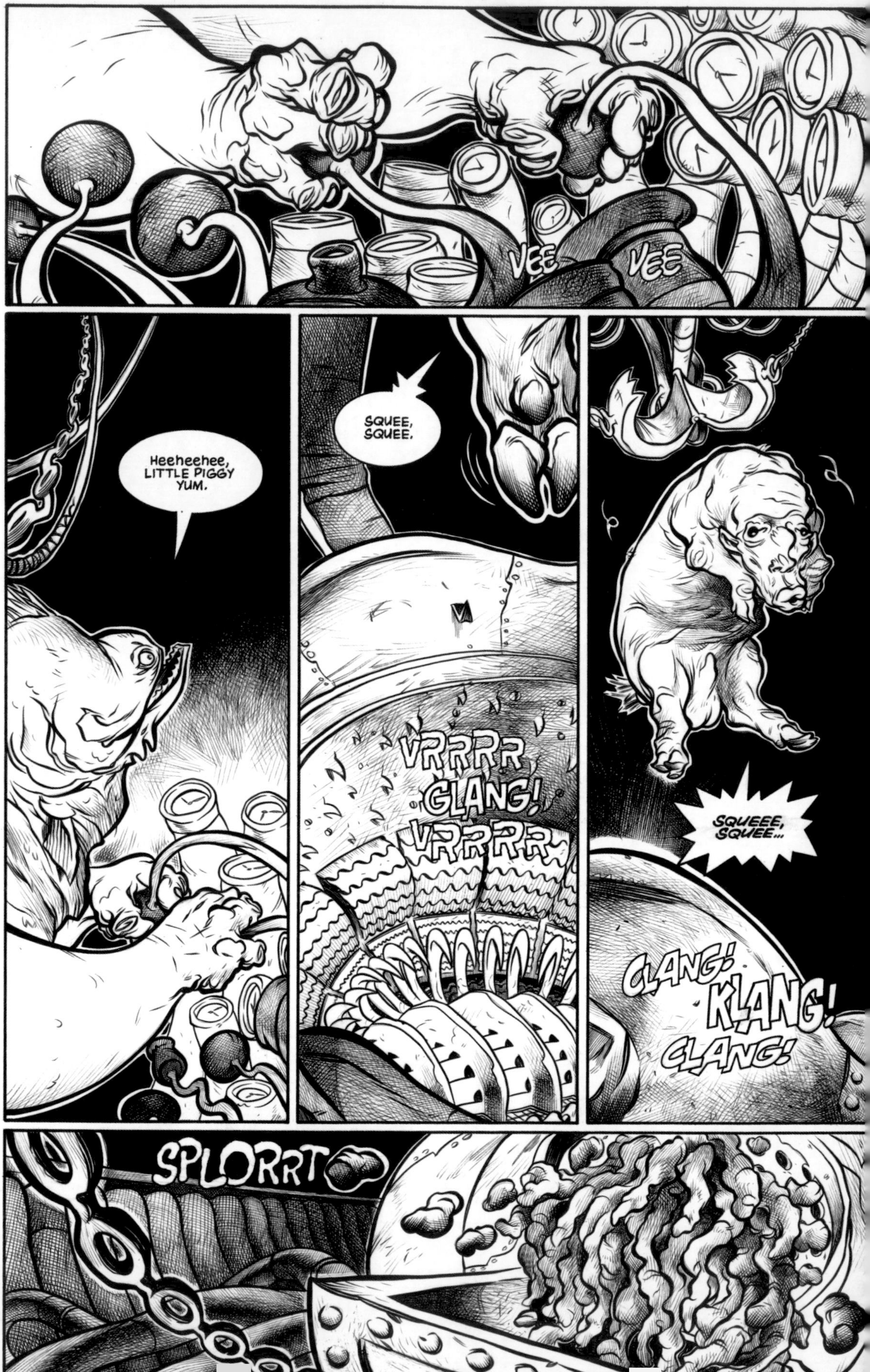
VEE
VEE
Heeheehee, LITTLE PIGGY YUM.
SQUEE, SQUEE.
VRRRRR
GLANG!
VRRRRR
SQUEEE, SQUEE...
CLANG!
KLANG!
CLANG!
SPLORRT

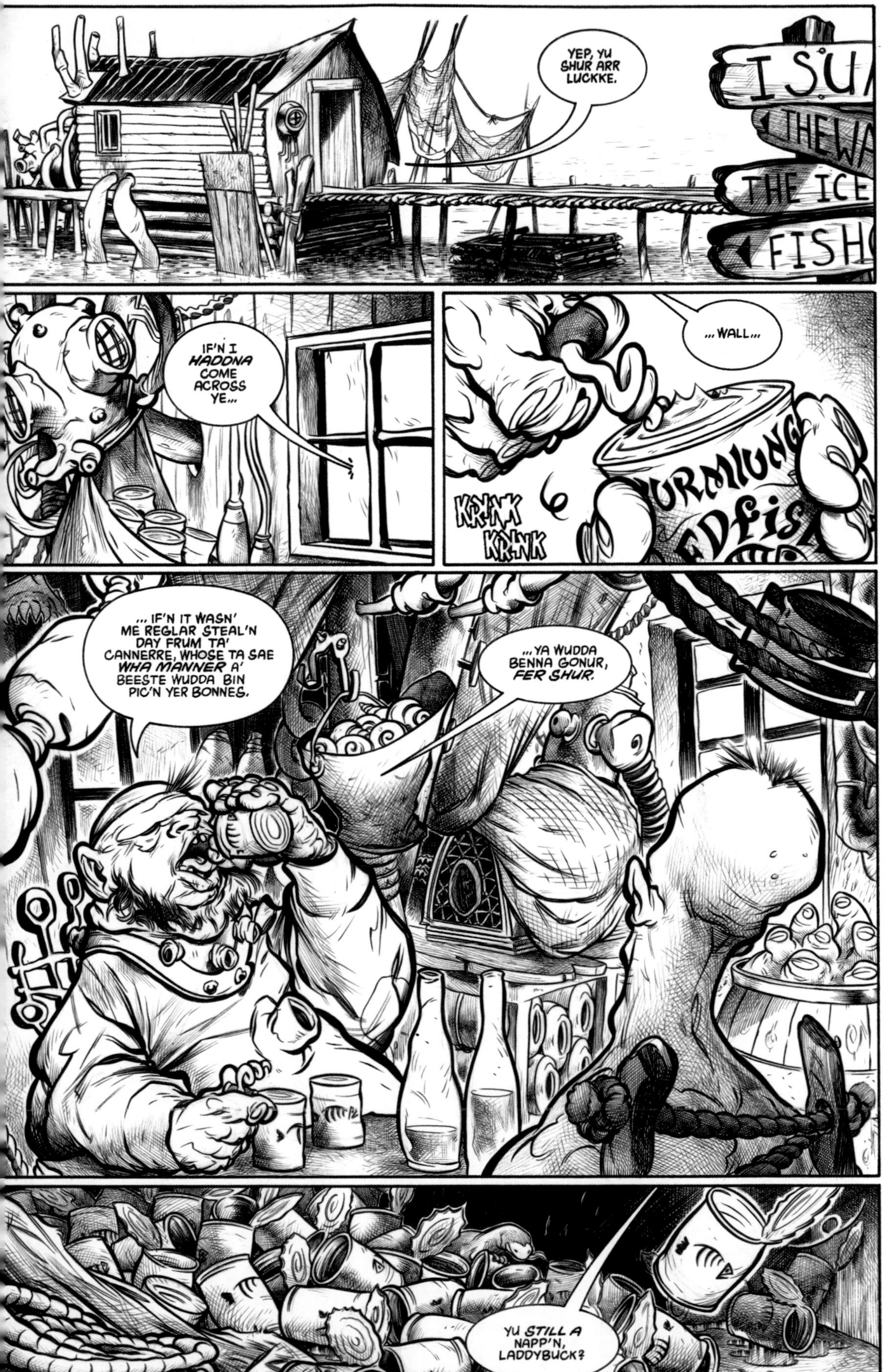
YEP, YU SHUR ARR LUCKKE.
I SU
THE WA
THE ICE
FISH
IF'N I HADDNA COME ACROSS YE...
...WALL...
KRANK KRANK
URMIUNG
EDFIS
... IF'N IT WASN' ME REGLAR STEAL'N DAY FRUM TA' CANNERRE, WHOSE TA SAE WHA MANNER A' BEESTE WUDDA BIN PIC'N YER BONNES.
...YA WUDDA BENNA GONUR, FER SHUR.
YU STILL A NAPP'N, LADDYBUCK?

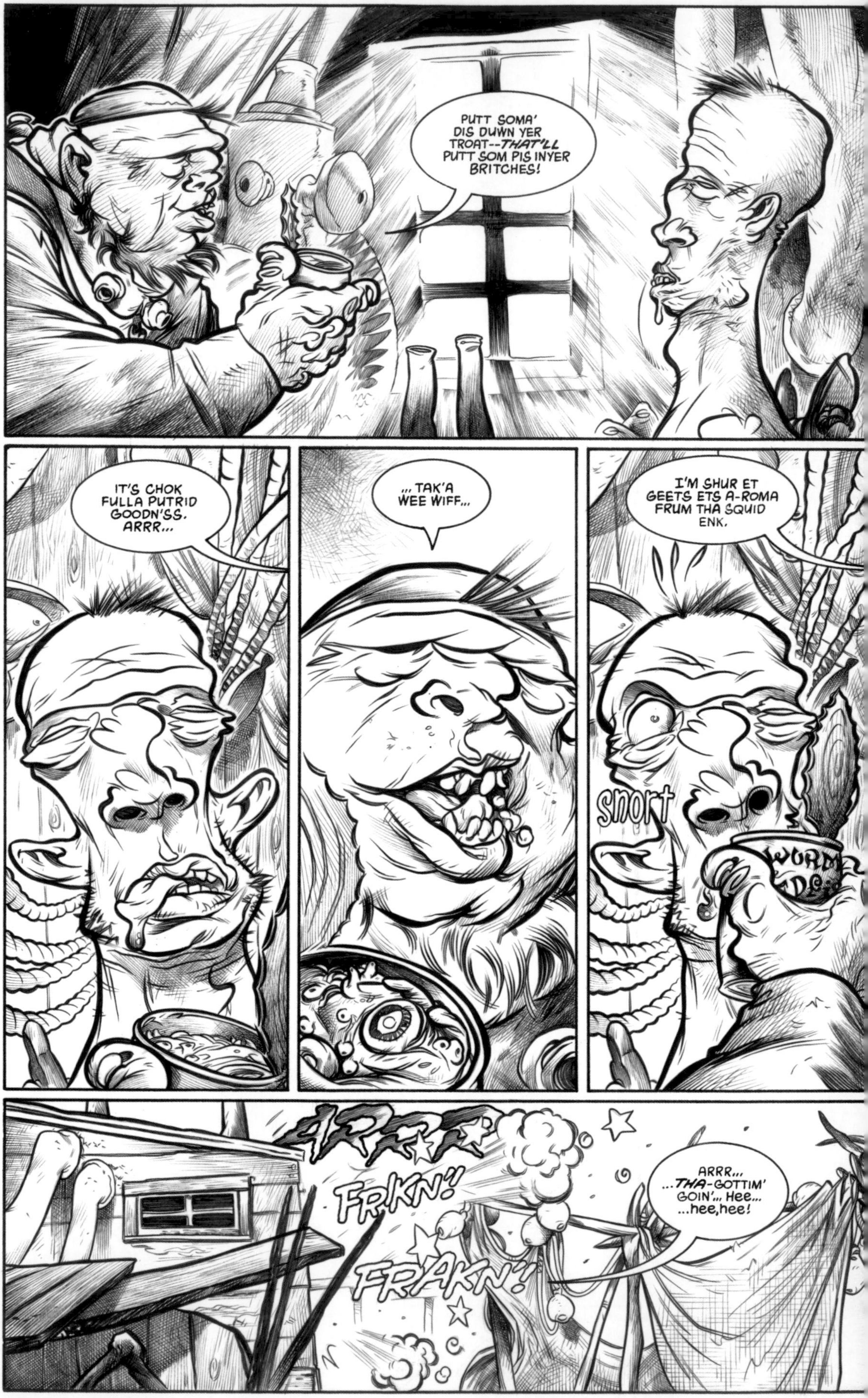
PUTT SOMA' DIS DUWN YER TROAT--*THAT'LL* PUTT SOM PIS INYER BRITCHES!
IT'S CHOK FULLA PUTRID GOODN'SS. ARRR...
...TAK'A WEE WIFF...
I'M SHUR ET GEETS ETS A-ROMA FRUM THA SQUID ENK.
snort
ARRRR
FRIKN!
FRAKN!
ARRR... ...*THA*-GOTTIM' GOIN'... Hee... ...hee,hee!

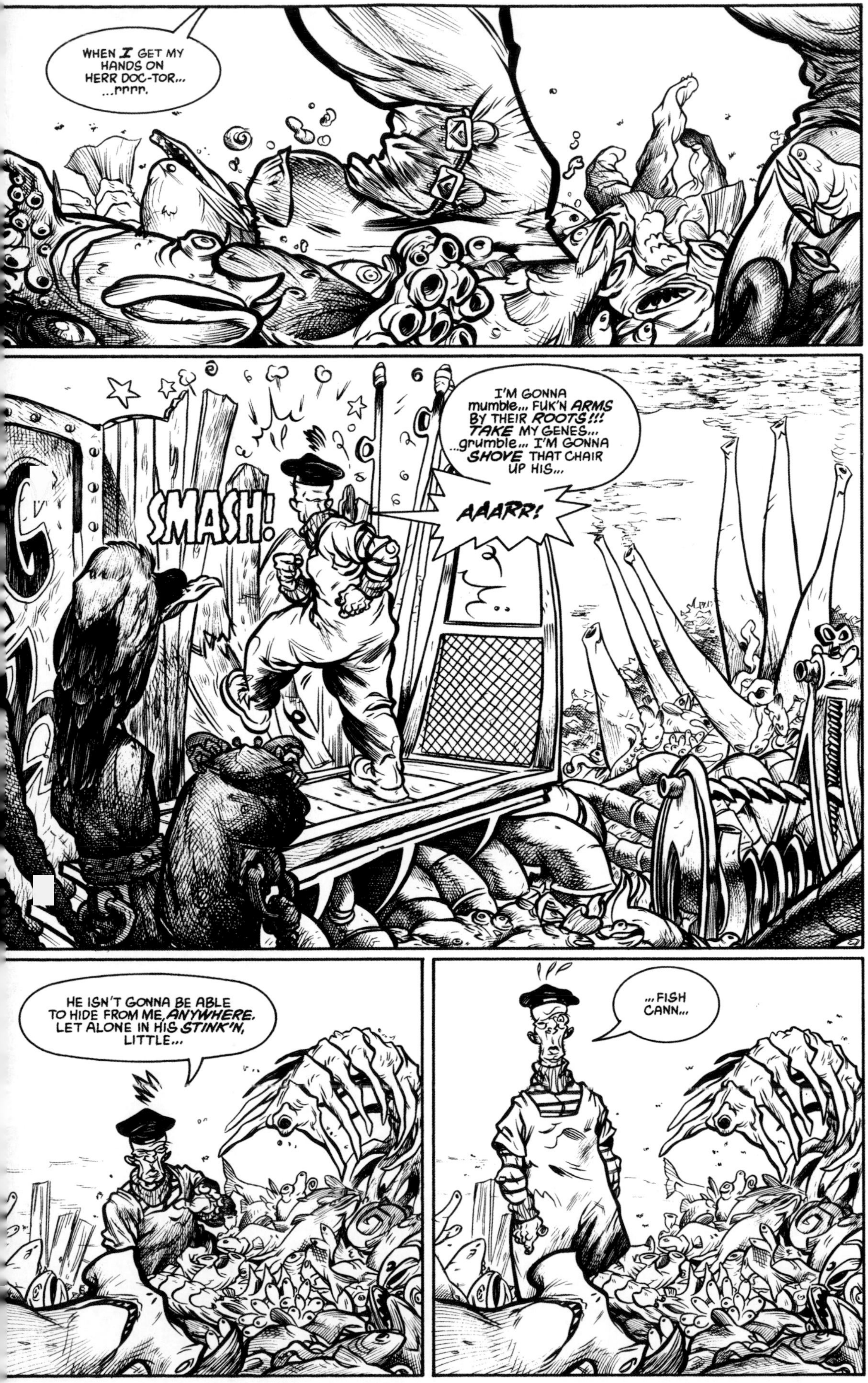
WHEN I GET MY HANDS ON HERR DOC-TOR... ...rrrr.
SMASH!
I'M GONNA mumble... FUK'N ARMS BY THEIR ROOTS!!! TAKE MY GENES... ...grumble... I'M GONNA SHOVE THAT CHAIR UP HIS...
AAARR!
HE ISN'T GONNA BE ABLE TO HIDE FROM ME, ANYWHERE. LET ALONE IN HIS STINK'N, LITTLE...
...FISH CANN...

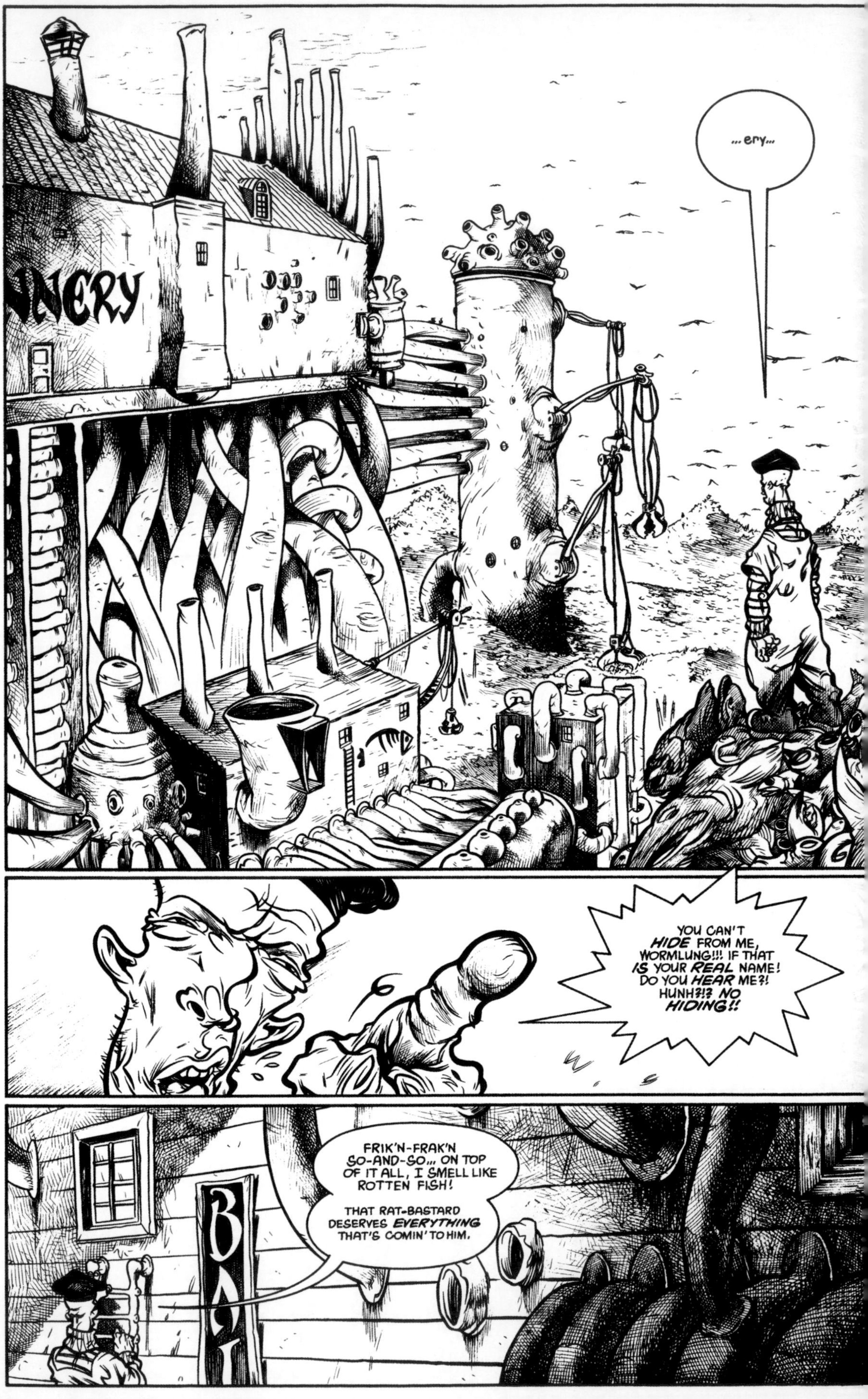
NNERY
...ery...
YOU CAN'T HIDE FROM ME, WORMLUNG!!! IF THAT IS YOUR REAL NAME! DO YOU HEAR ME?! HUNH?!? NO HIDING!!
FRIK'N-FRAK'N SO-AND-SO... ON TOP OF IT ALL, I SMELL LIKE ROTTEN FISH!
THAT RAT-BASTARD DESERVES EVERYTHING THAT'S COMIN' TO HIM.

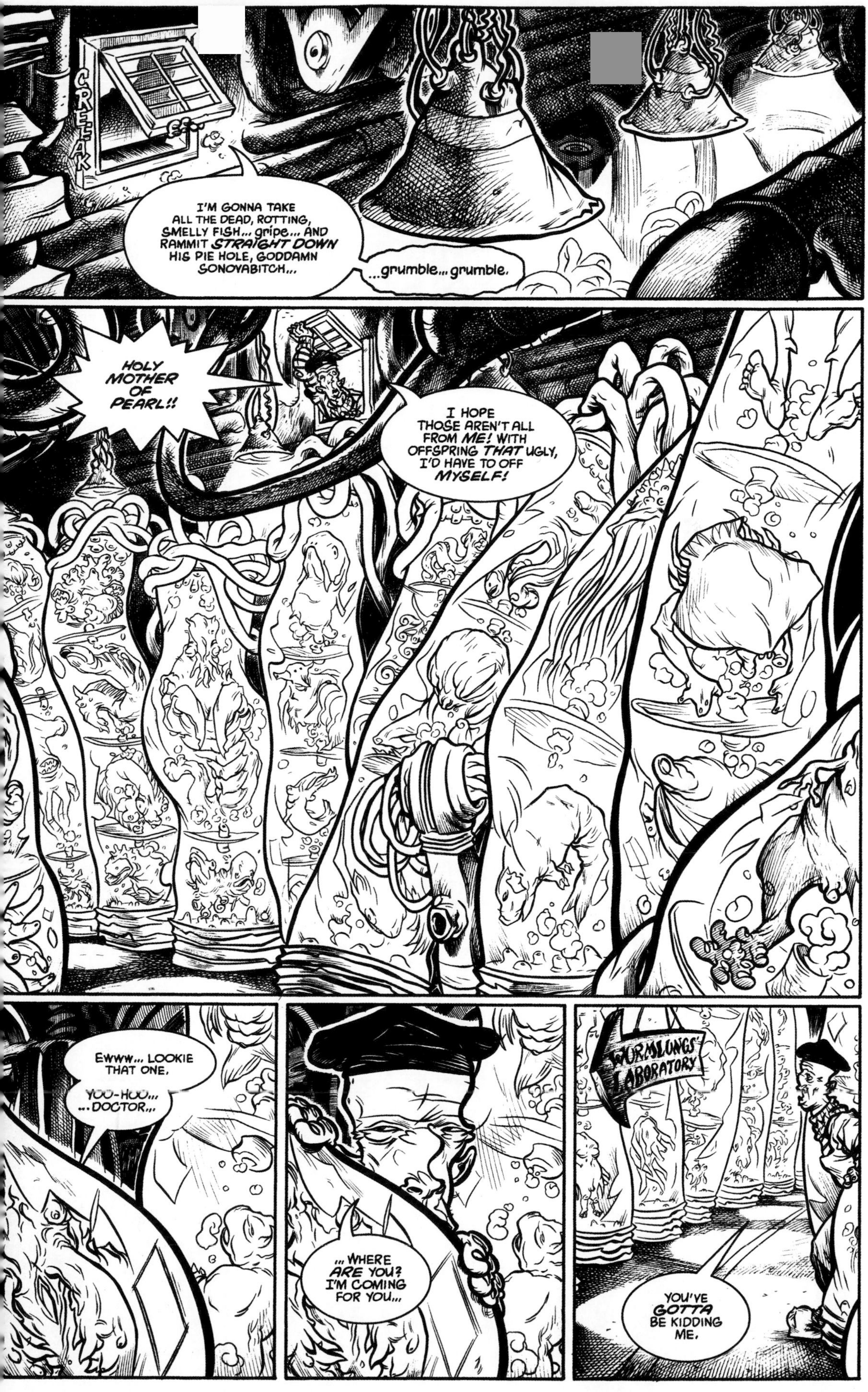

CREEAK
I'M GONNA TAKE ALL THE DEAD, ROTTING, SMELLY FISH... gripe... AND RAMMIT STRAIGHT DOWN HIS PIE HOLE, GODDAMN SONOVABITCH...
...grumble... grumble.
HOLY MOTHER OF PEARL!!
I HOPE THOSE AREN'T ALL FROM ME! WITH OFFSPRING THAT UGLY, I'D HAVE TO OFF MYSELF!
EWWW... LOOKIE THAT ONE.
YOO-HOO... ...DOCTOR...
...WHERE ARE YOU? I'M COMING FOR YOU...
WURMSLUNGS' LABORATORY
YOU'VE GOTTA BE KIDDING ME.

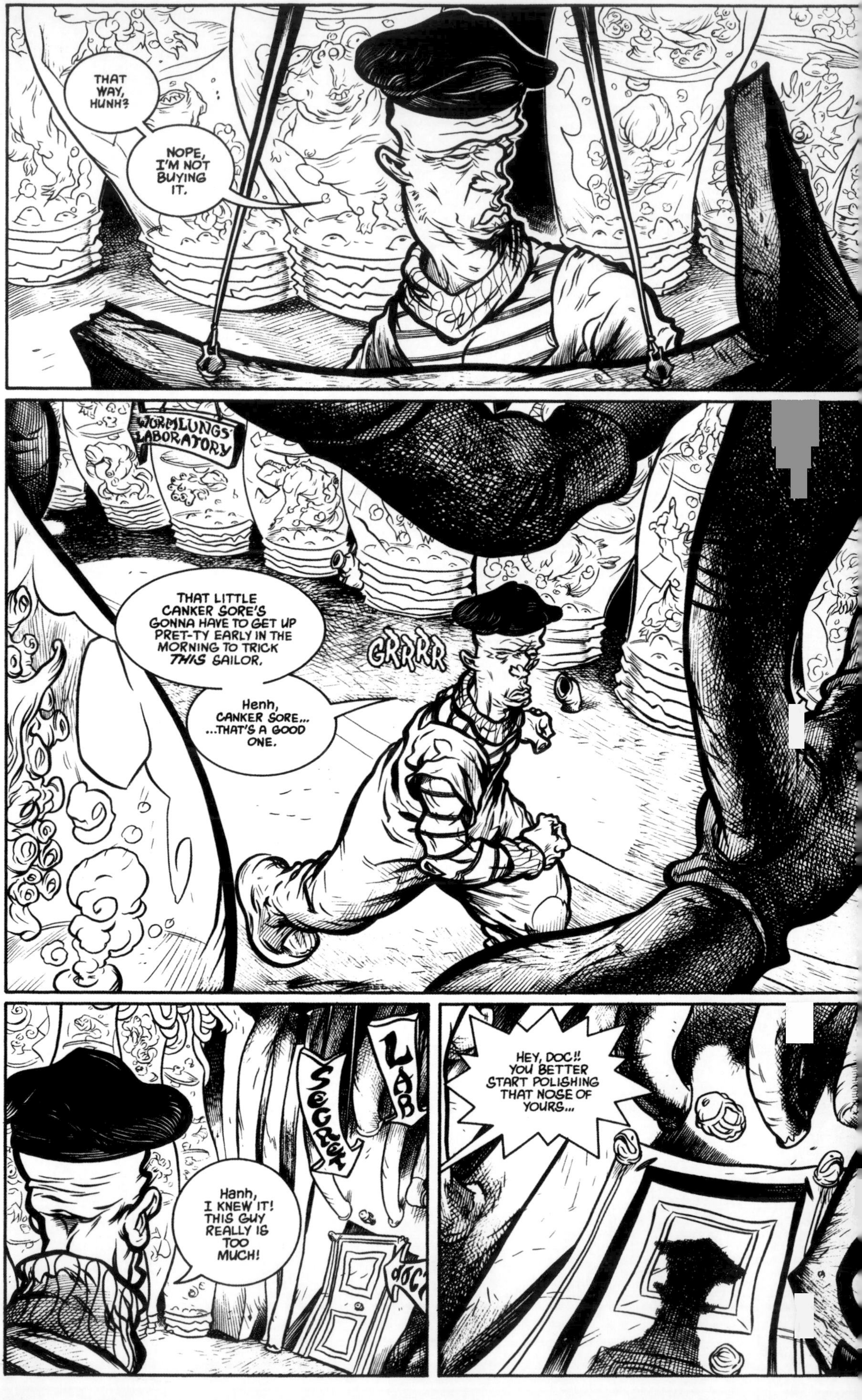
THAT WAY, HUNH?
NOPE, I'M NOT BUYING IT.
WORMLUNGS' LABORATORY
THAT LITTLE CANKER SORE'S GONNA HAVE TO GET UP PRET-TY EARLY IN THE MORNING TO TRICK *THIS* SAILOR.
GRRRR
Henh, CANKER SORE... ...THAT'S A GOOD ONE.
SECRET
LAB
Hanh, I KNEW IT! THIS GUY REALLY IS TOO MUCH!
HEY, DOC!! YOU BETTER START POLISHING THAT NOSE OF YOURS...

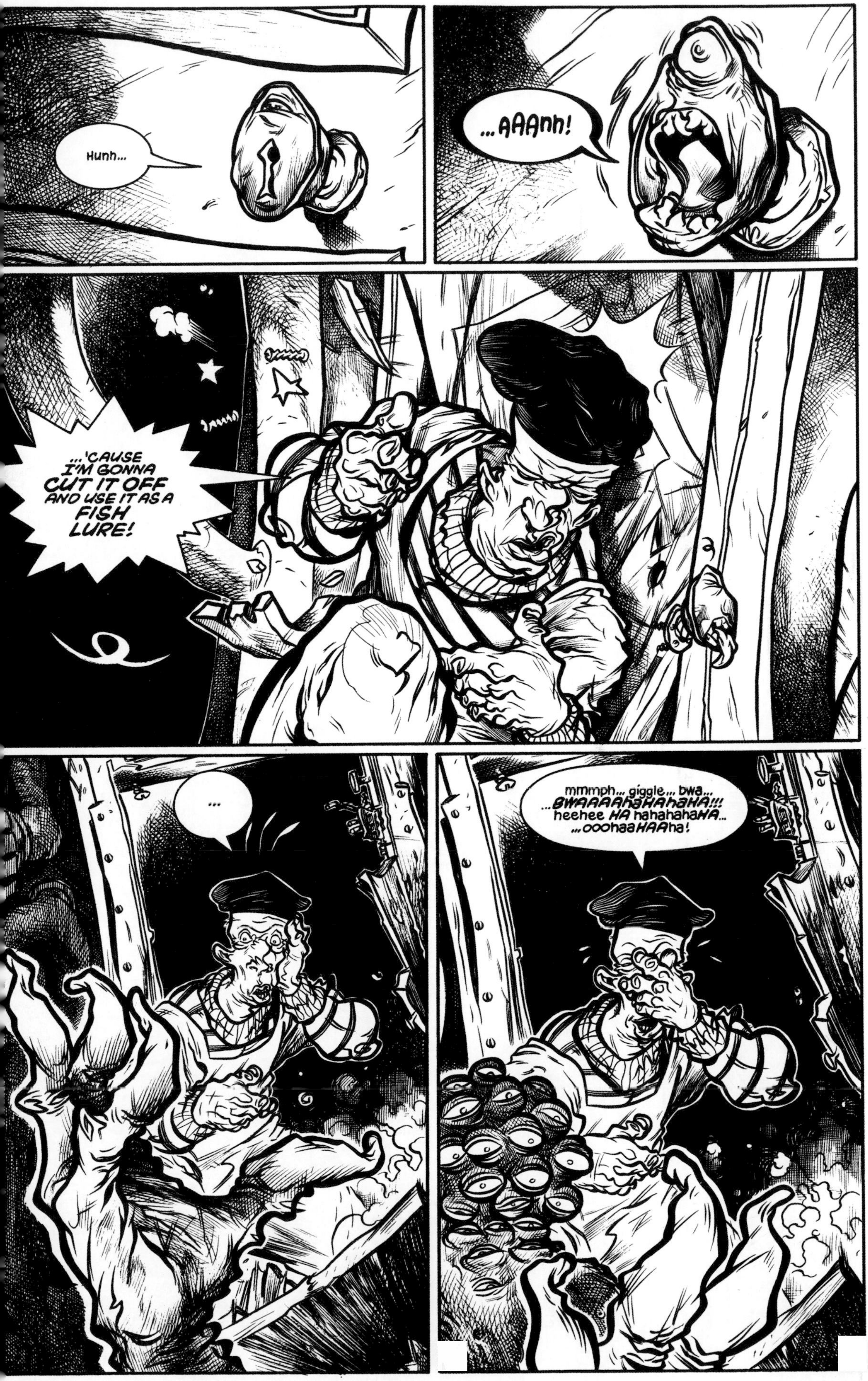
Hunh...
...AAAnh!
...'CAUSE I'M GONNA CUT IT OFF AND USE IT AS A FISH LURE!
...
mmmph... giggle... bwa... ...BWAAAAAhaHAHAhaHA!!! heehee HA hahahahahaHA... ...ooohaaHAAha!

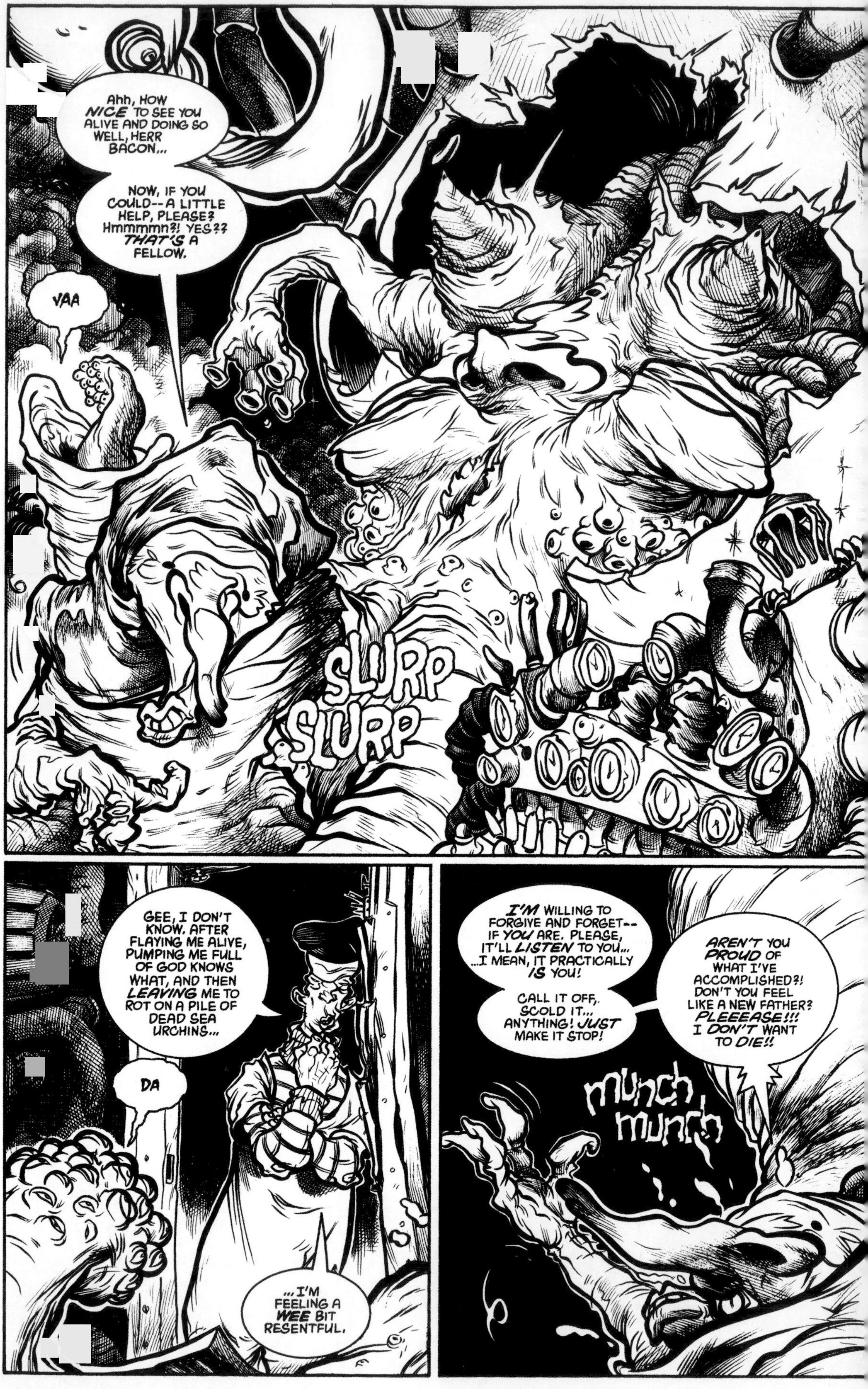
Ahh, HOW NICE TO SEE YOU ALIVE AND DOING SO WELL, HERR BACON...
NOW, IF YOU COULD--A LITTLE HELP, PLEASE? Hmmmmn?! YES?? THAT'S A FELLOW.
VAA
SLURP SLURP
GEE, I DON'T KNOW. AFTER FLAYING ME ALIVE, PUMPING ME FULL OF GOD KNOWS WHAT, AND THEN LEAVING ME TO ROT ON A PILE OF DEAD SEA URCHINS...
DA
...I'M FEELING A WEE BIT RESENTFUL.
I'M WILLING TO FORGIVE AND FORGET--IF YOU ARE. PLEASE, IT'LL LISTEN TO YOU... ...I MEAN, IT PRACTICALLY IS YOU!
CALL IT OFF, SCOLD IT... ANYTHING! JUST MAKE IT STOP!
AREN'T YOU PROUD OF WHAT I'VE ACCOMPLISHED?! DON'T YOU FEEL LIKE A NEW FATHER? PLEEEASE!!! I DON'T WANT TO DIE!!
munch munch

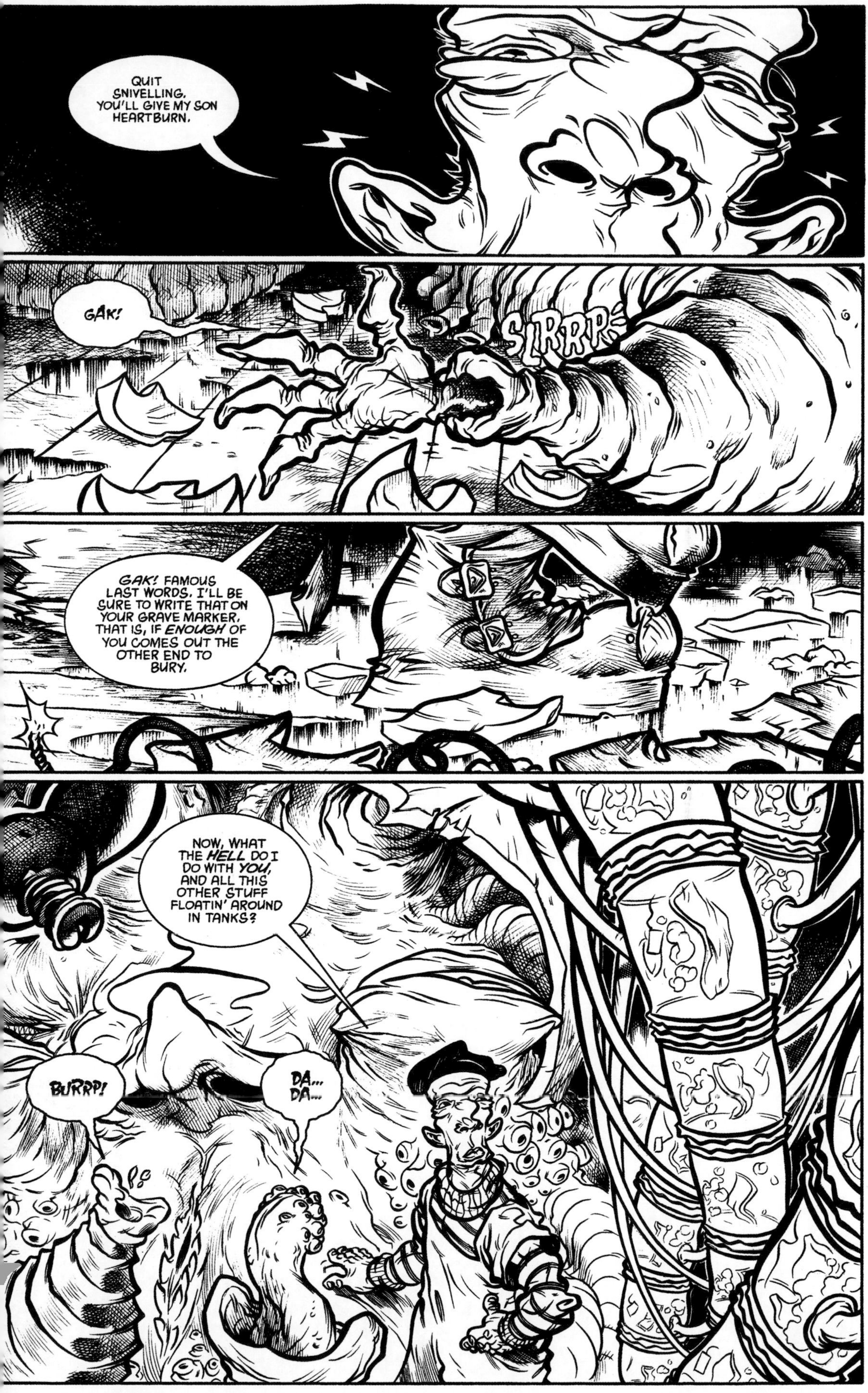
QUIT SNIVELLING. YOU'LL GIVE MY SON HEARTBURN.
GAK!
SLRRP
GAK! FAMOUS LAST WORDS. I'LL BE SURE TO WRITE THAT ON YOUR GRAVE MARKER. THAT IS, IF ENOUGH OF YOU COMES OUT THE OTHER END TO BURY.
NOW, WHAT THE HELL DO I DO WITH YOU, AND ALL THIS OTHER STUFF FLOATIN' AROUND IN TANKS?
BURRP!
DA... DA...

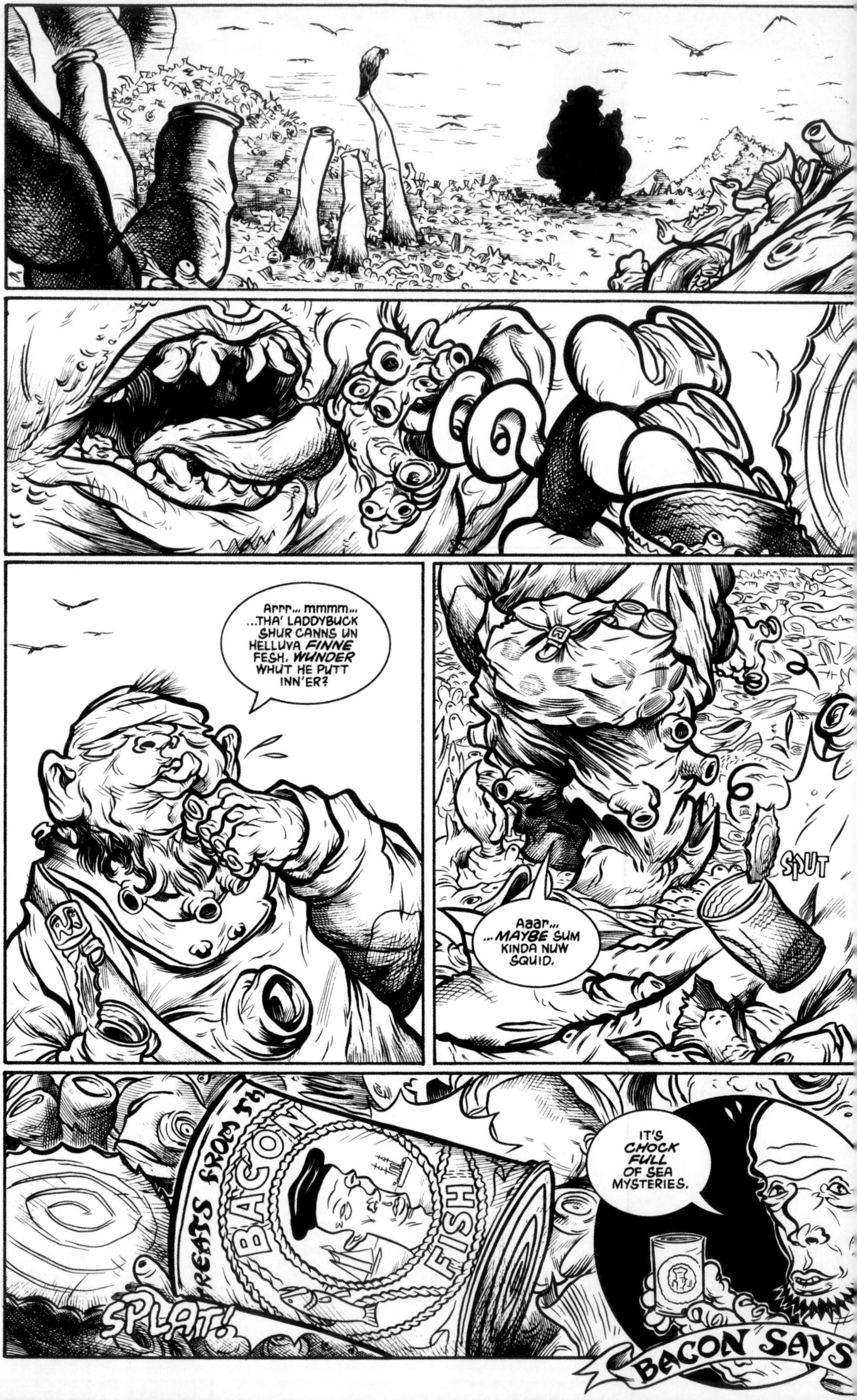
Arrr... mmmm... ...THA' LADDYBUCK SHUR CANNS UN HELLUVA FINNE FESH. WUNDER WHUT HE PUTT INN'ER?
SPUT
Aaar... ...MAYBE SUM KINDA NUW SQUID.
BACON
FISH
IT'S CHOCK FULL OF SEA MYSTERIES.
SPLAT!
BACON SAYS

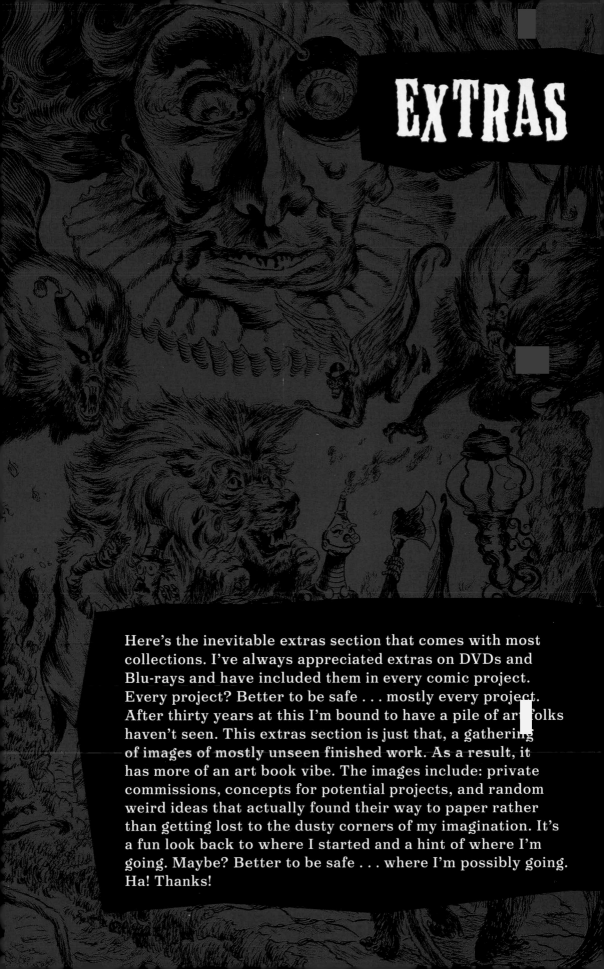

EXTRAS

Here's the inevitable extras section that comes with most collections. I've always appreciated extras on DVDs and Blu-rays and have included them in every comic project. Every project? Better to be safe . . . mostly every project. After thirty years at this I'm bound to have a pile of art folks haven't seen. This extras section is just that, a gathering of images of mostly unseen finished work. As a result, it has more of an art book vibe. The images include: private commissions, concepts for potential projects, and random weird ideas that actually found their way to paper rather than getting lost to the dusty corners of my imagination. It's a fun look back to where I started and a hint of where I'm going. Maybe? Better to be safe . . . where I'm possibly going. Ha! Thanks!

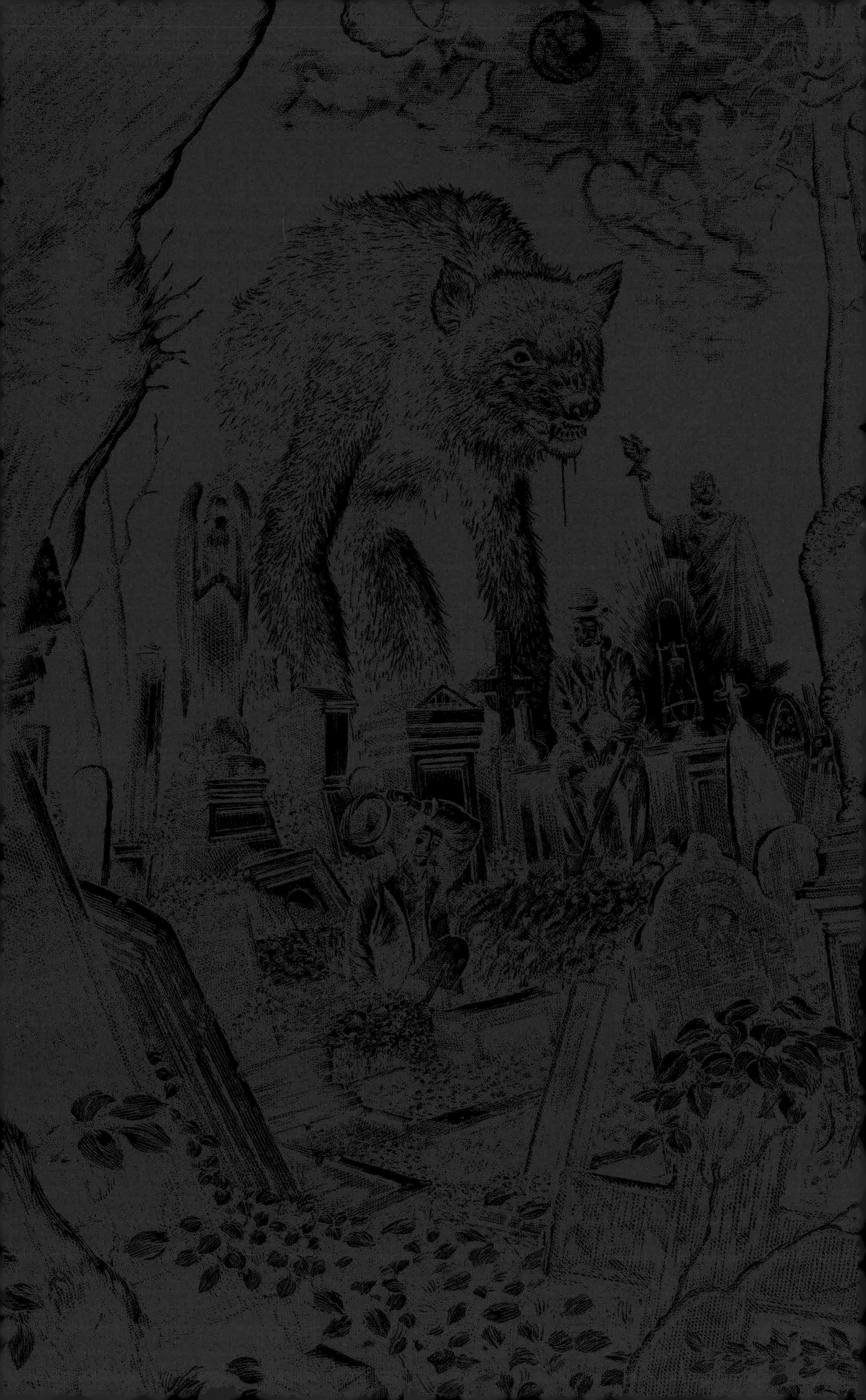

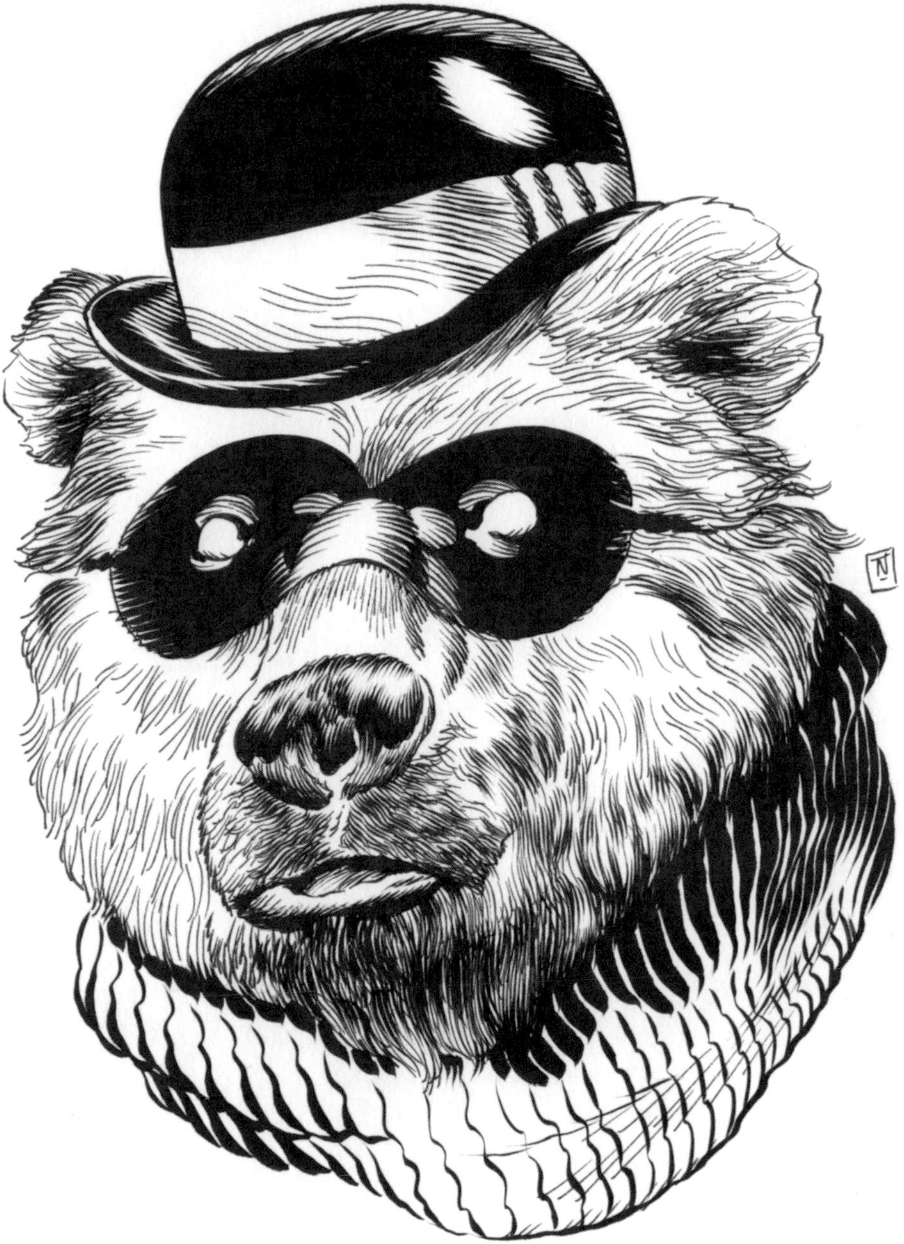

BURGLAR BEAR

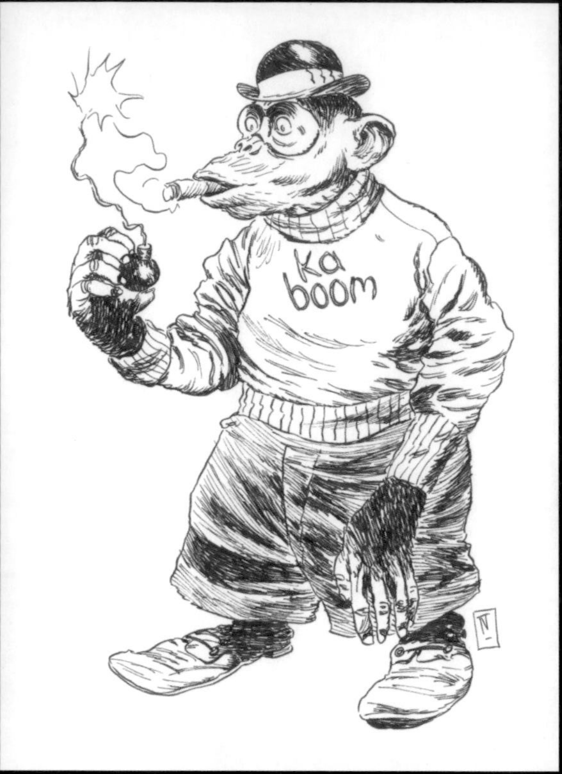
ka
boom

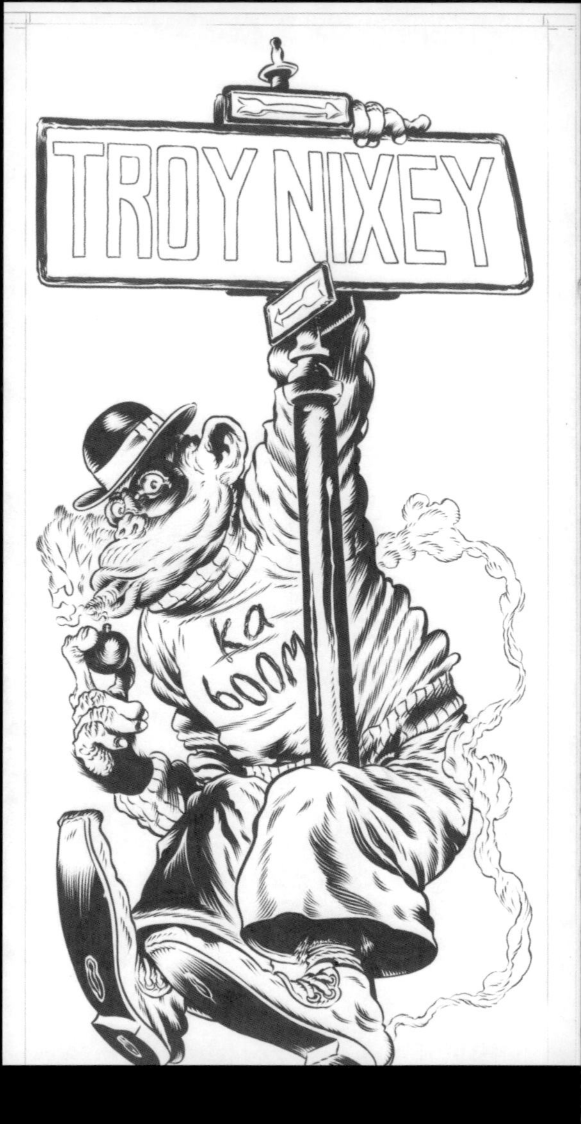
TROY NIXEY
ka
boom

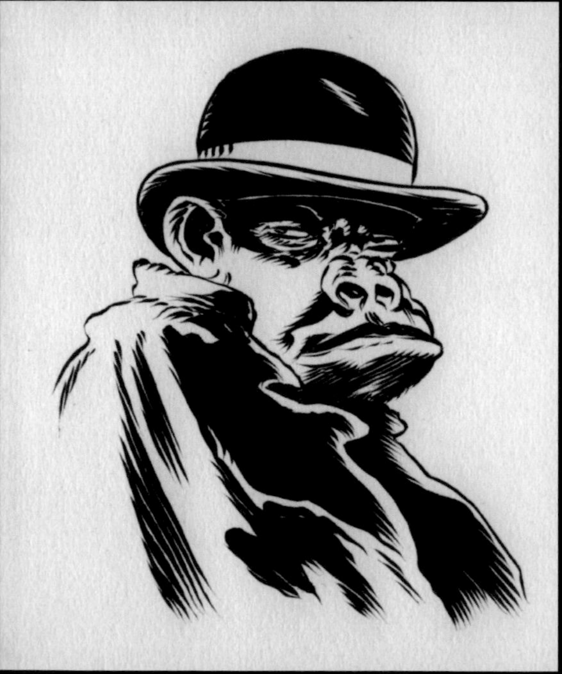

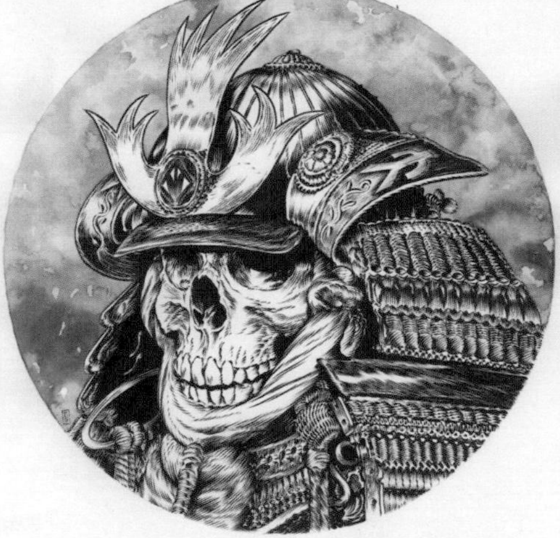

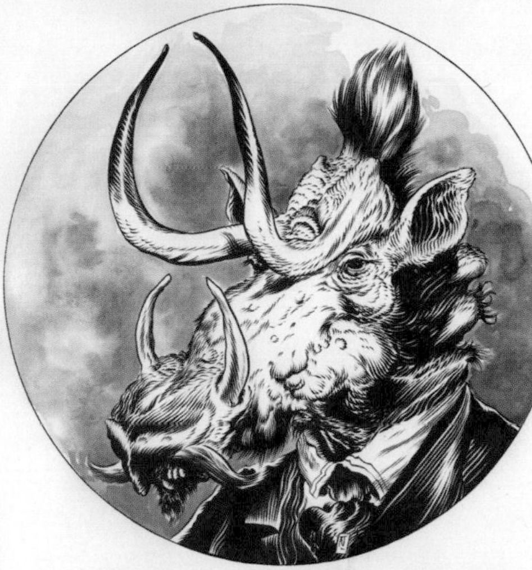

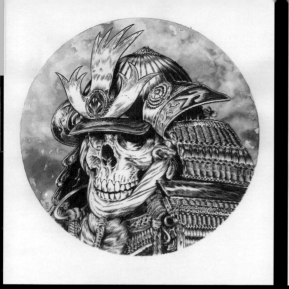

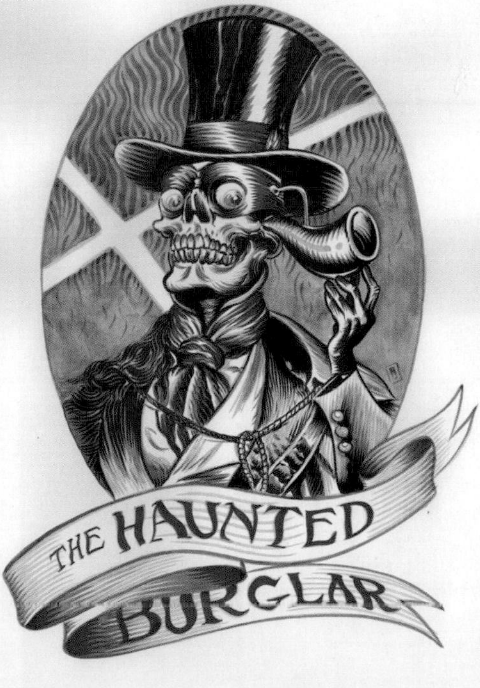
THE HAUNTED
BURGLAR

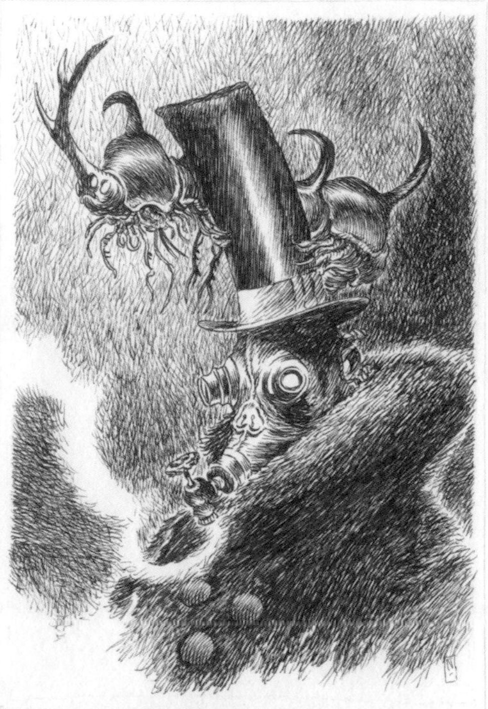

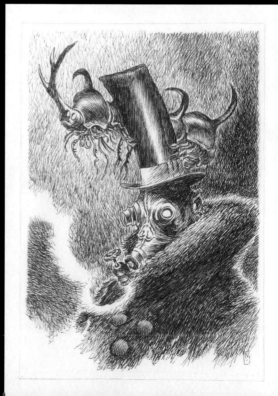

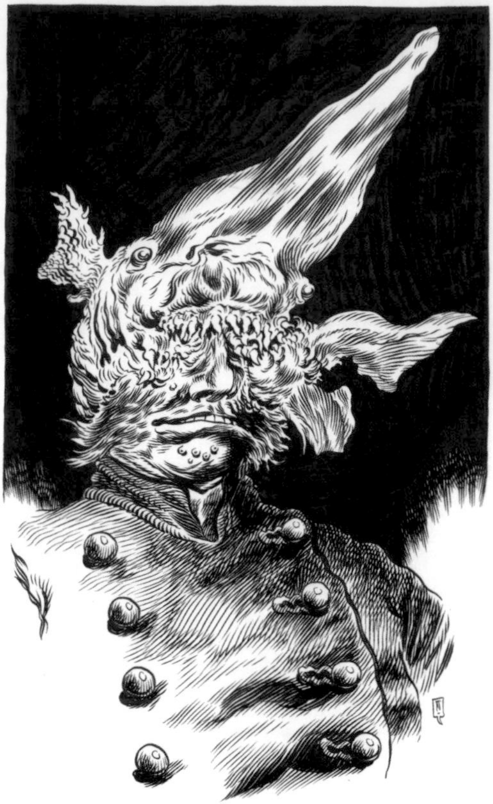
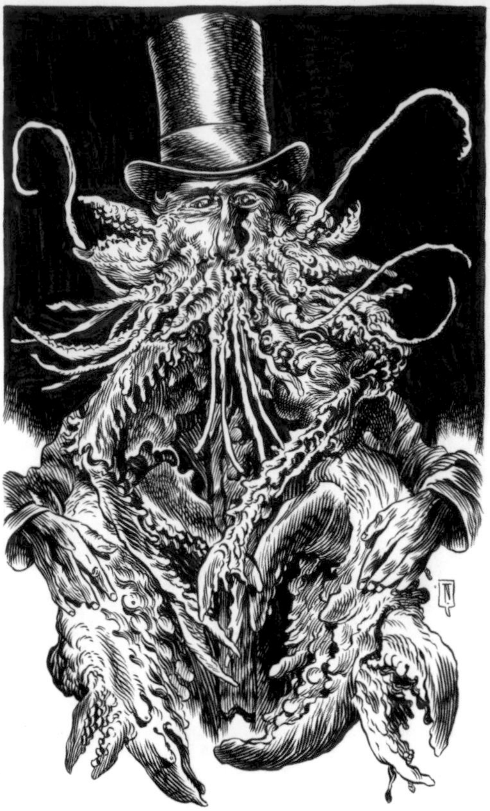
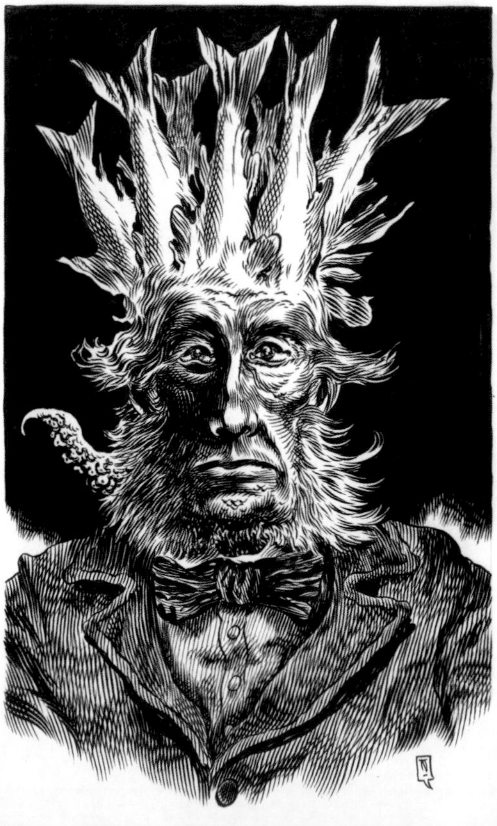
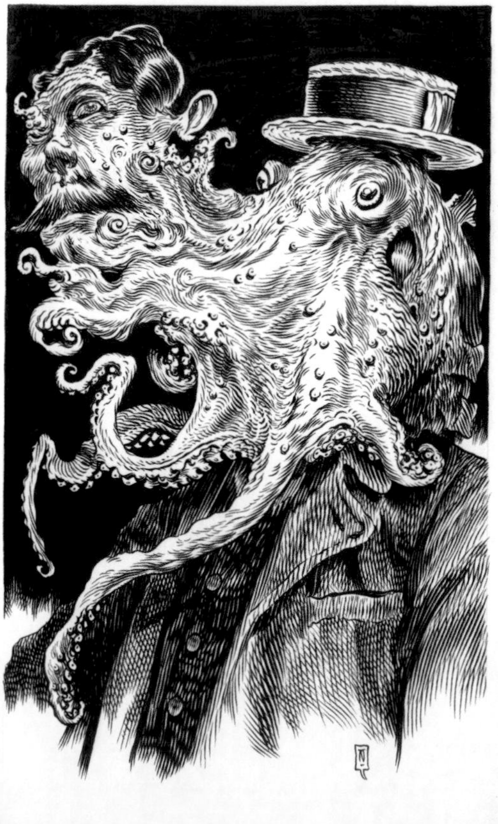

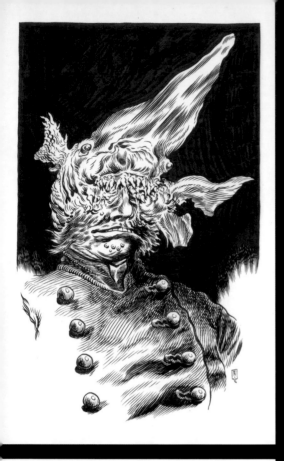

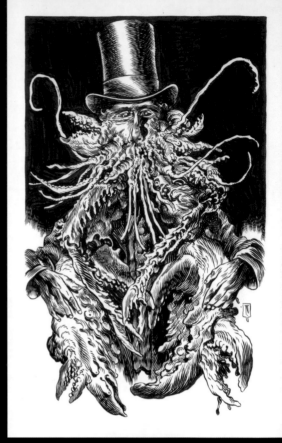

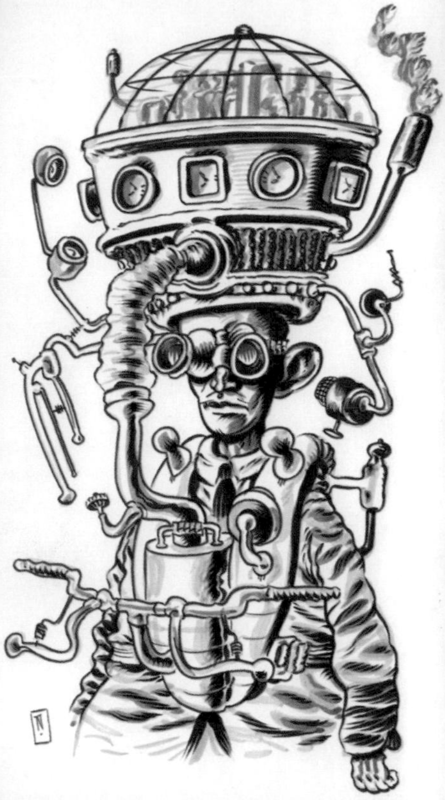

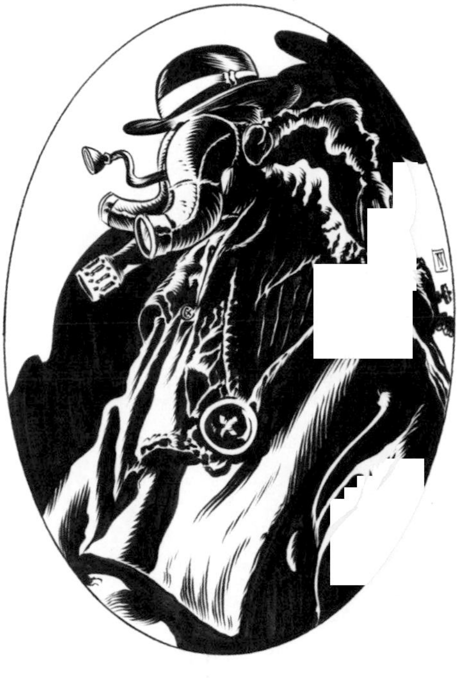

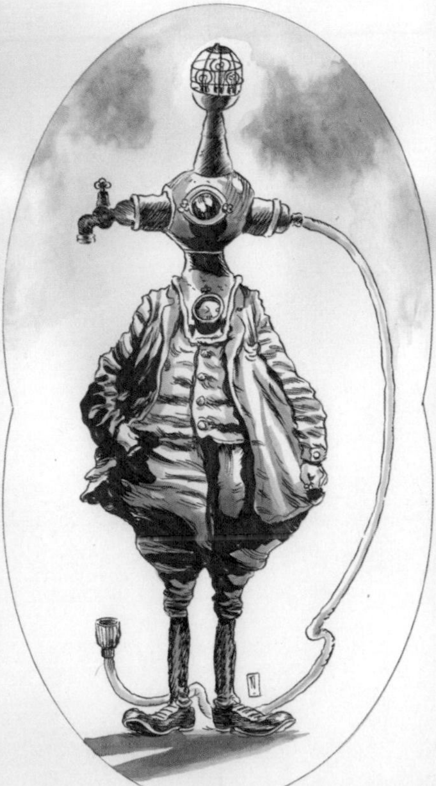

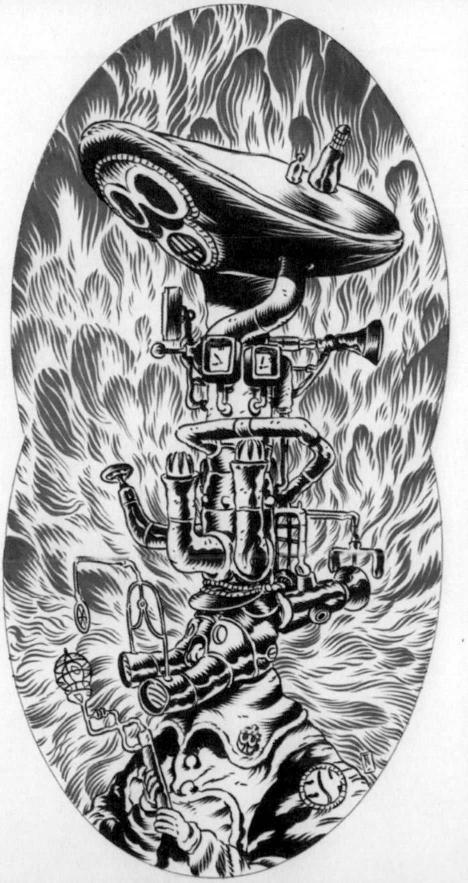

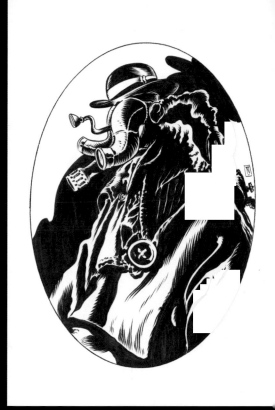

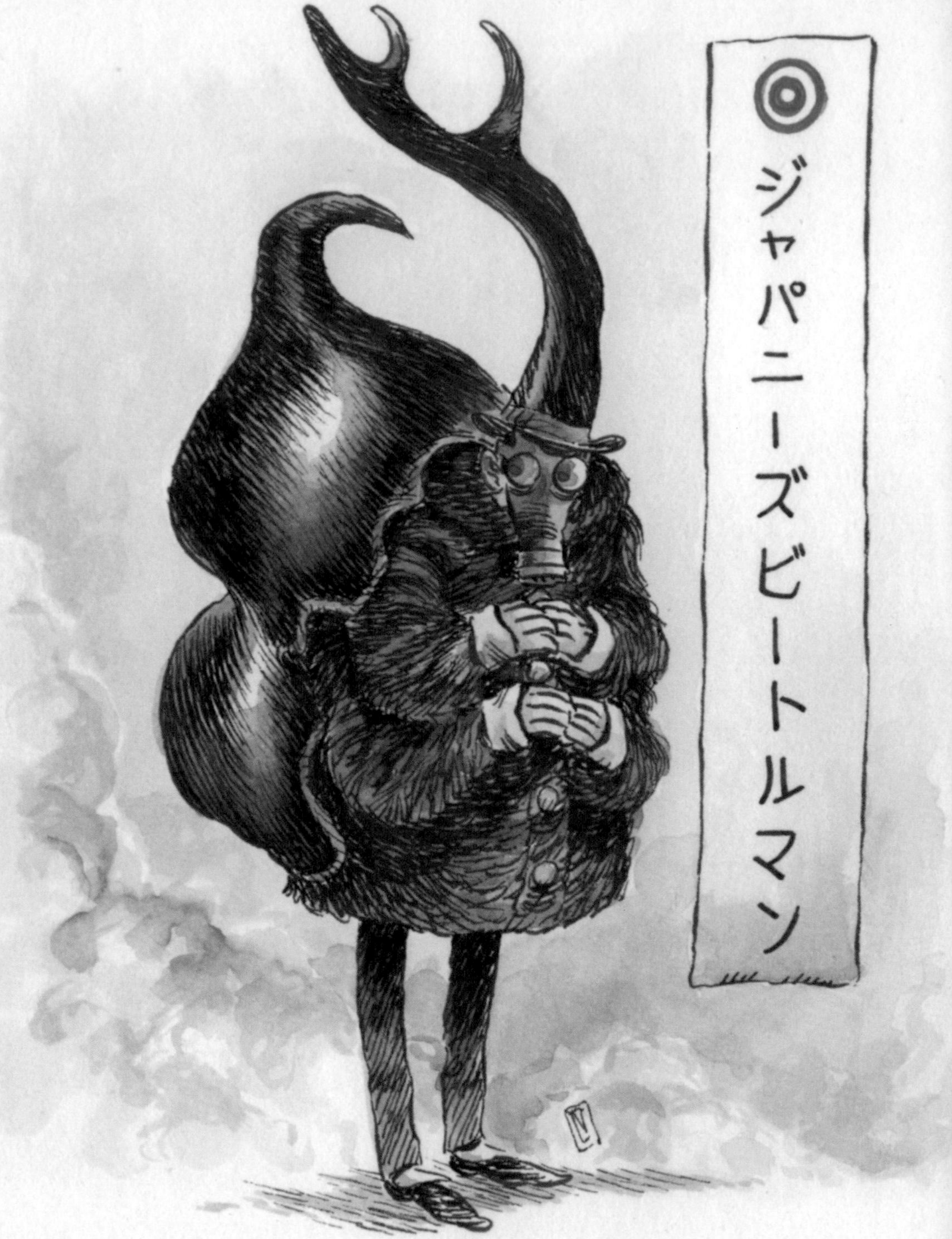
ジャパニーズビートルマン

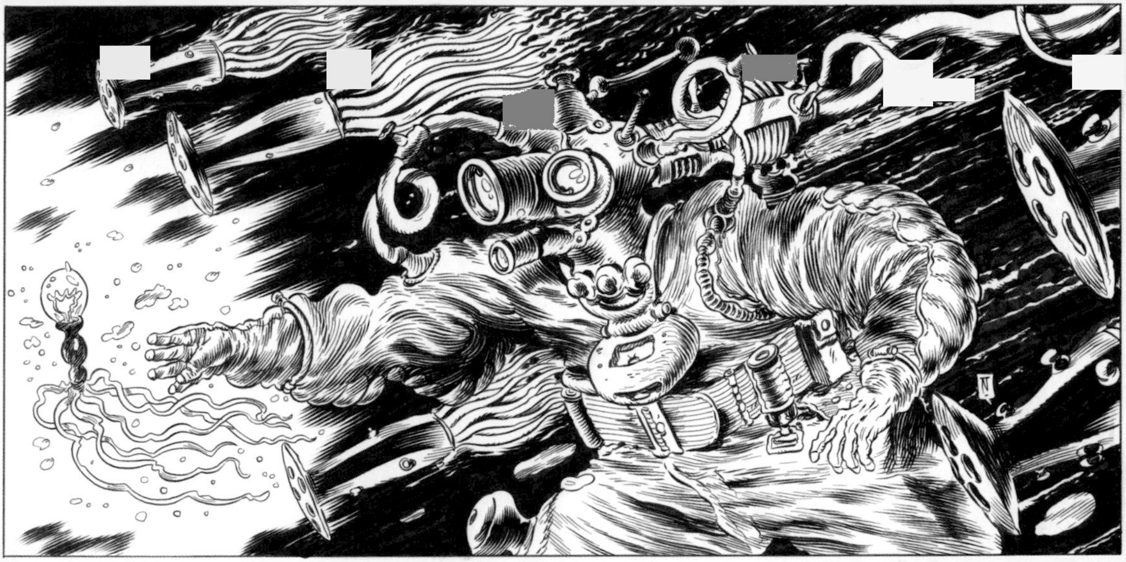

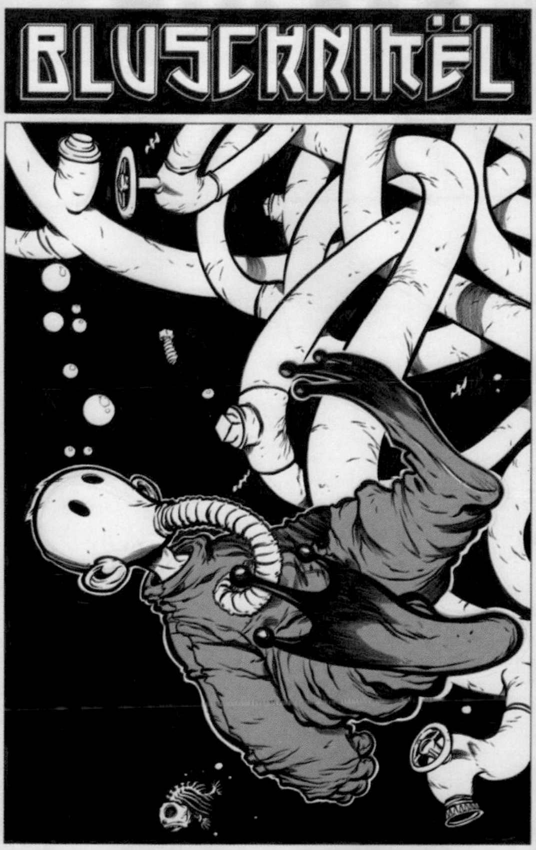
BLUSCHNIKËL

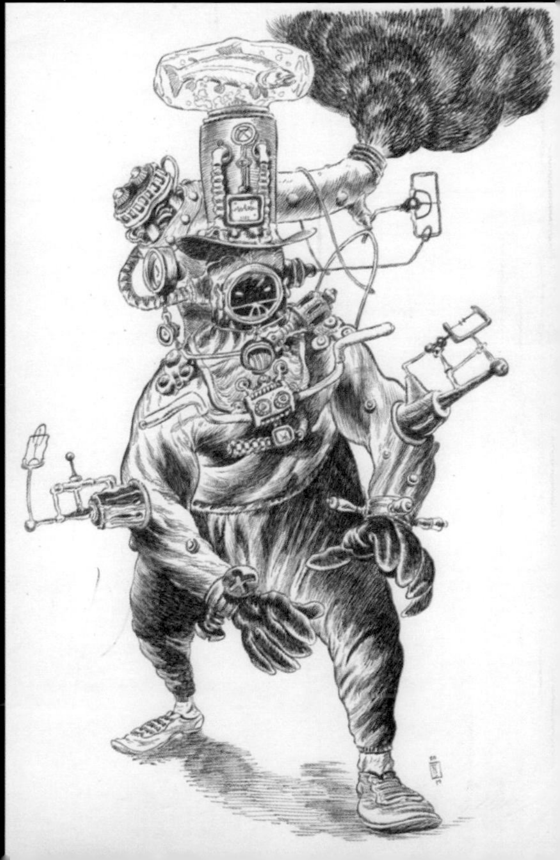

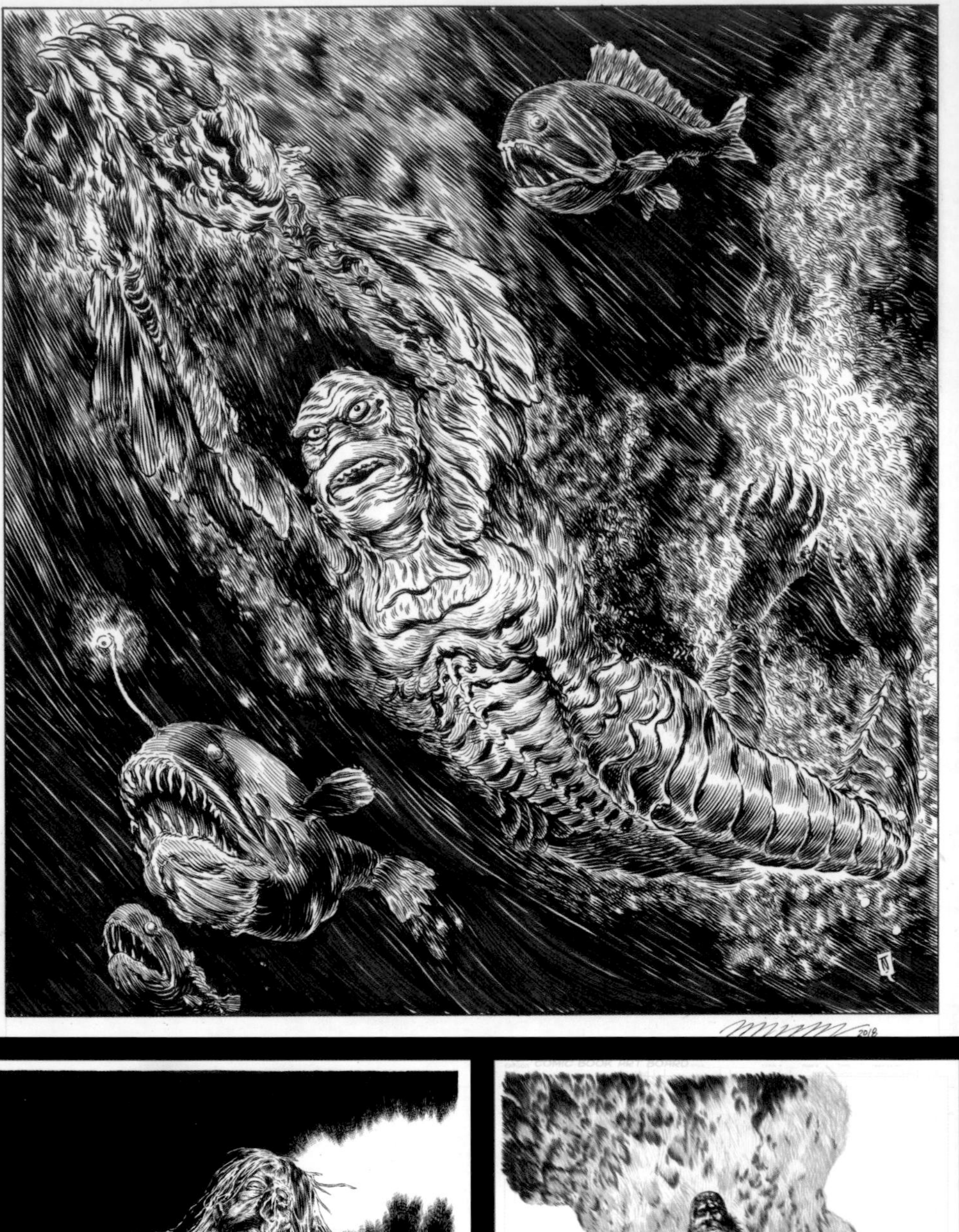

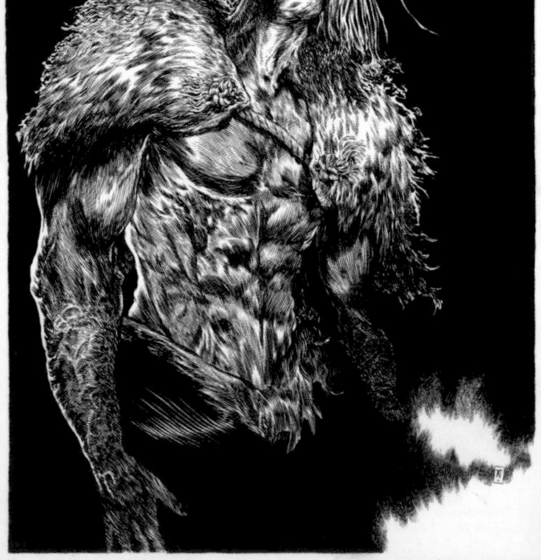

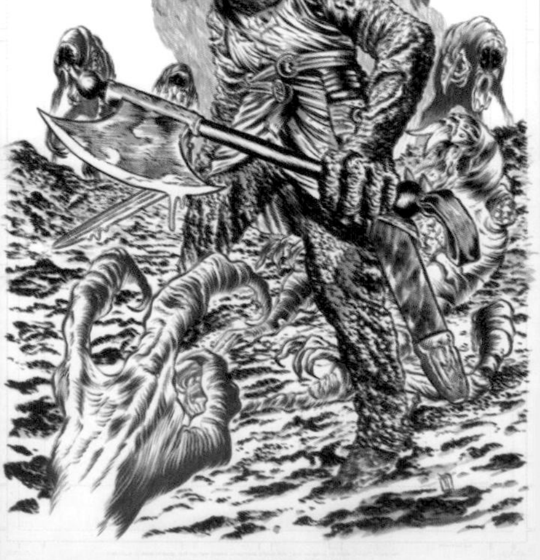

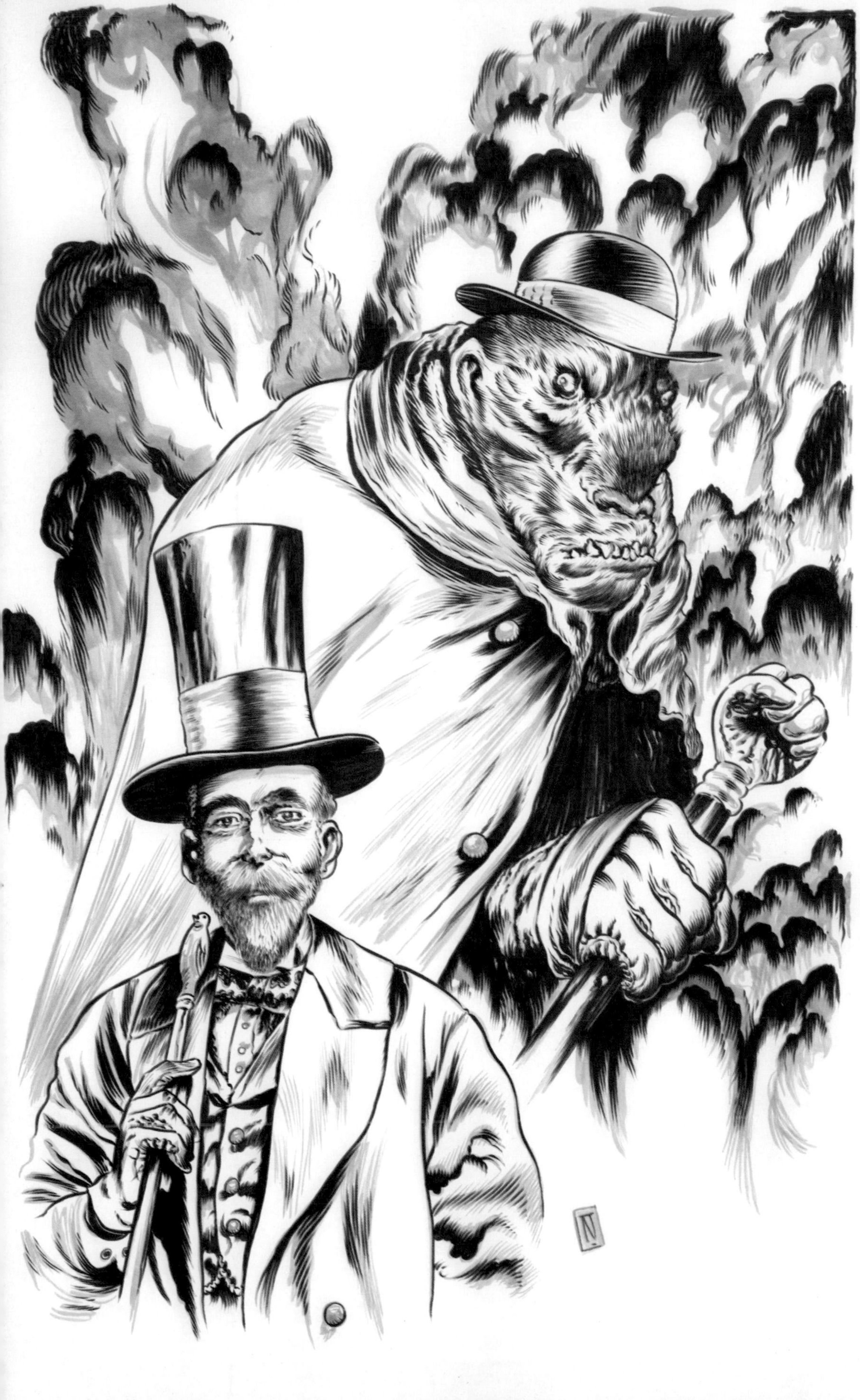

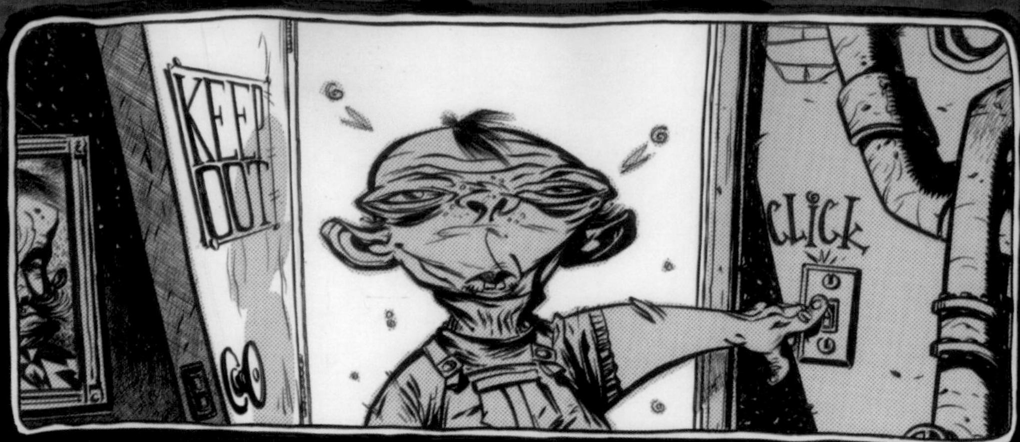
KEEP OUT
CLICK

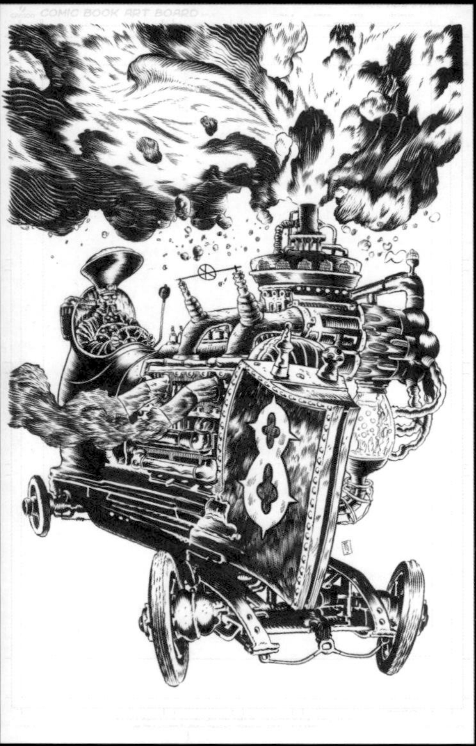

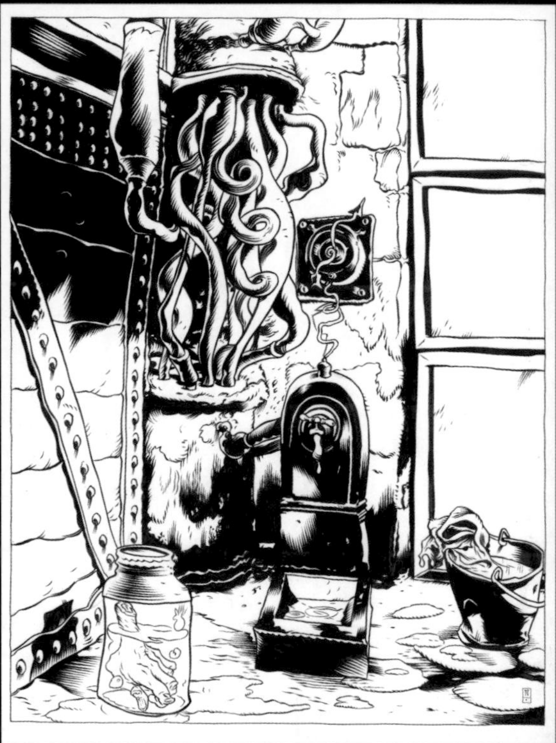

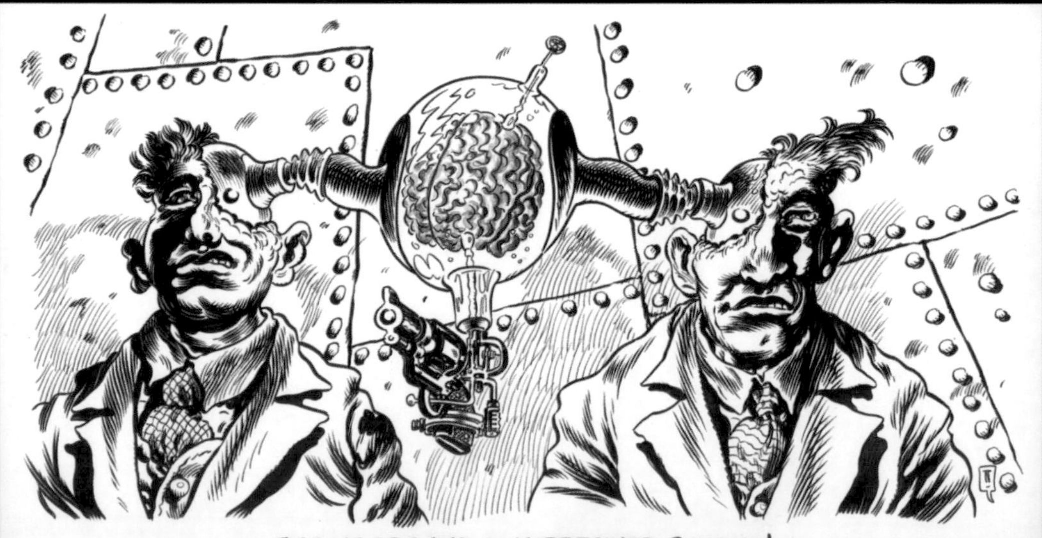

TWO HOODS AND A HAIRBRAINED SCHEME!

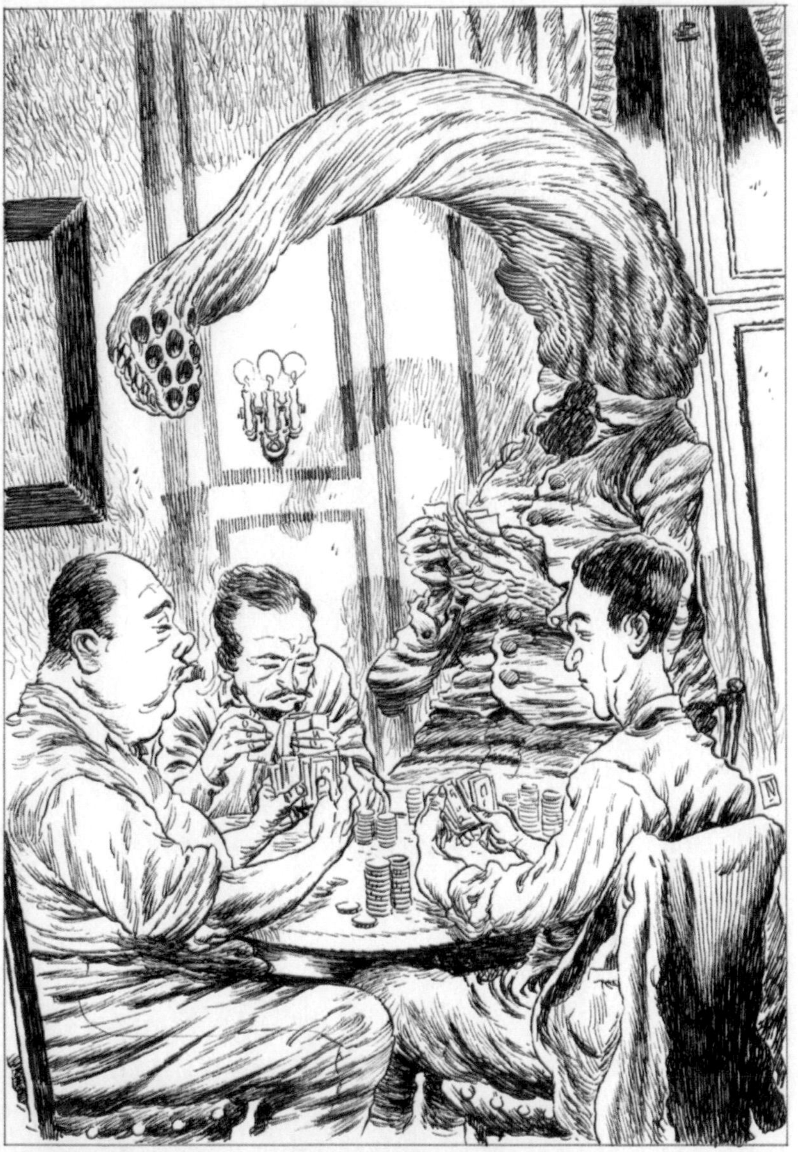

- THE CHEAT -

2015

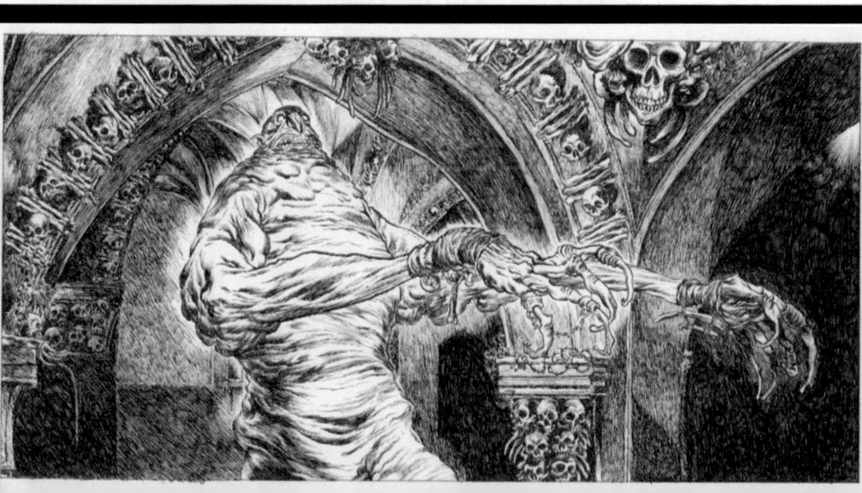

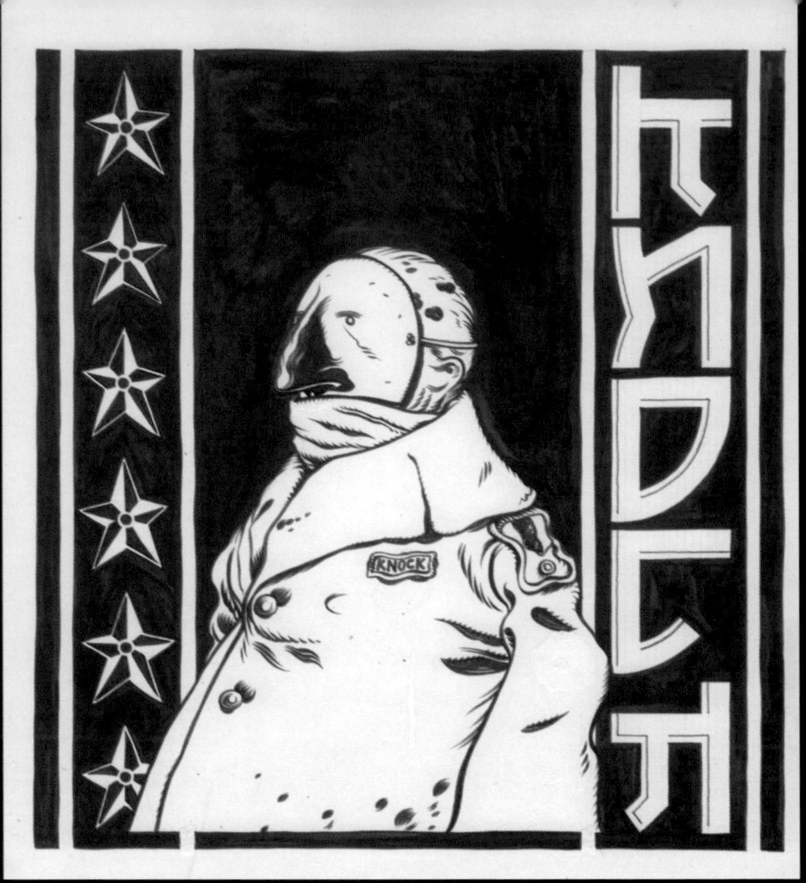
KNOCK
KNOCK

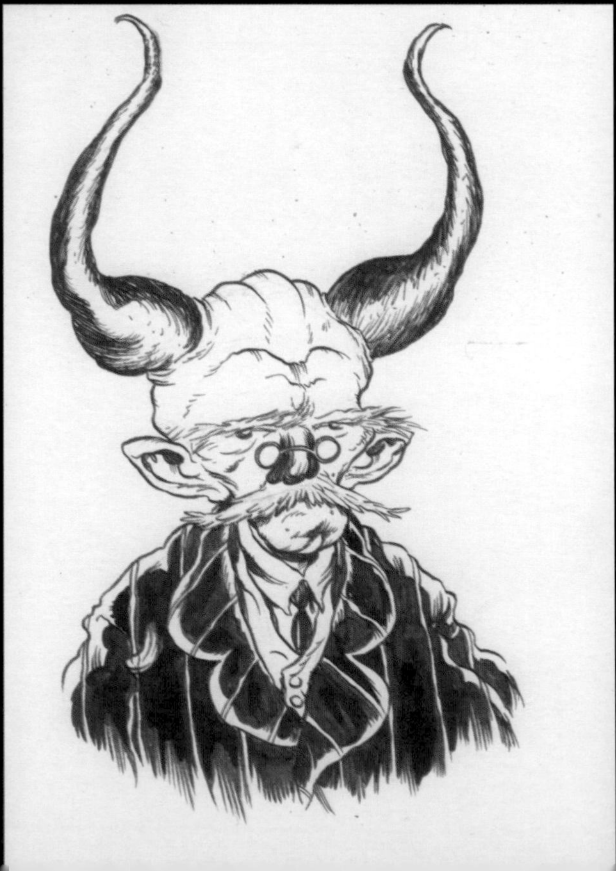

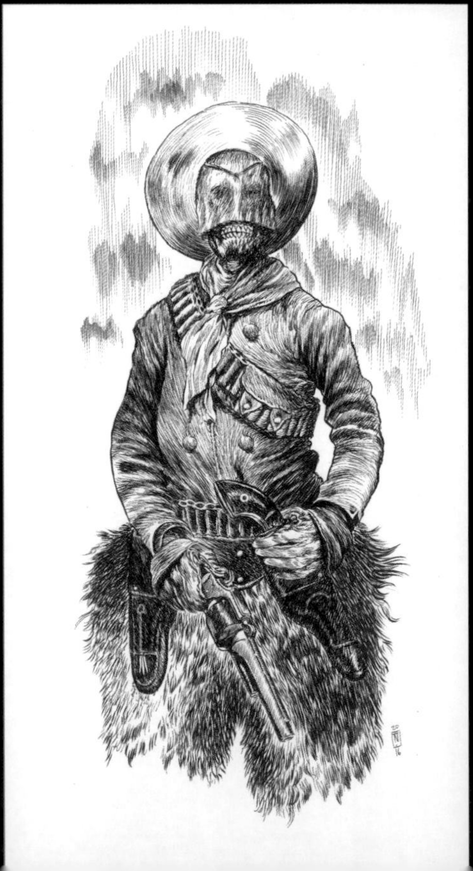

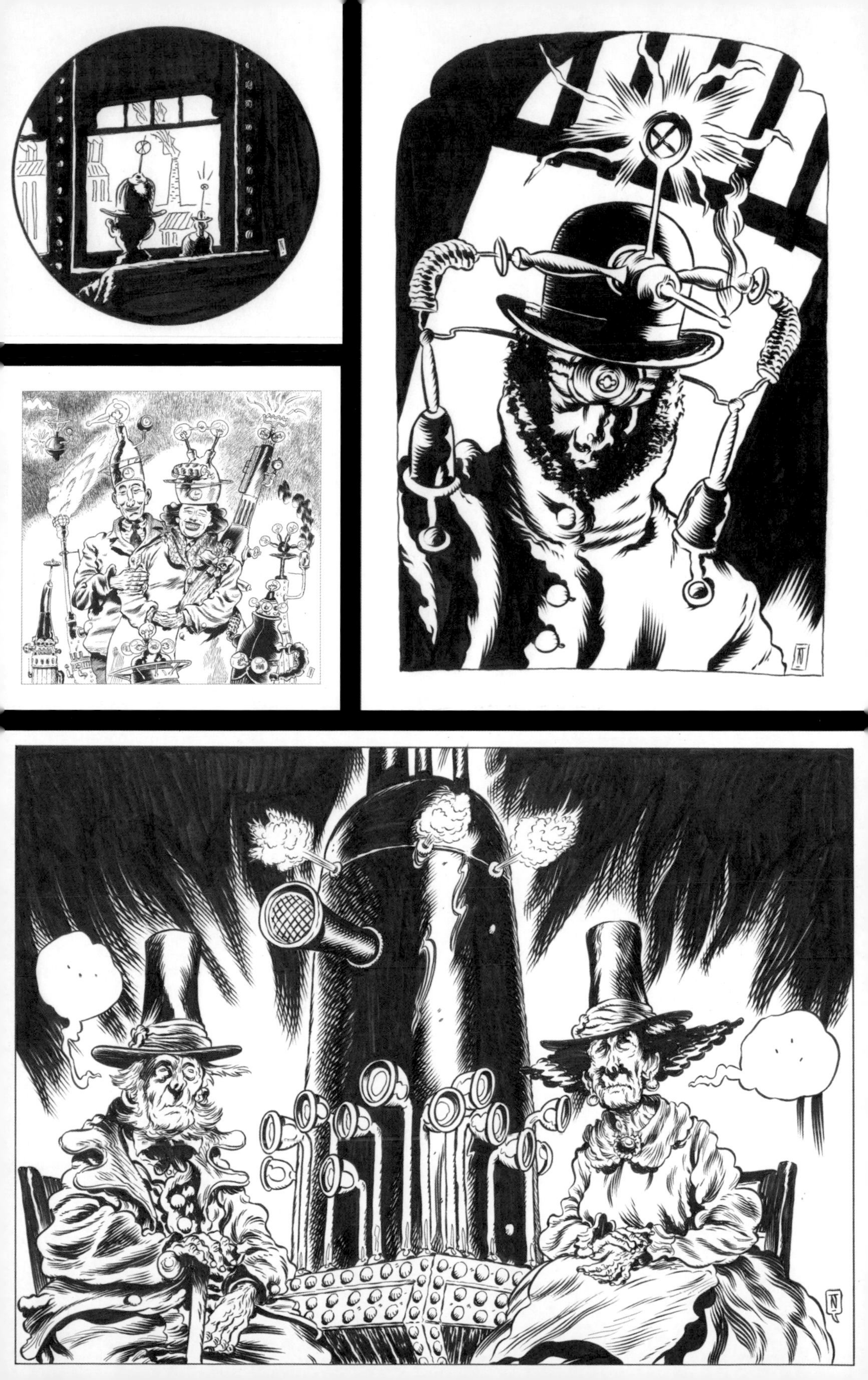

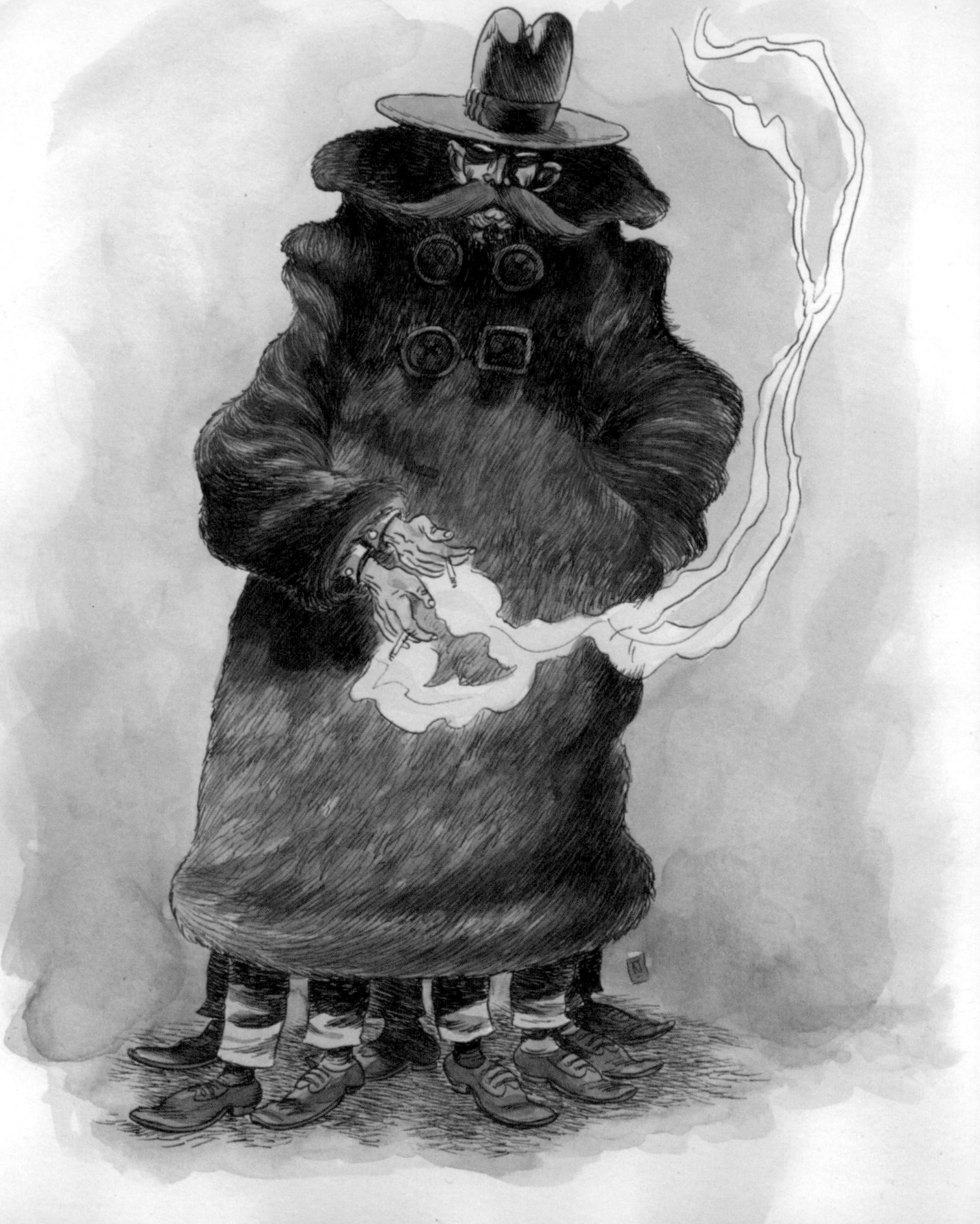

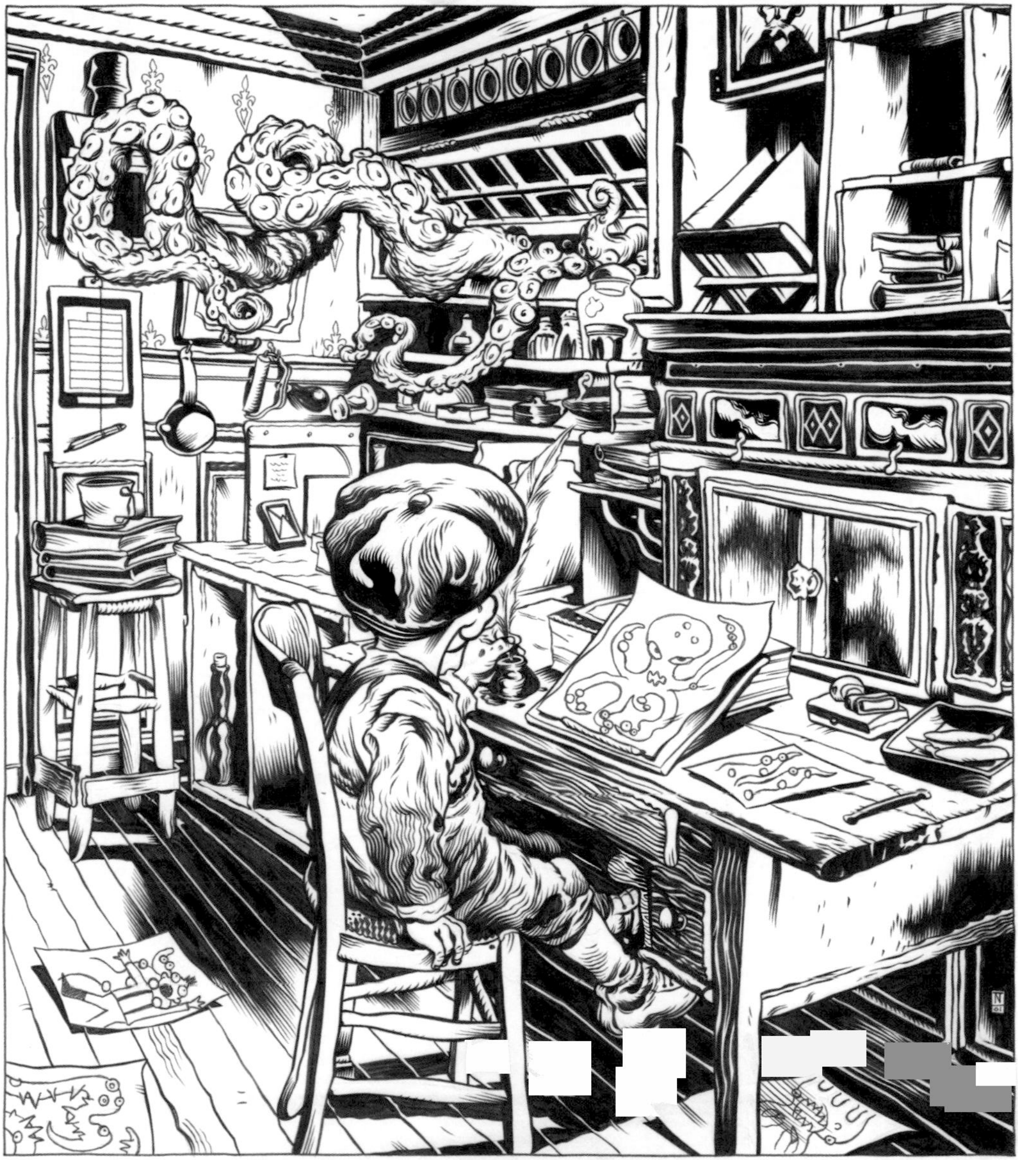

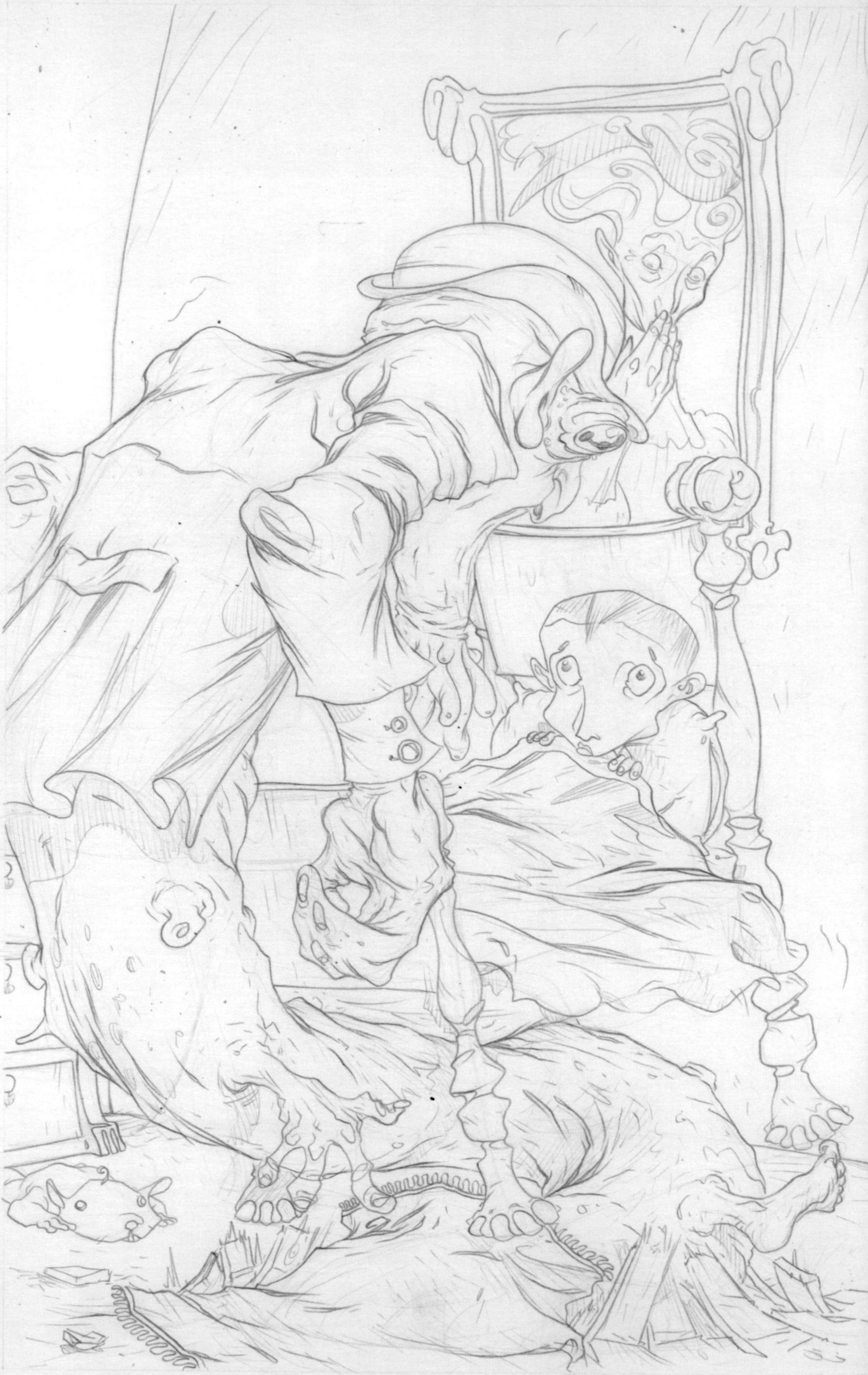

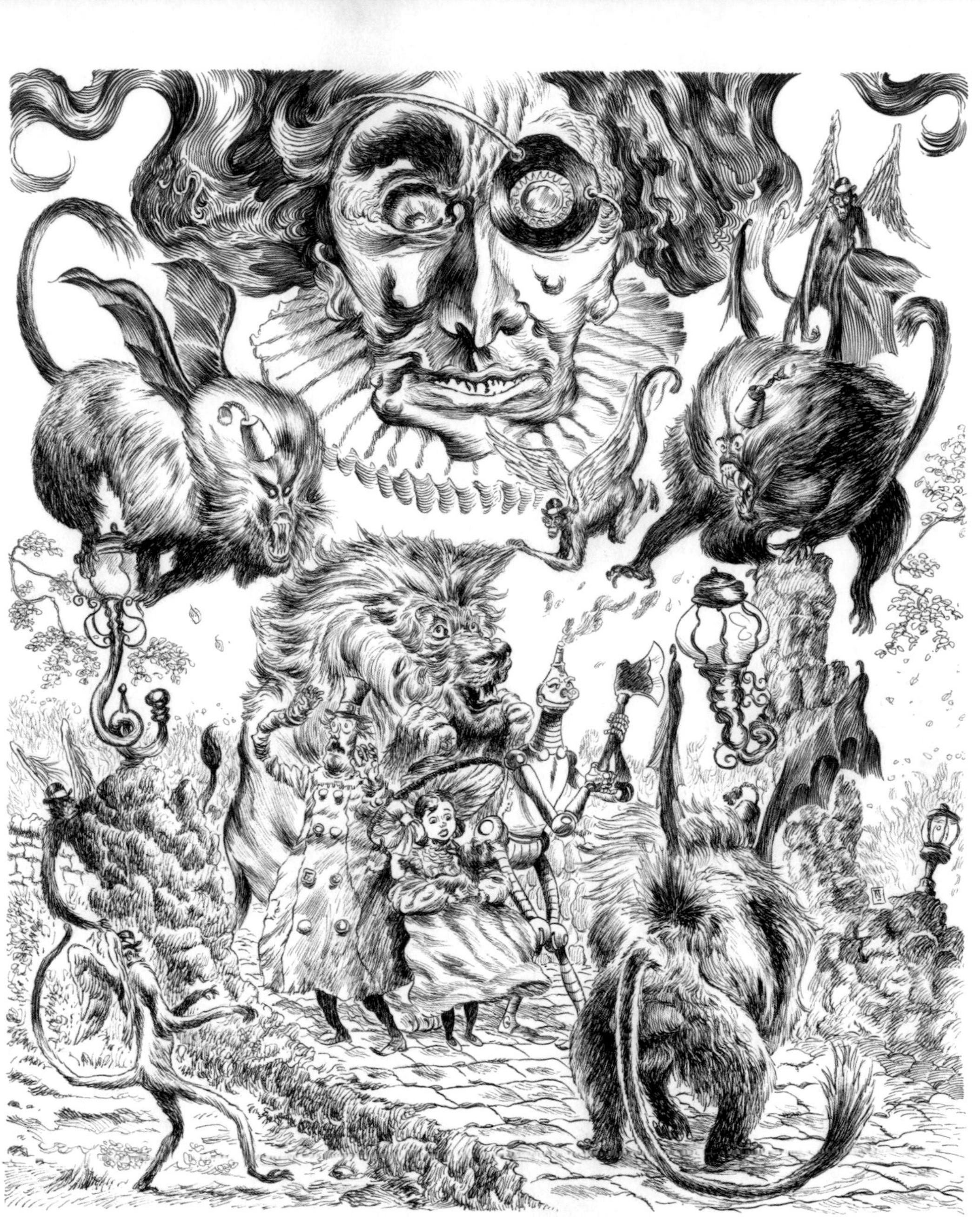

MORE FROM TROY NIXEY AND DAMON GENTRY!

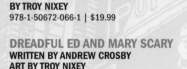

BACON AND OTHER MONSTROUS TALES
BY TROY NIXEY
978-1-50672-066-1 | $19.99

DREADFUL ED AND MARY SCARY
WRITTEN BY ANDREW CROSBY
ART BY TROY NIXEY
978-1-50671-330-4 | $19.99

TROUT VOLUME 1: BITS & BOBS
WORDS AND ART BY TROY NIXEY
COVER BY MIKE MIGNOLA
978-1-50671-259-8 | $14.99

TROUT VOLUME 2: THE HOLLOWEST KNOCK
WORDS AND ART BY TROY NIXEY
978-1-50671-260-4 | $17.99

VINEGAR TEETH
WRITTEN BY TROY NIXEY AND DAMON GENTRY
ART BY TROY NIXEY AND GUY MAJOR
978-1-50670-714-3 | $14.99

COLORADO JONESY
As seen in VINEGAR TEETH! Find it at
https://store.cdbaby.com/cd/coloradojonesy

JENNY FINN
WRITTEN BY MIKE MIGNOLA AND TROY NIXEY
ART BY TROY NIXEY AND FAREL DALRYMPLE
COVER BY MIKE MIGNOLA
978-1-50670-544-6 | $17.99

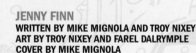

SABERTOOTH SWORDSMAN VOLUME ONE (Second Edition)
WRITTEN BY DAMON GENTRY
ART BY AARON CONLEY
978-1-50670-302-2 | $17.99

ONLY THE END OF THE WORLD AGAIN
WRITTEN BY NEIL GAIMAN AND P. CRAIG RUSSELL
ART BY TROY NIXEY
978-1-50670-612-2 | $19.99

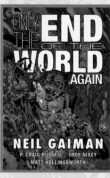

THE BLACK SINISTER
WRITTEN BY KAARE ANDREWS
ART BY TROY NIXEY AND DAVE MCCAIG
978-1-50670-337-4 | $9.99

LOBSTER JOHNSON: A CHAIN FORGED IN LIFE
WRITTEN BY MIKE MIGNOLA AND JOHN ARCUDI
ART BY BEN STENBECK, TROY NIXEY,
TONI FEJZULA, AND OTHERS
978-1-50670-178-3 | $19.99

AVAILABLE AT YOUR LOCAL COMICS SHOP OR BOOKSTORE

TO FIND A COMICS SHOP IN YOUR AREA, VISIT COMICSHOPLOCATOR.COM. FOR MORE INFORMATION OR TO ORDER DIRECT:
On the web: darkhorse.com · E-mail: mailorder@darkhorse.com

Dreadful Ed™ and Mary Scary™ © Andrew Cosby and Troy Nixey. Trout™ © Troy Nixey. Vinegar Teeth™ © Troy Nixey and Damon Gentry. Jenny Finn™ © Mike Mignola and Troy Nixey. The Sabertooth Swordsman™ © Damon Gentry and Aaron Conley. Only the End of the World Again™ © Neil Gaiman, P. Craig Russell, and Troy Nixey. The Black Sinister © Troy Nixey, Kaare Andrews, and Dave McCaig. Lobster Johnson™ A Chain Forged in Life © Mike Mignola. Bacon™ & Other Monstrosities © Troy Nixey. Hunger and Brooklyn 1950 © New Comic Co. LLC, reprinted with permission. Dark Horse Books® and the Dark Horse logo are registered trademarks of Dark Horse Comics LLC. All rights reserved. (BL 5084)

DarkHorse.com

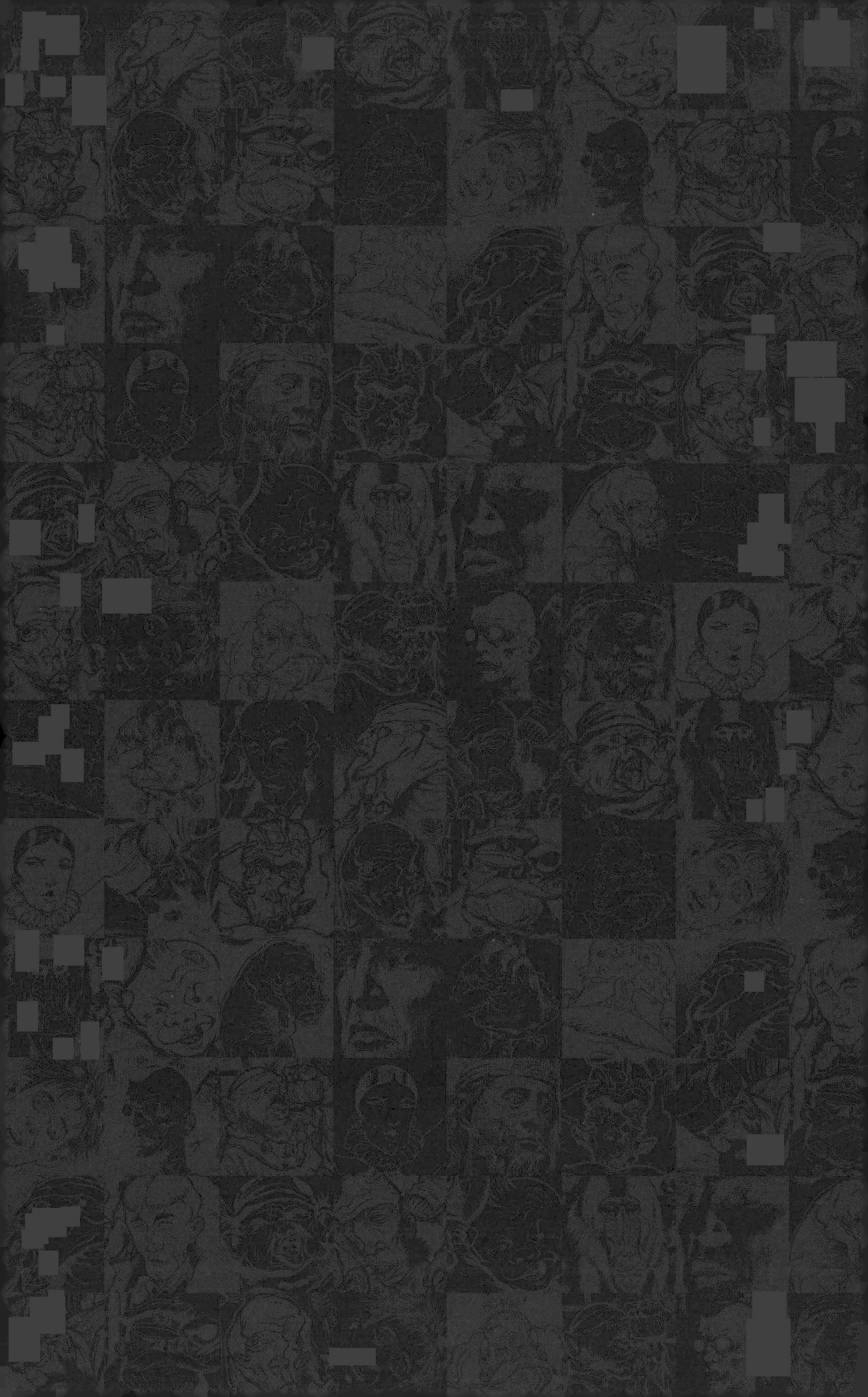